HS.

Britain Before the Reform Act

Britain Before the Reform Act, Politics and Society 1815–1832

Second edition

Eric J. Evans

PEARSON
Longman

Harlow, England • London • New York • Boston • San Francisco • Toronto
Sydney • Tokyo • Singapore • Hong Kong • Seoul • Taipei • New Delhi
Cape Town • Madrid • Mexico City • Amsterdam • Munich • Paris • Milan

PEARSON EDUCATION LIMITED

Edinburgh Gate
Harlow CM20 2JE
Tel: +44 (0)1279 623623
Fax: +44 (0)1279 431059
Website: www.pearsoned.co.uk

First published in 1989
Second edition published in Great Britain in 2008

ISBN: 978-0-582-29908-5

British Library Cataloguing-in-Publication Data
A catalogue record for this book is available from the British Library

Library of Congress Cataloging-in-Publication Data
Evans, Eric J., 1945–
    Britain before the Reform Act : 1815–1832 / Eric J. Evans. — 2nd ed.
        p. cm.
    Includes bibliographical references and index.
    ISBN 978-0-582-29908-5 (pbk.)
    1. Great Britain—Politics and government—1800–1837. I. Title.
    DA535.E86 2008
    941.07—dc22
                                            2008001879

10 9 8 7 6 5 4 3 2 1
12 11 10 09 08

Typeset in 10/13.5pt Berkeley Book by 35
Printed and bound in Malaysia (CTP-VVP)

The publisher's policy is to use paper manufactured from sustainable forests.

Introduction to the Series

History is a narrative constructed by historians from traces left by the past. Historical enquiry is often driven by contemporary issues and, in consequence, historical narratives are constantly reconsidered, reconstructed and reshaped. The fact that different historians have different perspectives on issues means that there is also often controversy and no universally agreed version of past events. *Seminar Studies in History* was designed to bridge the gap between current research and debate, and the broad, popular general surveys that often date rapidly.

The volumes in the series are written by historians who are not only familiar with the latest research and current debates concerning their topic, but who have themselves contributed to our understanding of the subject. The books are intended to provide the reader with a clear introduction to a major topic in history. They provide both a narrative of events and a critical analysis of contemporary interpretations. They include the kinds of tools generally omitted from specialist monographs: a chronology of events, a glossary of terms and brief biographies of 'who's who'. They also include bibliographical essays in order to guide students to the literature on various aspects of the subject. Students and teachers alike will find that the selection of documents will stimulate discussion and offer insight into the raw materials used by historians in their attempt to understand the past.

Clive Emsley and Gordon Martel
Series Editors

Contents

PART TWO   DOCUMENTS

Preface

It is nearly 20 years since the first edition of this book was published. A new edition is, therefore, overdue. I am grateful for the opportunity both to incorporate some of the results of the research done over the past two decades and, in doing so, to reflect on how far my own views have altered since 1989. As the further reading will indicate, I have continued to publish on the early nineteenth century in the interim, so this volume can be seen as a consolidating, rather than an undermining, enterprise. My views about the period have not fundamentally altered. However, perceptions have been sharpened and emphases changed. This edition is larger than its predecessor. Every section has been changed to a greater or lesser extent. Substantial revision is necessary to do justice to the findings of much first-rate work, particularly that by Boyd Hilton and Peter Jupp. Their work has shed important new light, both on the structure of politics and also on how economic ideology influenced the formation of policy. I am grateful to them for the excellence of their scholarship and the immense fruitfulness and originality of their insights. Many others, too numerous to mention here, have helped me reshape and refine my views. Whether or not they are aware of the influence they have had, I am immensely grateful to them.

Experts in the period 1815–32 are now much more likely to stress that contemporary politicians were not absorbed with the issue of parliamentary reform for much of the time. They were certainly not hanging about waiting for a Great Reform Act to drop from the sky! They were wrestling with other aspects of what might be called 'the pressures of modernity'. It will surprise many readers to learn that religious controversies were generally seen as more fundamental to the way contemporaries saw their world than were those relating to representation in Parliament. Ordinary people – or the 'lower orders', as contemporaries called them – might come out on to the streets in support of reform but they were more exercised most of the time by the availability of jobs, by the level of wages and prices and, if they lived in the new industrial towns, by just how filthy they were and how many of their children disease and poor sanitation carried off long before their time. Radical politicians saw it as their job to alert people to the part played by taxation in determining the price and affordability of food and drink and to the extent to which legislation was 'fixed'. A landowners' parliament would pass laws which benefited landowners. All of this might heighten political consciousness, but threatening mass meetings could only be organized in times of poverty and deprivation. The huge political crisis of 1830–32, which was defused by parliamentary reform, should not colour our understanding of the whole period.

It is, I think, a matter of regret that so little serious work is now done on the foreign policy and diplomatic history of the period. Devotees of the 'linguistic turn' stop short at deconstructing political treaties and diplomatic notes, it seems. It is difficult to understand why since so much attention has been directed towards what, in the great order of things, seems relatively trivial and, when written up – as it so often is – in exclusivist, lazy and ugly jargon, even less appealing. It is surely time for the research councils to institute a rigorous cost–benefit analysis of post-structuralism and for research students to cast their nets somewhat wider. Whatever, there is little to change to reflect in the area of foreign policy, although we do have a more developed understanding now of the extent to which Britain's overall strategy was influenced by formal or informal imperial objectives.

Readers will also note that this edition includes a Glossary of terms and a Who's who? that offers brief portraits of the leading characters. Both are intended to help the acclimatization of students unfamiliar with early nineteenth-century British history. The author believes that an understanding of this period is crucial to explaining both Britain's transition to a modern, industrial state and how that transition was effected without a revolution. If this introduction to its key themes encourages readers to dig deeper in what is a very rich and diverse literature, then it will have served its purpose.

Acknowledgements

The publishers are grateful to the following for permission to reproduce copyright material:

Plate 1 courtesy of Private Collection/The Bridgeman Art Library; plates 2, 5, 6, 7 and 9 courtesy of the National Portrait Gallery, London; plate 3 courtesy of the Manchester Art Gallery, UK/The Bridgeman Art Library; plate 4 courtesy of Museum of London, UK/The Bridgeman Art Library; plate 8 courtesy of Bristol Museums and Art Galleries; plate 10 courtesy of Graeme Peacock Photographic Imagery (www.graeme-peacock.com).

In some instances we have been unable to trace the owners of copyright material, and we would appreciate any information that would enable us to do so.

Chronology

1815

March Corn Law passed which restricts import of foreign corn until domestic price reaches 80s a quarter. Provokes riots in London

March Newspaper Stamp Duty increased to 4d per copy in an attempt to restrict readership of radical papers

March On Tyneside, keelmen involved in disturbances during labour dispute

15 June Battle of Waterloo ends Napoleon's '100 days' campaign and signals final defeat of France in wars which had begun in 1792

April First British army Gurkha regiments founded. Became King's Own First Gurkha rifles

June Congress of Vienna signed

6 July Samuel Whitbread commits suicide

October A strike by seamen is accompanied by some violence

20 November Second Treaty of Paris imposes harsher terms on France than the First (signed on 30 May 1814) because of '100 days' campaign. France's territory reduced to its 1789 boundaries and it had to pay a 700 million franc indemnity and house an army of occupation

5 November 'United States of the Ionian Islands', created under British protection, established

9 November Humphry Davy announces to Royal Society invention of the first oil-burning miners' safety lamp

1816

April Income Tax (introduced in 1799) abolished

April–June Widespread disturbances involving rural labourers in East Anglia

June George Canning enters Liverpool's Cabinet as President of Board of Control. Economic crisis precipitates numerous bank failures

July–August	Food riots
November–December	Further food riots
October	First cheap (2d) edition of Cobbett's *Political Register* published
2 December	Spa Fields Riots in London
	Jane Austen's *Emma* is published

1817

28 January	Crowds attack Prince Regent's coach after State Opening of Parliament, provoking restrictions on public meetings and suspension of Habeas Corpus
February–March	Further food riots
10 March	Troops end the radical 'March of the Blanketeers'
9 June	'Pentrich Rising' in Derbyshire
18 July	Death of Jane Austen
	William Grenville retires from leadership of the Whig party. His grouping in Parliament breaks up, paving the way for its assimilation with the Tory party
6 November	Princess Charlotte, the Prince Regent's only legitimate child, dies aged 21
21 December	Sir Thomas Hyslop defeated an Indian Maratha army at Mahidput. This action increases British control in India
	High Tory Magazine *Blackwood's Edinburgh Magazine* founded
	David Ricardo's *Principles of Political Economy and Taxation* published
	Trustee Savings Banks established by Act of Parliament

1818

January	F.J. Robinson (later Goderich) becomes President of the Board of Trade
13 January	In India, treaty of mutual friendship signed between British and Maharana Bhim Singh. Rajputana states come under British protection. Most of India now under British influence
	Vestries Act (Sturges Bourne Act) establishes a new system of electing parish officials on basis on landownership
2 June	Surrender of the Marathas to British forces at end of Anglo-Maratha war begun in 1817. Maratha Empire in India comes to an end
	Habeas Corpus Act re-established
July–August	Manchester spinners strike; several disturbances take place

August	General Election gives Liverpool's Tories a majority in the Commons
	Foundation of the Church Building Society. Parliament grants £1 million for building of Anglican churches
27 September– 15 November	Congress of Aix-la-Chapelle held. Army of occupation withdrawn from France
15 November	Quadruple Alliance of Britain, Russia, Austria and Prussia renewed
2 November	Death of Samuel Romilly; George Tierney becomes opposition leader in the Commons
	Mary Shelley's *Frankenstein* published
1819	Factory Act prohibits children under nine years from working in cotton factories and prescribed maximum 12-hour working day for children of 9–13, but no inspection regime to supervise or ensure compliance
	Poor Relief Act (Sturges Bourne Act) enables parishes to appoint a poor law committee. Voting powers would be determined by amount of land ratepayers held
July	Anti-Catholic riots take place in Liverpool, where there has recently been substantial Catholic Irish immigration
16 August	'Peterloo Massacre' by yeomanry in Manchester
	'Peel's Act' recommends return to the Gold Standard by 1823
	Singapore is founded as a commercial outpost by the East India Company
1820	
29 January	Death of George III, aged 81; his eldest son, the Prince Regent, succeeds him as George IV
February	Cato Street conspiracy uncovered
March	Disturbances in Ross-shire and Sutherland in protest against the forcible movement of peasants and smallholders out of large landed estates in the Highlands: the Highland Clearances
April	General election, necessitated by the King's death, confirms majority for Liverpool's Tory government
5 May	Castlereagh's 'State Paper' attacks the idea that one state can forcibly interfere in the affairs of another. The Paper was a criticism of the 'Holy Alliance' of established European powers trying to prevent nationalist activity in smaller states or would-be states
June	Caroline returns to England to take up her duties as Queen. Wins much popular support, especially in London

23 October–
17 December Congress held at Troppau. Britain decided to send only observers

November King's attempt to divorce Queen foiled when Liverpool abandons the Bill of 'Pains and Penalties' in face of dwindling parliamentary support

12 December Canning resigns from Cabinet over Caroline affair

1821

May Bank of England resumes cash payments and effects a return to the Gold Standard

July George IV crowned; Caroline unsuccessfully attempts a forced entry

August Queen Caroline dies. Riots in London as her funeral cortege passes

12 January–12 May Congress of Laibach (a reconvening of Troppau) held

Small parliamentary borough of Grampound (Cornwall) disfranchised for bribery in the 1820 general election. Its two members were transferred to Yorkshire, England's largest county

Constable's *The Hay Wain* is painted

Census reveals that population of England and Wales has increased from 10.2 million to 12.0 million since 1811

1822

January Peel succeeds Sidmouth as Home Secretary

May Lord John Russell introduces a parliamentary reform bill. It would have removed one of the two MPs from smallest boroughs and transferred the seats to larger towns. Defeated by 269 votes to 164

June Amendment of Navigation Acts to reduce protection given to British shipping

10 June World's first iron steamship, the *Aaron Manby*, recently launched on the Thames crossed the Channel to Le Havre under command of Captain Charles Napier

12 August Viscount Castlereagh commits suicide; Canning replaces him in September and returns to Liverpool's Cabinet

20 October Congress of Verona opens; wider splits within the system are revealed

Widespread agricultural distress affects numerous smaller landowners and tenant farmers

1823

January Huskisson becomes President of the Board of Trade (and enters Cabinet in November); Robinson replaces Vansittart as Chancellor of Exchequer

January   Reciprocity of Duties Act passes. It permits reductions of duties with other countries on a reciprocal basis

March   Greeks revolt against Turkish (Ottoman) rule

May   Daniel O'Connell forms the Catholic Association to press for greater civil liberties for Roman Catholics there

July   Death penalty abolished as penalty for a number of relatively minor offences

Gaols (Prison) Act begins reform of prison system by consolidating and amending previous laws on building and regulating prisons

Anti-Slavery Society founded to press for the abolition of slavery throughout the British empire. Brougham and Wilberforce are among prominent members

1824

5 February   Britain declares war on Burma in response to Burmese threat to invade India. This first Anglo-Burmese war lasts until 1826

February   Combination Acts, prohibiting working men from combining to pursue their interests together, abolished

19 April   Death of Lord Byron at Missolonghi, Greece, aged 36. Byron was there to support Greeks in their struggle for independence

Canning recognizes the independence of Buenos Aires, Mexico and Colombia from Spain

Huskisson and Robinson begin process of reducing customs and excise duties to an average maximum of 20 per cent

Prison Discipline Act establishes further rules for prison management with Justices of the Peace supposed to inspect to ensure that these are being implemented

Royal National Lifeboat Institution founded

Royal Society for the Prevention of Cruelty to Animals founded

National Gallery founded

1825

July   Rights of trade unionists, expanded by 1824 legislation, restricted. Combinations of workmen or masters now only legal if concerned just with wages or hours of work

September   First public steam railway opened; it runs between Stockton and Darlington

November	Banking crisis begins; many private banks go bust
December	Full-blown economic crisis, caused by over-consumption, is under way

1826

24 February	Treaty of Yandaboo ends first Anglo-Burmese War. Burmese territories of Arakan and Tenassarim became part of British empire
April	By the St Petersburg Protocol, Britain and Russia agree the principle of Greek independence
May	Government permitted the Bank of England to establish provincial branches
July	General election confirms a majority for Tory government of Lord Liverpool but many MPs favouring Catholic Emancipation elected in Ireland
December	Canning sends British troops to the River Tagus to defend Portugal from attack by Spain and thus helps to preserve the balance of power
	Attacks on power looms in weaving towns in Lancashire and Yorkshire

1827

5 January	Prince Frederick, Duke of York, heir to the throne, dies aged 63. His younger brother William, Duke of Clarence, becomes heir
17 February	Liverpool suffers a paralytic stroke
February	Peel further consolidates the criminal law, making its operation more consistent
28 March	Illness forces Liverpool to resign
12 April	George Canning appointed prime minister
6 July	Treaty of London signed. Britain, Russia and France agree to support Greeks fighting for independence
8 August	Canning dies; is succeeded by Viscount Goderich
20 October	At naval Battle of Navarino, British, Russian and French fleets destroy Turkish fleet

1828

8 January	Goderich resigns as prime minister; a more purely Tory government under the Duke of Wellington is formed
May	Government reshaped as 'Liberal Tories' or 'Canningites' leave Wellington's administration

May   Test and Corporation Acts repealed by House of Commons; Nonconformists gain equality of political rights

July   Daniel O'Connell elected MP for County Clare but is prohibited by his Catholic religion from taking his seat

    Operation of the corn laws modified with the introduction of a 'sliding scale' which reduced the amount of protection

·   Length of polling in parliamentary elections reduced to eight days; polling stations may be established in more places to speed up the process

    University College, London, founded. Unlike the Universities of Oxford and Cambridge, it is open to Dissenters

1829

April   Roman Catholic Emancipation passed; furious opposition to Wellington and Peel from 'Ultra Tories'

    Duke of Norfolk becomes the first Roman Catholic to sit in the House of Lords

June–July   Food disturbances in Lancashire as prices begin to rise

September   Metropolitan Police Act brings a professional, preventive police force into operation for the first time. Police force operates only in London area but not in the historic City itself

    General Union of Spinners formed in Lancashire by John Doherty

1830

January   Birmingham Political Union founded; other provincial Unions pressing for parliamentary reform rapidly follow

3 February   Britain and France sign a Protocol confirming support for Greek independence

26 June   George IV dies; is succeeded by his brother William IV

July   General election, necessitated by King's death, is held. Whigs make some gains amid revival of pressure for parliamentary reform

August   Beginning of 'Swing Riots' by agricultural labourers (these continue until middle of 1831)

15 September   Opening of the Liverpool to Manchester railway. William Huskisson, MP for Liverpool, becomes the first person to die as a result of an accident on a passenger railway when he was killed on the line's inaugural run

November   Wellington declares government against parliamentary reform. This precipitates a crisis which leads to fall of the government. A Whig/

Liberal-Tory coalition takes over with Earl Grey as prime minister. Government pledges itself to introduce parliamentary reform

National Association for the Protection of Labour attempts to produce more integrated pro-union activity across the trades

Cobbett's *Rural Rides* published

1831

20 January	British government signs Protocol supporting the separation of Belgium from the Netherlands
May	National Union of the Working Classes founded
2 June	Riots in Merthyr begin – the so-called 'Merthyr Rising'
29 June	British and Foreign Temperance Society founded to press for the abolition of alcohol sales
March	Government parliamentary reform bill introduced. Passed by only one vote in the Commons
April	When an amendment to the Reform Bill is passed, government persuades the King to dissolve parliament and call fresh elections
June	General Election produces huge gains for reformers. Government certain of large majorities in the Commons
7 October	House of Lords rejects reform bill. Pro-reform riots ensue in Nottingham, Derby and Bristol
17 October	First case of cholera reported in Sunderland, beginning a national outbreak. Disease reaches epidemic proportions in Britain over the next 15 months
	Vestries Act (Hobhouse Act) – new system for electing members of parish vestries. Election could be by secret ballot if ratepayers agree
	Truck Act passed, prohibiting workers to be paid in goods or in tokens issued by employers
	Census reveals that population of England and Wales has increased from 12.0 million to 13.9 million since 1821

1832

January	King agrees to Grey's request to create pro-reform peers if the House of Lords continues to block parliamentary reform
17 March	Establishment of the Carlton Club to coordinate Tory/Conservative party both in Westminster and outside
22 March	Third reading of Reform Bill passes with majority of 116 in the Commons

8 May   After defeat on a vote in the Lords, the government resigns

9–15 May   'The May Days' are a political crisis over reform with much agitation and many disturbances in British towns. King asks Duke of Wellington to form a government but he is unable to do so

17 May   Grey resumes as prime minister with a further pledge from the King to create peers if the government needs it

4 June   House of Lords finally passes Reform Bill

7 June   Royal assent given to Representation of the People (Reform) Act in England and Wales

July   Representation Act for Scotland receives royal assent

August   Representation Act for Ireland receives royal assent

    Poor Law Commission set up. Its report will heavily influence the Poor Law Amendment Act (1834) which radically altered the principles governing the granting and distribution of poor relief

December   General election gives reformers a parliamentary majority of about 300 over Tories who opposed reform

Who's Who

Addington, Henry: See Sidmouth.

Althorp, Viscount (John Charles, 3rd Earl Spencer) (1782–1845): Whig politician. Born into one of the most aristocratic families in Britain, he followed family tradition by becoming a Whig politician. As Chancellor of the Exchequer and leader of the Whigs in the House of Commons, he did much to facilitate parliamentary reform during the crisis of 1830–2. He also piloted slavery reform through the Commons in 1833 and helped to draft the Poor Law Amendment Act of 1834.

Attwood, Thomas (1783–1856): Radical politician and currency reformer. He founded the Birmingham Political Union early in 1830 to press for parliamentary reform, particularly in order to improve representation of the wealth-creating middle classes. He was an effective speaker and contributed substantially to the success of the reformers' campaign. He served as MP for Birmingham from 1832–9 and promoted local government reform in the 1830s before declaring his support for universal manhood suffrage. He presented the first Chartist petition to Parliament.

Bamford, Samuel (1788–1872): Weaver, writer and radical politician. He was born in Lancashire and became a radical during the trade depression at the end of the Napoleonic wars. He was a strong supporter of 'Orator Hunt', with whom he was imprisoned after Peterloo. He became less active after 1820, devoting more of his attention to journalism and other writing. Later he supported Chartist objectives but opposed the use of physical force. His *Passages in the Life of a Radical* (1840–4) has become an important source for historians of radicalism in the first half of the nineteenth century.

Bentham, Jeremy (1748–1832): Political philosopher. He was much influenced by the ideas of the European enlightenment and published an *Introduction to the Principles of Morals and Legislation* in 1789. He is best known for developing 'utilitarianism', a political philosophy which judged the appropriateness of systems according to their practical utility. He also influenced the development of classical economics. He founded the *Westminster Review* in 1823 to argue for radical reform. Parliamentary reform, which he supported for most of his life, received royal assent the day after his death.

Brandreth, Jeremiah (1788?–1817): Born at Wilford, near Nottingham, he was a hosiery worker or 'stockinger' by trade. He led the Pentrich Rising in 1817. Little is known about his background but he was literate and able to rouse fellow workers with passionate speeches and promises of much better things if they followed him to revolutionary glory. When the Rising failed, he was arrested, charged with treason and hanged.

Brougham, Henry Peter, 1st Baron (1778–1868): Whig politician, lawyer and writer. He helped found the intellectual journal *Edinburgh Review* in 1802, writing large numbers of articles for it. He took up a range of reformist causes, including Catholic emancipation and the abolition of slavery in British colonies. He was also legal adviser to Queen Caroline and acted in her defence during the trial for divorce in 1820. He joined Grey's cabinet as Lord Chancellor in 1830. His keen wit, frequently wounding words and taste for manipulating public opinion all made him a difficult colleague.

Burdett, Sir Francis (1770–1844). Radical politician. He entered Parliament in 1796. His commitment to a range of reforms irritated more conservatively minded MPs, including the Younger Pitt. After 1815, he was accused by more extreme radicals, such as Hunt, of not being wholehearted in the cause, but he did introduce a bill calling for manhood suffrage and annual parliaments in 1818. As he grew older he became yet more cautious and made numerous attacks on those he called 'demagogues' who led the people astray.

Canning, George (1770–1827): Tory politician and journalist. He entered Parliament in 1793 on the younger Pitt's recommendation and remained intellectually and practically indebted to Pitt for inspiration and guidance. He served as Foreign Secretary under Portland (1807–9) and, after a long period either out of office or in junior posts, he became Foreign Secretary again in 1822. In this post, he supported the aspirations of nationalists seeking to break free from continental European empires. He served in Liverpool's Cabinet until the latter's stroke and succeeded him in April 1827. He was prime minister for only four months, dying in office on 12 August. He was a controversial figure. Many of Liverpool's ministers opposed his liberal policies, not least concerning Catholic Emancipation, and refused to serve under him. He was a brilliant speaker and had a waspish wit. The former made him one of the most popular politicians of his day outside Westminster; the latter brought him envy, suspicion and dislike inside Parliament.

Carlile, Richard (1790–1843): Radical journalist and tinplate worker. His journalism was strongly influenced by Thomas Paine, whose *Age of Reason* began his intellectual journey towards freethought. Much of his writing was irreligious, bringing him into conflict with other radicals. He was arrested for making blasphemous statements in 1819 and imprisoned for six years. From prison, he published the weekly journal *Republican*. During the Reform crisis, he took over the Rotunda in London which, with Robert Taylor, he made into an important radical centre. He was arrested again, charged with seditious libel and imprisoned for 30 months.

Caroline of Brunswick-Wolfenbüttel (1768–1821): Queen from 1820–21. She married Prince George, heir to the British throne, in 1795 but the couple were never compatible. They largely ignored each other after their daughter Charlotte was born in the following year. Caroline left England in 1813 and toured Europe, famously returning in 1820 to begin her duties as Queen, though George IV had stated his intention of divorcing her. The ensuing 'divorce scandal' made both far-from-innocent parties a laughing stock. Caroline avoided divorce when the prime minister, to the King's disgust, abandoned proceedings to strip her of the title in the face of rapidly diminishing parliamentary support. George refused his unwanted Queen admittance to his coronation in June 1821, though she attempted forcible, and farcical, entry. She died six weeks later.

Castlereagh, Viscount (Robert Stewart) (1769–1822): Tory politician. He was instrumental in formulating policies, and negotiating details, for the Act of Union of Ireland with Britain in 1800. He impressed the younger Pitt early in his career and subsequently held government office for virtually the whole of his career: as President of the Board of Control (1802–9), Secretary for War (1809–12) and Foreign Secretary (1812–22). An able man, with a keen eye for detail, he was a firm anti-reformer. He was intimately involved both in the management of the French wars and, from 1814, the 'Congress' diplomacy which followed them. His main objective was a stable balance of power between European states to preserve peace and aid Britain's commercial development. His mental health was more fragile than appeared on the surface and he committed suicide in August 1822.

Chandos, Viscount (Richard Temple, 2nd Duke of Buckingham and Chandos) (1797–1861): Tory politician. From an established landed family, he opposed Catholic Emancipation and was a staunch defender of agricultural protection. His parliamentary career was not distinguished and his extravagance precipitated a series of financial crises, most notably in 1848 when the entire contents of the family home at Stowe was put up for auction. He is best known for 'the Chandos Amendment' to the Whigs' parliamentary reform bill. The government reluctantly accepted it in the hope of easing their bill's passage through the House of Lords. It gave votes to tenants of medium-sized and larger farms and was to prove a significant factor in the Tories' political revival of the 1830s and early 1840s.

Cobbett, William (1763–1835): Radical journalist and parliamentary reformer. His early writings were anti-reformist and he was scathing in his attacks on Thomas Paine. He was converted to radicalism by the effects of the financial policies adopted by the younger Pitt. These, he believed, massively increased the National Debt and led to increased tax burdens for ordinary folk. Cobbett matured into the most prolific, and probably most influential, of radical journalists. His best-known journal was the weekly *Political Register*, published almost continuously from 1802 to 1832, and *Rural Rides* (1830), the result of extensive tours through the agricultural areas of southern England from 1825. He correctly predicted the outbreak of rural distress known as the Swing Riots. He became MP for the newly enfranchised borough of Oldham in 1832.

Doherty, John (1797–1854): Radical politician and trade union organiser. He attempted to establish general unions of working men across the trades. He was an active factory reformer and became influenced by the cooperative movement. He was instrumental in organizing the Grand General Union of Operative cotton spinners in 1829. This was an important landmark in the development of national, rather than merely local, trade unions. He tried to establish a 'General Union of Trades' and published a *United Trades Co-Operative Journal* in 1830, which publicized the activities of his National Association for the Protection of Labour. The strikes he organized often failed and his ideas for national unions proved both premature and grandiose.

Durham, Baron (John George Lambton) (1792–1840): Whig politician from a wealthy landed family in County Durham. Known by the nickname 'Radical Jack', he made many reformist speeches after he entered Parliament in 1813 and produced his own parliamentary reform proposals in 1816. He became Lord Privy Seal in Grey's Cabinet of 1830 and was one of the Committee of Four who drafted the Whig reform bill. He favoured the introduction of a secret ballot but was outvoted.

Eldon, 1st Earl (John Scott) (1751–1838): Tory politician and lawyer. His father was a prosperous coal merchant from Newcastle-on-Tyne. Eldon was first appointed Lord Chancellor in 1801 and held that office continuously from 1807 to 1827. Politically, he was noted for his resistance to reform and his antipathy to extra-parliamentary reformers. In 1819, he introduced the Six Acts to the House of Lords with relish. He also opposed the repeal of the Test and Corporation Acts and Catholic Emancipation and had little time for the Canningite wing of the Tory party. He spoke vigorously against parliamentary reform in 1831–2 and spent his later years opposing Whig legal reforms and their proposals for Irish church reform.

George III (1738–1820): George was the son of Frederick Prince of Wales and Princess Augusta of Saxe-Gotha. His father having died in 1751, he succeeded his grandfather, George II, in 1760. He was the first Hanoverian monarch to be born in England. Aware that the Hanoverian, and therefore German, monarchy had never been popular, he emphasized his Britishness. Indeed, he was frequently portrayed as a symbol both of national unity and the virtues of an established monarchy in the war against revolutionary France, which began in 1793. He was a dutiful, conscientious monarch if one who lacked imagination and, sometimes, insight. He had numerous blind spots. He was stubborn and did not like challenges to his authority. As a Protestant monarch, he was deeply suspicious of Roman Catholicism. In 1801, he broke with his long-serving prime minister, the Younger Pitt, over the latter's proposals for Catholic emancipation. From the late 1780s onwards, he suffered bouts of mental instability and was finally declared unfit to discharge his duties in 1811. His eldest son took over as Prince Regent.

George IV (1762–1830): He was the eldest son of George III and his wife, Charlotte Sophia of Mecklenburgh-Strelitz. As a young man, he was wilful, extravagant and dissolute and age did not mellow him much. He was a man of some aesthetic sensibility but little political sense. A tendency to posture and a notoriously short temper reduced his influence further. He contracted an unwise, and illegal, marriage to a Catholic commoner, Maria Fitzherbert, in 1785 and a contrived and loveless, yet legal, one to a Protestant Princess, Caroline of Brunswick, in 1795. Their only child, Charlotte, predeceased him in 1817. He discharged the duties of a monarch from 1811 when he was created Prince Regent because of his father's mental incapacity. He frequently disagreed with his long-serving prime minister, Lord Liverpool, and tried to dismiss him when Parliament would not agree to his divorce from Caroline after he finally became King in 1820. He was especially unpopular in London, though post-Coronation tours to Ireland (1821) and Scotland (1822) increased his standing in those countries and showed at least some awareness that he was trying to rule over a United Kingdom comprising four nations. He meddled in the formation of ministries although, once established, increasingly cohesive Cabinets were able to ignore both his wishes and his tantrums. Towards the end of his life, religious reforms were effected against his rooted opposition.

Goderich, Viscount: See Robinson.

Grenville, William Wyndham (1759–1834): Pittite and Whig politician. His early career was strongly linked to that of the Younger Pitt, of whom he was an exact contemporary. He headed the brief so-called 'Ministry of All the Talents' in 1806–7, After it fell, he never held office again, though he remained at the centre of political life till 1822. He was, in effect, leader of the Whig party from 1807–17 although he was far less keen on parliamentary and economic reforms than the Foxite Whigs who comprised the majority of the party. He formally resigned in 1817 and most of his followers reconnected with their Tory past when they joined Liverpool in government in 1822.

Grey, 2nd Earl (Charles Grey, Lord Howick) (1764–1845): Whig politician. He was a leading member of the Foxite Whigs who maintained a reformist course in the 1790s. He introduced two reform bills into the Commons in 1793 and 1797, both of which were defeated by large majorities. He was briefly in Cabinet during the Talents Ministry of 1806–7 as First Lord of the Admiralty and Foreign Secretary, after which he remained in opposition for 23 years. He became leader of the Whigs on Grenville's resignation in 1817 but achieved little. It was only the extraordinary set of circumstances which deprived Wellington of a sufficiently broad range of support during his government of 1828 to 1830 which finally brought Grey back into office. As prime minister, he displayed a single-mindedness and determination which had rarely been a feature of his earlier political career in steering a highly controversial parliamentary reform bill on to the statute book. It was his great achievement and is marked by a large monument which stands at the top of Grey Street in Newcastle-on-Tyne. He remained prime minister until 1834.

Hume, Joseph (1777–1855): Radical MP. He made a reputation for himself by arguing that the government's handling of Peterloo and other political disturbances had been heavy-handed. On policy, he was heavily influenced by the ideas of Jeremy Bentham. He played a key role in establishing the Select Committee which recommended the repeal of the Combination Acts and he supported both religious toleration and parliamentary reform. During the reform crisis, he acted as an intermediary between Whig politicians at Westminster and extra-parliamentary reformers.

Hunt, Henry ('Orator') (1773–1835): Radical politician from a farming background. Following William Cobbett, his political leanings were originally loyalist. By the end of the French Wars, however, he had established himself as a vigorous speaker, well known both in Bristol and London, in defence of the interests of ordinary people against a corrupt political elite. He also attacked the smaller shopkeepers and tradesmen who saw themselves as a 'privileged class above . . . the labourer'. He developed the peaceful mass meeting into a key feature of radical protest. He addressed the Spa Fields Meeting in London in December 1816 but is best known for his role as key speaker at the meeting in St Peter's Fields, Manchester, in August 1819 which became known as the 'Peterloo Massacre'. He was imprisoned for two years and, from prison, developed his literary talents as a writer of radical pamphlets. He was radical MP for Preston from 1830–2. He opposed the Whig reform bill as insufficiently radical and damaging to the interests of the working man. He also introduced one of the first petitions for female suffrage. His stance, as one of the very few radical MPs, brought him much criticism and split radical opinion. It contributed to his defeat in the general election of 1832.

Huskisson, William (1770–1830): Pittite Tory politician. In the 1810s, with government debt high and the currency often unstable, Liverpool relied on Huskisson for advice on financial and economic matters. He entered Liverpool's Cabinet in 1823. His trade liberalization policies as President of the Board of Trade made him distrusted and unpopular with many landowning Tories. He also served in Canning and Goderich's governments but resigned from Wellington's government, with other 'liberal' colleagues, in 1828. Out of office, he supported Catholic Emancipation. He retained political ambitions and had visions of leading a coalition government of Liberal Tories and old Whigs. This might have happened had Huskisson not been killed in an accident at the opening of the Liverpool–Manchester railway in September 1830.

Liverpool, 2nd Earl of (Robert Banks Jenkinson, Lord Hawkesbury) (1770–1828): Pittite politician. He held a series of major government posts, including Foreign Secretary, Home Secretary and Secretary for War and the Colonies, becoming prime minister in 1812. He had a high reputation for efficiency and was one of the best speakers in the House of Lords. In office, he built on the legacy of the Younger Pitt. He favoured modest, cautious reforms in administration and the reduction of tariffs to boost trade and enhance national prosperity. Like Pitt, he opposed parliamentary reform and followed repressive policies when radicalism appeared to be building up a dangerous head of steam, as it did from 1815 to 1820. Knowing that Roman Catholic emancipation was divisive, he refused to commit his government one way or the other. Though this led to his being criticised for lack of leadership, keeping emancipation an 'open question' probably extended his government's life. Liverpool held the prime ministership for longer than anyone except Walpole. His long tenure of power helped to develop the concept of collective Cabinet responsibility for policies. Cabinet solidarity, backed by usually secure parliamentary majorities, was one of many factors which explain the declining powers of the monarchy in this period.

McCulloch, John Ramsay (commonly J.R.) (1789–1864): Political economist. Largely self-taught in economics, he became one of the most influential political economists of the age. His concern was to apply general ideas about economics to the solution of practical problems, such as the size of the national debt and the cost and alleged inefficiency of the English poor law system before 1834. He was Professor of Political Economy at London University from 1828 to 1837 and influenced Peel's thinking on economic issues.

Mackintosh, Sir James (1765–1832): Whig politician and writer. Born near Inverness, he became an MP in 1813 after service in India. He was friendly with Lord Byron, and became an influential figure among the Whig intellectuals and politicians who congregated at Holland House. He wrote many articles for *Edinburgh Review* which advocated moderate reform and, especially, the need for a free press. He also advocated Catholic Emancipation, law reform and independence both for Latin American countries and for Poland.

Melbourne, 2nd Viscount (William Lamb) (1779–1848): Whig and Canningite politician. Although he became an MP in 1806, he made little impact at Westminster until the later 1820s. He began his political career as a Whig but transferred his allegiance to the Canningite group of Tories from about 1816. Canning made him Chief Secretary for Ireland in 1827. He did not support parliamentary reform but resigned from Wellington's government with other Liberal or Canningite Tories in May 1828. He came into Cabinet as Home Secretary in Grey's coalition government of 1830. He was firm in his policies to put down the Swing Riots in 1830–1. He went along with parliamentary reform only because he believed it would restore public confidence in government. He was prime minister in 1834 and from 1835–41.

O'Connell, Daniel (1775–1847): Irish nationalist. After practising successfully as a barrister, he founded the Catholic Association in 1823, which called for Catholic Emancipation, Repeal of the Act of Union, an end to tithe payments to the Anglican church and wider Catholic landownership. He forced the first of these issues when he won the County Clare by-election in 1828. As a Roman Catholic, he was ineligible to take up his parliamentary seat. He supported parliamentary reform in the early 1830s as a means of increasing Irish nationalist influence at Westminster.

Owen, Robert (1771–1858): Manufacturer, philanthropist and socialist thinker. He set up a model cotton factory at New Lanark, with good quality housing and a new system of education for factory children. He believed that society could only advance if masters and workmen cooperated for mutual benefit. His ideas, which challenged the capitalist system, formed the basis of the nineteenth-century Co-Operative movement.

Palmerston, 3rd Viscount (Henry John Temple) (1784–1865): Liberal Tory, then Whig, politician. Palmerston's background was Tory and he was in minor office as early as 1807. He was Secretary at War from 1809–27. He favoured Roman Catholic emancipation and became increasingly frustrated during the 1820s with those Tories who believed that repression was the only way of keeping the old order. He entered the Cabinet under Goderich and resigned from Wellington's government with the Canningites in 1828. His break with the Tories proved to be permanent. In Grey's ministry he became Foreign Secretary, a post he held whenever the Whigs were in office, until 1851. He was prime minister twice, in 1855–8 and 1859–65.

Peel, Sir Robert (1788–1850): Tory politician. Peel came from an industrial family, his father having made a fortune as a cotton manufacturer. Once in parliament, his rise was swift. He was Chief Secretary for Ireland from 1812–18, where he was staunchly pro-Protestant. As Home Secretary under Liverpool, he pursued a range of administrative reforms. He also persuaded Wellington of the need for Catholic emancipation in 1829, which provoked deep divisions within the Tory party and much personal hostility towards Peel. He refused to join a Tory government pledged to parliamentary reform in 1832, though he emerged as leader of the Tory opposition (1835–41) and prime minister (1834–5 and 1841–6). His attempts to appeal to a wider section of society helped to modernize the Tory party, which was increasingly known as the Conservative party from the 1830s. Peel was methodical, organized, always sure of his facts and tended to dominate in debates. He was perhaps the most effective, and certainly one of the most controversial, politicians of the age.

Place, Francis (1771–1854): Radical politician. He was born into humble circumstances and apprenticed as a tailor. He was a leading radical organizer in the 1790s, helping to found the London Corresponding Society. He became a prosperous master-manufacturer working in Charing Cross but retained both his radical views and his talent for organization and lobbying. With Joseph Hume, he organized the campaign to get the Combination Acts repealed and was also active during the reform crisis of 1830–32. He later helped to draft the People's Charter.

Ricardo, David (1772–1823): Political economist. Born into a family of Jewish bankers, he was influenced by Adam Smith's views about free trade and became one of his most distinguished and influential disciples. He argued that the poor laws impoverished rural society, operating inefficiently, depressing rental values and therefore inhibiting investment. The Corn Law of 1815, he argued, engendered social tensions by advantaging landowners at the expense of both manufacturers and labourers. These and other views developed in the *Principles of Political Economy* (1817) influenced economic reformers in Liverpool's government, particularly Huskisson and Robinson. He became an MP from 1819 and was thus in a good position to put his case to ministers. His ideas underpinned trade liberalization policies in the 1820s.

Robinson, Frederick John (also Viscount Goderich and 1st Earl of Ripon) (1782–1859): Tory politician. Robinson, who became an MP in 1806, occupied a number of offices, mostly concerned with economic affairs. He was responsible for piloting the new Corn Law through the Commons in 1815. As Chancellor of the Exchequer from 1823, he developed reformist economic policies alongside Huskisson. A friend of Canning, he served in his brief ministry and became ennobled as Viscount Goderich. George IV, knowing his limited leadership skills, asked him to form a government when Canning died but his motive was to increase his own influence. Goderich's ministry was a failure, lasting only five months. It never faced parliament. Like other 'Liberal Tories', Goderich left Wellington's government in May 1828. He returned to office in Grey's coalition government of 1830. He was created an Earl in 1833 and was a cabinet minister again under Peel from 1841 to 1846.

Romilly, Samuel (1757–1818): Whig politician. He only held government office once, as Solicitor-General in the Talents Ministry of 1806–7 but he was an influential and highly principled figure. He carried a number of important law reforms not least on debt and against excessive punishments for criminal offences. He was also vocal in support of the abolition of the slave trade. Respect for his abilities grew in the Whig party and it is possible that he might have become its leader. However, his mental health was not robust and he committed suicide in 1818.

Russell, Lord John (1792–1878): Whig politician. A member of one of the great Whig families, he had a long career, and was prime minister from 1846–52. In the early nineteenth century, he was notable mainly for parliamentary reform proposals. He introduced an unsuccessful reform bill in 1822 and was one of the four members of the Committee selected by Earl Grey which drafted the Reform Bill in early 1831. His determination to redistribute a large number of parliamentary boroughs caused massive alarm in parliament when the Bill was presented. Russell was anxious to pass a major reform, believing that it might settle the Reform question for a generation. He said at the time that he anticipated parliamentary reform would be a 'final solution' to a great constitutional question. This explains his nickname of 'Finality Jack'.

Sidmouth, Viscount (Henry Addington) (1757–1844): Tory politician. As Henry Addington, he was George III's choice to replace the Younger Pitt as prime minister in 1801 but his tenure of office was not successful. He served under Grenville as Lord President of the Council, a post he also held very briefly just before Perceval's assassination. He was Home Secretary from 1812–22 in Liverpool's government. Here he faced numerous challenges, largely because of the rapid growth of radical politics after the war, and especially the large public meetings which he believed were a threat to public order and a cloak for revolutionary activity. He responded by introducing restrictions on meetings and taxes on the press. Radicals considered him repressive. He was certainly no administrative reformer.

Spence, Thomas (1750–1814): Bookseller and author. Although he died before our period begins his ideas remained influential. He believed that, originally, men had held land in common and should now reclaim their rights. He believed in land nationalization or a form of agrarian communism. From 1815–20, some of the most violent radicals, such as Arthur Thistlewood, were attracted by his ideas. Land reform movements were a feature of radical politics in Britain throughout the nineteenth century and testify further to the abiding influence of his thinking.

Taylor, Robert (1784–1844): Deistical writer, lecturer and radical politician. He was strongly influenced by Richard Carlile in the 1820s. He was imprisoned both for debt and for blasphemy in the late 1820s and used prison as a place in which to write and publish radical material. He preached regularly on deistical themes at the Rotunda in Blackfriars. This activity led to further imprisonment for blasphemy in 1831. His unorthodox religious views alienated him from many radical politicians.

Thistlewood, Arthur (1774–1820): Revolutionary. He become involved with Spencean land reformers in 1814 and was a member of the committee which organised the Spa Fields demonstration in 1816. He was also involved in the disturbances that followed. He is best known for his involvement in the Cato Street conspiracy, which was infiltrated at an early stage by a government spy. Thistlewood was arrested on a charge of high treason. He was convicted and suffered both hanging and decapitation at Newgate.

Vansittart, Nicholas (1st Baron Bexley) (1766–1851): Tory politician. He entered parliament in 1796 and supported both Pitt's wartime policies and his suppression of radical politics. He is best known as Liverpool's Chancellor of the Exchequer from 1812 to 1823. Here he inherited a massive debt but his attempts to improve national finances were ham-fisted and he lost the support both of the Bank of England and of many in his own party. After being replaced at the Exchequer by Robinson, he stayed in government as Chancellor of the Duchy of Lancaster and with a peerage.

Victoria (1819–1901): Victoria's reign would last from 1837 to 1901 and become the longest in British history. She came to the throne only as the result of fortuitous deaths during our period. She was the daughter of the fourth son of George III, Edward Augustus, Duke of Kent, and his wife, Mary Louisa Victoria of Saxe-Coburg Gotha. Her father died in 1820 but she would in any case have given precedence in succession to her father's three elder brothers and their legitimate children. Of these brothers in order of their birth, George IV died in 1830, Frederick Augustus in 1827 and she succeeded William IV on his death in 1837. None of them had surviving legitimate children. George IV's only legitimate child, Princess Charlotte, died two years before Victoria was born. Frederick had no children and William IV's ten known children by Dorothea Jordan were all illegitimate. To compound all of this fortuity, there are strong reasons for believing that the Duke of Kent was not Victoria's father anyway. Hereditary succession is subject to any number of quirks of fate and unwittingly supposititious progeny. In coming to the throne at all, Victoria benefited from many of these.

Wellington, 1st Duke of (Arthur Wellesley) (1769–1852): Soldier and Tory politician. Wellington had enormous prestige as the hero of the Battle of Waterloo. This made him an important member of every Tory government (except the two brief ones headed by Canning and Goderich) from 1819 to 1846. He was prime minister from 1828–30. Wellington was instinctively conservative and experience tended further to confirm his instincts. He could, however, see the need for careful reform when occasion demanded. He therefore changed his mind on Catholic Emancipation and reluctantly saw the necessity for some kind of parliamentary reform, though he considered the Whigs' Reform Act dangerously radical. He was a hard-working prime minister but, being used as a military man to giving orders, found the political arts of compromise and dissimulation difficult to master.

William IV (1765–1837): He was the third son of George III and his wife, Caroline of Mecklenburgh-Strelitz and, as such, did not expect to become King. For most of his life, he had been a sailor. He had limited talent but, as a member of the royal family, he rose high, becoming Admiral of the Fleet in 1811 and Lord High Admiral in 1827. He did not become heir to the throne until his elder brother, Frederick Augustus, died in 1827. He was unfortunate in coming to the throne in 1830 just as the parliamentary reform issue was becoming critical for the first time in a decade. He handled the crisis poorly. Political insiders frequently commented not only on his inexperience but his ineptitude. He was disrespectfully known as 'silly Billy'. He was fundamentally opposed to reform but lacked both the ability and power to prevent its passing. He had some success, however, in persuading anti-reformers that their attempt to delay the inevitable was not only futile but dangerous to the established order. He had married Princess Adelaide of Saxe-Meiningen in 1818 but the marriage was childless.

Glossary

Absolute government: A form of government in which there is no limit or restraint on the power that can be exercised by a leader or leading group. Someone exercising such rule, or supporting it, is often called an 'absolutist'.

Agnostic: One who feels that there is not enough evidence to determine whether God exists or not, or that nothing can be known about the existence of God. It follows that an agnostic would not (for other than cynical reasons) be a member of any orthodox church.

Anglo-American War, 1812–15: A conflict which is now little remembered in Britain, but which significantly added to the economic difficulties the country experienced towards the end of the Napoleonic Wars. It was caused by a number of disputes between the two nations, including American attempts to break Britain's naval blockade of France and border disputes between the United States and British Canada. The conflict was bitter on America's northeastern seaboard but neither country could establish a decisive advantage before the Treaty of Ghent brought the war to a close.

Arable farming: The farming of crops. In Britain, arable farming usually refers to the cultivation of corn, especially wheat, barley or oats. In England, the most corn is grown in the south and east of the country where the predominant weather is sunnier and drier.

Arbitrary government: Government in which the exercise of authority is unrestrained. In some contexts, the phrase can also imply government which depends on particular prejudices or whims rather than on the outcome of rational deliberation between alternative policies.

Atheist: A person who denies the existence of God. In this period, atheists could not become members of parliament or hold government office.

Backbench member of parliament: In this period, an adult male elected to, or selected for, parliament who does not hold any government office or act as a senior figure in the opposition. Some backbenchers in the early nineteenth century were independent of any political party and refused to accept party labels; others were happy to be known as 'Whigs' or 'Tories' but might exercise their own judgement on whether they supported their party on an issue or not.

Balance of power: In diplomacy, this phrase is used to describe a situation in which no one power, or group of allied powers, can exert undue pressure on other states on account of larger territory or greater resources. In our period, British politicians and diplomats were generally trying to ensure that no European power became too powerful, thus threatening the settlement which had been agreed at Vienna in 1814–15.

Cabinet: The collective name for a group of senior ministers who, between them, determine government policy. In our period the role of the Cabinet was becoming more sharply defined. Cabinet members were beginning to accept collective responsibility for decisions, whether or not individual members disagreed about specific policies. Also, the Cabinet could present to Parliament policies with which the monarch disagreed.

Catholic emancipation: By legislation passed in 1829, Roman Catholics in the United Kingdom were entitled to vote in parliamentary elections and to be elected or appointed to most local or national positions of responsibility.

Church of England: The official, or state, church of England, sometimes known as 'the Anglican church' or 'the Established Church'. It came into being during the Reformation of the sixteenth century and its status was ensured by the role of the monarch as the head of the church. Appointment of senior clerics also involved monarch and government. Bishops were members of the House of Lords and thus part of the process of making laws. In our period, many members of the Church of England saw the repeal of the Test and Corporations Acts and Catholic Emancipation both as direct attacks on the status and privileges of their Church and a means of weakening the established order.

City of London: The small area, towards the east of the modern capital city, around the old city walls. It housed the main financial and commercial structures not just of London but of England. Often referred to just as 'the City', its population was much smaller than that of London as a whole, though it generated a disproportionate amount of the capital's wealth.

Coalition government: A government in which power is shared and the ministers forming the government come from more than one party. This situation has been relatively rare since the late nineteenth century, although coalitions have been normal during wartime. In our period, when party allegiances were less tight, coalition governments were more common. Those formed by Canning (1827), Goderich (1827) and Grey (1830) were all coalitions.

Committee of secrecy: A committee consisting of members of parliament in effect appointed by the government to hear evidence about possible conspiracies and treasonable activity. After hearing the evidence, the committee reported its findings to parliament.

Constitution: The body of rules, codes and practices which govern how a state is organized, how power is exercised and how its laws are formulated and put into practice. In the United Kingdom, although codes and practices are extensive, there is no overall written constitution, as in the United States, which can act as a universal reference point to determine, for example, whether power is being properly exercised.

Cooperative movement: A movement, whose members were mostly from the working classes, which encouraged people to trade for their mutual benefit. In the case of one of the earliest Co-Operative Societies, founded in Rochdale in 1844, 28 working men each subscribed £1 to set up a fund for the purchase of essential items. Cooperative principles were advocated in the early nineteenth century, many of them deriving from the ideas of Robert Owen. Owen's schemes attempted to minimize the impact of competition which, he believed, favoured the stronger members of a community at the expense of those with less property and fewer resources.

Corn laws: Legislation designed to help British landowners and farmers against foreign competition. Such 'protective legislation' had been in force since the seventeenth century but the most important, and controversial, corn law was passed in 1815. It prohibited foreign corn being imported until the domestic price reached the very high level of 80s (£4) a quarter. The Corn Law was widely condemned by political radicals, and many other town dwellers, as imposing a tax on those least able to afford it – working people – because it kept the price of bread artificially high. Landowners were accused of passing laws which benefited only themselves.

Country banks: Local banks, often containing only a single branch, which sprang up in the eighteenth century. Their origins usually lay in other activities. Successful lawyers or traders might establish a private bank using funds paid in by their clients. They made use of 'bills of exchange' as forms of credit and could apply for licences to issue their own bank notes. At the beginning of our period, more than 300 were in existence. Some expanded and were very creditworthy. Others were very vulnerable to collapse during adverse trading conditions. The system was virtually destroyed by the banking crisis of 1825–6 and a system of 'joint-stock' banks (where the capital of the bank was held jointly) was encouraged by government legislation passed in 1826 and 1833.

County constituencies: In England, each county before the 1820s, irrespective of its size or population, sent two members to the House of Commons. All owners of land worth at least 40s (£2) were entitled to vote. County MPs were usually accorded higher status partly because they were nearly all substantial landowners themselves, and land was considered the pre-eminent form of property, but mostly because the electorates were larger than in most boroughs, so county members were directly representing more people.

Customs: Duties levied on goods produced or sold, particularly on goods or commodities coming into, or being exported from, a country. In our period, customs were a major source of revenue for the government.

Democratic government: A government based on the principle of full representation, in which virtually all adults in a state can participate (usually by means of an election) in the process of determining who shall rule. In our period, very few considered extending the vote to women. Radical parliamentary reformers were divided between those who wanted to see the principle of 'one man, one vote' and those who wanted far more to be able to vote but would restrict voters to those who were either property owners or who rented a house – the so-called 'householder franchise'. Almost all MPs were profoundly antagonistic to the idea of democracy.

Dissenters: Those Christians who were not members of the state church the Church of England – and who 'dissented' from its doctrines. In our period, Dissent was growing in both numbers and influence. The largest dissenting churches were the Methodist, Baptist and Congregationalist. Dissenters were particularly numerous in the larger towns.

Economic warfare: This phrase can be used metaphorically to describe any rivalry over trade or industrial production. In our period, however, it refers to the strategy adopted by Napoleon in order to defeat Britain after the Battle of Trafalgar in 1805. That defeat made it impossible for Napoleon to mount an invasion. Instead, he used his immense power in Continental Europe to try to prevent British imports reaching the Continent or raw materials and manufactured goods coming into Britain. Britain retaliated and the later stages of the war saw trade hostilities which led to depression and much unemployment.

Evangelical: A person subscribing to a Protestant Christian faith who believes that the Bible offers direct lessons in moral behaviour and that a Christian should undergo a process of 'conversion' (or rebirth) to a heightened spiritual awareness. In our period, evangelical Christians, both in the Church of England and in dissenting sects, were influential in concentrating attention on a range of moral and social issues, including slavery, poverty and the condition of prisons.

Excise: a tax or 'duty' levied on goods produced or sold *within* a country. In our period, excise duties were specially resented by ordinary people because they represented a tax which made food, drink and many other necessities more expensive than they would otherwise have been.

Freeholders: Literally, people who own land free of any restrictions, such as leases or covenants. In our period, it was an important term since the possession of freehold land was one of the key qualifications for the vote in parliamentary elections, especially in county constituencies.

Friendly Societies: Organisations which collect funds and pay out benefits. They were established to permit people of modest means to club together by paying in small amounts and then to draw on benefits when these were needed. They enabled many poor people to have the dignity of a respectable funeral, for example. Many had an insurance function. They originated in the late eighteenth century and grew fast in our period. Governments increasingly encouraged Friendly Societies as a means of promoting self-help and economic independence among working people.

Gentry: Collective term covering smaller landowners. The amount of land owned varied widely but gentry families were usually comfortably off. Heads of gentry families usually exercised local influence as Justices of the Peace.

Gold standard: Setting the value of paper money and gold against an agreed rate. Its purpose was to tie a nation's currency to the price of gold with the aim of preventing unpredictable fluctuations in the value of money. Britain was 'off the gold standard' from 1797–1821, during which time the Bank of England was permitted to issue notes not tied to any external value.

Government: The collective group responsible for devising policies at national level. In our period, it would be correct to include the monarch of the day in the government, since the monarch could refuse to give 'assent' to legislation proposed in Parliament and still had influence on which people became ministers. Members of the government are called 'Ministers'. However, only the more senior ones, who met regularly to discuss business, formed the Cabinet (see above). Ministers sat in both the House of Commons and the House of Lords.

Government ministers: Collective name given to those who served in central government and who received seals of office from the monarch. A small number of more senior ministers served in the Cabinet.

Grenvillites: Political grouping headed by William Wyndham Grenville. In our period the Grenvillites were closely linked to the Whigs until 1816; thereafter they veered increasingly towards the Tories. Grenvillites appeared in Liverpool's administration during the 1820s.

Habeas corpus: Technically, this was a writ requiring a person accused of a crime to be brought before a court which would determine whether the accused was guilty or not. This was an important civil liberty because otherwise suspected criminals could be kept in gaol indefinitely without the authorities having to produce evidence against the suspected person. During this period, the government suspended Habeas Corpus during periods of disturbance, thus enabling them to detain people without trial.

House of Commons: Collectively, the men elected, or selected, as members of parliament (MPs) to represent constituencies in each of the four countries which in our period comprised the United Kingdom. Their duties included debating issues brought forward by the government (see above) and voting on proposed legislation. Members of the Commons served until they resigned or until the next general election when they would need to seek re-election. The House of Commons from 1801–32 had 658 members: 489 from England, 100 from Ireland, 45 from Scotland and 30 from Wales.

House of Lords: Collectively 'the Lords Spiritual and Temporal'. In plain language, and in our period, these were the male members of the aristocracy, who either inherited their titles (often called 'peerages') from relatives (most usually they were their fathers' eldest sons) and the 26 bishops of the Church of England. Their duties were similar to those of members of the Commons but they either inherited their titles or were, as senior Anglican clerics, appointed. The monarch could create new peerages, so the size of the House of Lords was likely to grow, as it did in the late eighteenth and early nineteenth centuries when many new peerage creations were made on the recommendation of William Pitt the Younger as prime minister.

Indirect taxes: Taxes which are levied not 'directly' on a person's land, other property or income but on the goods which they buy. Such taxes could be a particular burden on those with limited incomes because the proportion of those incomes subject to a given indirect tax was much greater than on someone who was wealthy. In our period, taxes on malt (affecting the price of beer) and on newspapers were particularly resented.

Industrial Revolution: Name given to the development whereby the process of manufacturing was accelerated by more efficient means of production, especially by mechanization in new factories. There is no doubt that Britain underwent such a process in the eighteenth and nineteenth centuries but debate continues about how 'revolutionary' the process was and whether there was a 'take-off' point which can be identified with any chronological precision.

Justices of the Peace (JPs): People with authority in the local community who were expected to discharge a range of administrative duties. JPs had powers of arrest and could judge lesser crimes. In our period, they also supervised the poor law and levying of rates. JPs were normally appointed by the Lord Lieutenant, the monarch's representative at county level. Appointment was a mark of status; it was usually given to members of the gentry and to the more successful or substantial figures in the world of commerce.

Laissez-faire: Meaning literally to leave alone, the phrase became attached to an economic policy based on free trade, low taxation and limited role for the state as compared with private enterprise.

Liberal Tories: Name rather loosely applied to members of the Tory party who supported reformist policies, especially in the 1820s. The leading members of this group were Huskisson, Canning, Robinson and Peel. They were involved in administrative and legal reforms and the lowering of tariffs. Many supported Catholic emancipation and the nationalist aspirations of states wishing to be independent of the large continental empires which had ruled over them.

Limited monarchy: Term used when the monarchical powers are not absolute. In Britain in our period, although the monarchy possessed substantial theoretical powers including the appointment of ministers and the approval of all legislation passed by Parliament, monarchs could not govern without the consent of Parliament and Parliament controlled the raising of revenues through taxation. In this period, the powers of the monarch to appoint ministers who could not command a parliamentary majority were very limited and, wisely, no monarch attempted to veto legislation.

Luddism: The term originated from the name of the mythical figure 'Ned Ludd' who was supposed to have led workers to break machinery, especially in the West Riding of Yorkshire, Lancashire and the East Midlands in the years 1811–16. Modern usage has the term describing the mindless, indiscriminate violence by those trying to hold back the march of progress, but this is misleading. Luddites were very specific in their targets, attacking only those machines that threatened the livelihoods of skilled workers in the textile trades.

Master-manufacturers: Term applied usually to skilled men who set themselves up in business on their own account rather than being employed by an owner. Most manufacturers had served an apprenticeship in a given skill. Most employed only a small number of workmen and relied more on handcraft than on machinery. During the early nineteenth century, however, the size of such businesses tended to increase as ownership of productive capacity became rather more concentrated.

Middle classes: A rather vague term covering a wide variety of occupations and wealth. Broadly, the middle classes divide into two categories. The industrial/

commercial middle classes were in business. They chased markets, took risks and employed labour. The professional middle classes were experts trained in a particular form of service for which more sophisticated societies had increasing need. Among the oldest professions were the clergy, medicine and the law. During our period, the professions expanded greatly. Engineering, accountancy and other fields of specialist endeavour all became professionalized. Just as in the commercial middle classes, there could be huge discrepancies in scale and wealth, from humble shopkeepers to mighty overseas traders, so the professions rapidly established their own hierarchies. Professional societies restricted entry, defined seniority and, sometimes, differential levels of expertise.

Ministry: Name given to a group of ministers who had roles in government as officers under the crown. Thus when we refer to 'Liverpool's ministry' we mean the ministers who served in the government of Lord Liverpool, whether they were in the Cabinet or not.

National debt: Collective borrowing by government, both from individuals and from institutions at home or abroad. The national debt was formalized in 1694 and, over time, it both increased and included a larger proportion of longer-term obligations. Its size tended to increase hugely during wartime. In the years 1793–1815, for example, it more than tripled, before falling back, though to nowhere near pre-war levels. It was a key aim of government financial policy in the 1820s to spend less and rely less on loans, thus reducing the size of the debt.

Nationalism: The doctrine which believes in the integrity of the nation state as a political entity. In our period, it usually applied to nations attempting to break free from colonial rule, particularly those of the Spanish and Portuguese empires in South America and of the Ottoman (Turkish) Empire in South-East Europe. Irish nationalists sought the repeal of the Act of Union and the creation of a united, independent Ireland.

Navigation Laws: Legislation designed to advantage British trade over foreign competition by imposing duties on imports. Under the influence of Adam Smith's economic theories, these laws came under increasing attack in the early part of the nineteenth century. Levels of duty were steadily reduced from the 1820s and the Navigation Laws finally repealed in 1849.

Nonconformists: Literally, those who did not conform to the doctrines of the Established Church, which was in England and Ireland the Church of England. See also Dissenters.

Paper currency: The issuing of bank notes is a cheaper and easier process than dealings in large, heavy volumes of coin or metal as currency. However, the term was normally used to describe the situation when a government, or a bank, issued its own notes which were not anchored to an external source of value such as gold. The danger in the excessive issuing of paper currency was the depreciation of its value at home and also the fall of the value of a currency against international competitors.

Paper money: See paper currency.

Parliament: The legislative body of a nation. Britain's parliament had two chambers (in other words it is 'bi-cameral'), the House of Commons and the House of Lords. Before 1832, the former was elected, albeit on a very restricted franchise; the latter comprised members of the hereditary aristo- cracy, who served for life once they inherited their titles, and bishops of the Church of England. Proposals for new or amending laws were made in either House but needed to be passed by votes in both before being submitted to the monarch for the 'royal assent', after which they became law.

Parliamentary division: Name given to the procedure for taking votes. The House is formally said to 'divide', so that members can vote for or against a proposal.

Patronage: The links, often through families, by which support and opportun- ities for work are given by senior members to junior ones. In eighteenth- and early-nineteenth-century politics, posts in government were often filled, and candidates for Parliament nominated, through the influence and recom- mendation of powerful men, particularly the great landowners.

Pittite: Literally a supporter of William Pitt the Younger, prime minister from 1783–1801 and 1804–06. It can be used almost interchangeably with the term 'Tory' in our period since most of those who formed Tory governments had been supporters, or junior colleagues of Pitt. The main features of Pittite policy were resistance to extra-parliamentary agitation, the maintenance of public order at times of disturbance and trade liberalization by reducing tariffs and tolls.

Plebiscite: The putting of a specific political question to the people at large. Figuratively, it means the formal sounding out of public opinion. Literally, it requires a voting process. There was no provision for a plebiscite in the British political system in our period.

Pocket borough: Term used to indicate that a borough was, in effect, owned – usually by a member of the aristocracy or the crown. Elections in such boroughs were rare because the outcome was so often a foregone conclusion. Pocket boroughs could even be bought and sold.

Political economy: The branch of economics which deals with issues relating to government including, for example, taxation policies and how government revenues are spent.

Poor law: From early in the seventeenth century, it had been the responsibility of each parish in England and Wales to 'relieve' (or provide for) the needs of those unable to provide for themselves. An individual showing that he or she was in need had a right to relief in the parish of birth or where he or she could show a 'settlement', usually defined as continuous residence over a period of a year. This system came under increasing attack from the end of the eighteenth century as a result of a growing population, poor harvests and periods of unemployment. The cost of poor relief nationally rose from £2 million to nearly £8 million in the years 1775 to 1818. This stimulated much debate about reducing costs by radical reform of the law. The views of the political economists proved most influential here. In the 1810s and 1820s, the poor law was administered more harshly as ratepayers tried to save money. A royal commission was established in 1832 to investigate the operation of the laws and its report heavily influenced the legislation of 1834 (Poor Law Amendment Act) which imposed both more uniform and more stringent conditions for relief.

Poor Law Overseers: Those responsible for the day-to-day administration of the poor law at parish level. They were unpaid but their expenses were defrayed by local ratepayers. The work of the overseers was strongly criticised by the Royal Commission on the Poor Laws, which found that many overseers were appointed not for their expertise but just because it was their turn. There was little incentive for them to work professionally and many inconsistencies of practice were uncovered.

Private member's bill: A proposal for legislation which is presented not by a political party but by an individual member of parliament (MP). Most legislation until the middle of the nineteenth century came about in this way.

Radicalism: This term derives from the Latin word meaning 'root'. Radical policies, therefore, were designed to be far-reaching and to get to the root of a given problem. In our period, radical politicians were those who called for extensive reform, particularly but not exclusively, of the political system. The term 'radical' was often used disapprovingly by members of parliament who, if they were reformers at all, favoured much more cautious change which was designed to preserve the stability of the old order rather than to undermine it. The term 'philosophical radical' was used to describe those who wanted major reforms in the role and functions of government, particularly along the lines suggested by Jeremy Bentham.

Reactionary: The term is normally used to describe those resistant to change or who wish to re-establish an older policy or form of government. It derives from 'reaction'. In other words, reactionaries react adversely to proposals for change or to new systems of government. In our period, the 'Ultra Tories' of the late 1820s and 1830s might properly be described as reactionaries.

Regent: In monarchical terms, someone performing the role and duties on behalf of another. Regencies were common when the monarch was an infant or child. In our period, the 'Prince Regent' assumed the role of a monarch from 1811–20 because of his father's mental incapacity.

Representative government: Government based on the idea that those in authority have legitimacy because they can show that they represent the interests and needs of others. Radicals in our period increasingly believed that such a government would emerge only when those in the legislative assembly were directly elected by all, or at least all male, citizens. On the other hand, opponents of parliamentary reform argued that the unreformed parliament was representative since MPs were the key, propertied, interests of the nation – via land, commerce and industry.

Republican: Someone who does not believe in the principle of monarchy. Following Tom Paine, most republicans reject the idea of hereditary succession.

Retrenchment: Originally a military term, this refers to government policy designed to reduce expenditure and produce better balanced budgets. It was a policy advocated by political economists, especially after the massive expenditure incurred by the French wars, and it greatly influenced the policies of Huskisson and Robinson in the 1820s.

Select committees: Committees appointed by either House of Parliament to investigate an issue and to make recommendations which might lead to proposals for legislation. Parliament determines the composition and terms of reference of these committees.

Sinking fund: A sum set aside by government to reduce the size of the National Debt. It was established in 1717 but reorganized by Pitt in 1786, with the creation of an independent body of National Debt Commissioners. Largely because of the needs of war, the sums set aside proved inadequate. In 1819, the government addressed the problem by determining that government revenue should exceed expenditure by £5 million a year. The system was further reorganized in 1823 when the Commissioners were to receive £1.25 million a quarter to reduce debt.

Sunday schools: Schools which provided religious instruction and which are associated with the Evangelical revival in the 1770s and 1780s. The schools developed by Robert Raikes of Gloucester took children out of church during adult worship and provided separate instruction. As they grew in number, many provided basic instruction in literacy and numerous. They were a means of providing basic education for many children from poorly-off families.

Tariffs: The collective name for duties (taxes) paid on imports or exports. Tariffs were one of the main sources of revenue for government. In the

1820s, many tariffs were reduced in order to stimulate trade and national prosperity.

Tory: Name of a political party originating in the late seventeenth century which was politically in eclipse for much of the eighteenth century. The party revived after a coalition of Whigs and supporters of William Pitt the Younger was formed in 1794 to resist radicalism and calls for parliamentary reform during the wars against revolutionary France. For most of our period, many associated with this coalition resisted the name 'Tory', preferring 'Pittite'. Tory principles in this period included: support for existing authority; presenting the monarch, and the institution of monarchy, as a symbol of national unity; resistance to reform; support for the Church of England as an important pillar of the state and for its status as the 'established' or 'national' church; and, for many, opposition to religious toleration. Support for the Tories was usually much stronger in England than in the other nations of the United Kingdom and stronger in the country and small market and cathedral towns than in the main commercial and industrial centres. The party was the fore-runner of the Conservative party. Some called the modernized Tory party under Peel in the 1830s a 'Conservative' party.

Trade liberalization: The process whereby tariffs on trade were reduced with the purpose of increasing trade volumes and, thereby, the wealth of the nation. Liberalization was a reaction to policies which depended on protecting the trade of a nation by imposing protective duties.

Ultra-Tories ('Ultras'): Name given to 'extreme' Tories who opposed almost all reforms. Most were especially antagonistic to the religious reforms of 1828–9 which gave greater civil liberties to Dissenters and Roman Catholics, although opposition to parliamentary reform was also widespread within this group. Ultras believed themselves to have been betrayed by Wellington and Peel over Catholic Emancipation. Many retained a resentment towards Peel which lasted to the end of his career.

Utilitarianism: Philosophy which holds that the purpose of government should be to secure the maximum happiness and benefit for the largest number of citizens. Legislation should be judged on how effectively it meets this criterion. Originating in ancient Greece, the modern philosophy was developed by Jeremy Bentham and, later, John Stuart Mill. It guided the formulation of much social policy from the 1830s.

Wage differentials: Differences in the wages paid. The term is mostly used to describe how wage levels differ between one occupation and another or by how much they differ between skilled, semi-skilled and unskilled workers in the same trade.

Whig: Name of a political party originating in the late seventeenth century which was politically dominant for much of the eighteenth century. It was, however, normally out of office in our period. It was organized by inter-locking groups of aristocrats and other large landowners who were often related to one another. The party increasingly gained support among the commercial and professional classes in the towns, many of whom were Dissenters. It was associated with policies which included: limiting the powers of the monarchy; religious toleration; support for a range of reforms, including parliamentary reform. It was the forerunner of the modern Liberal party.

Whips: In political terms, those with a responsibility for ensuring party discipline. Whips seek to ensure that their party registers its maximum voting strength in parliamentary divisions. This could involve argument, persuasion, inducement or even threats.

Working classes: As with 'middle classes', definitions are never water-tight. However, most would accept that a defining characteristic is that its members subsist by selling their labour for wages. In our period, they had little, or no, property or investments. During the industrial revolution, the nature of work was undergoing rapid change. A larger proportion of the population became engaged in repetitive work either in factories or in unskilled labouring in dockyards or in the building trade.

Yeomanry: Mounted troops who supported the regular soldiery. Their main purpose was national defence and they were organized into county regiments during the French wars. It was the yeomanry who mounted the attack on the massed crowd at St Peter's Fields, Manchester, in August 1819 precipitating what is usually called the 'Peterloo Massacre'.

Part 1

ANALYSIS

1

Introduction

1815 AND ALL THAT

There is no denying that 1815 is an important date in British history. On 18 June the **Duke of Wellington**, with vital help from the Prussian army at a late stage, defeated Napoleon Bonaparte, Emperor of France, at the battle of Waterloo, fought just south of Brussels on the road to Paris. Defeat at Waterloo ended Napoleon's phenomenal military and political career. The 67,000 troops who fought under Wellington's command in that bloody, decisive engagement seemed to have settled the fate of Europe. They had ended the longest war in which Britain had been engaged since the fifteenth century and the most costly war yet fought. Britain's victory over the French gave her a commanding influence in European diplomacy which would not be lost for over a century.

Britain was the only nation which had kept up the European fight against first revolutionary, then Napoleonic, France from the time it entered the war in February 1793 to its end, with only a brief truce in 1802–3. Britain, alone among the significant European powers, had not been defeated or overrun by French armies. From being commercially important, and growing in influence, but nevertheless often in the second half of the eighteenth century of relatively limited significance in European diplomatic affairs, Britain's influence was transformed by war. In 1815 it was clearly the leading power in Europe and thus, still, in the world. Its naval power was not to be directly challenged in battle for more than a century and, the brief Crimean conflict of 1854–6 apart, its armies fought no wars on European soil until the First World War which began in 1914. If the emphasis is placed on diplomatic and military history, therefore, it remains logical to begin a study of Britain's century of pre-eminence in 1815.

Many historians in the early twenty-first century, however, would challenge such an emphasis, deriding it as 'drum-and-trumpet' history. Fashions for historical study change and foreign policy, in particular, receives far less

Wellington, 1st Duke of
Soldier and Tory politician. Wellington was the hero of the Battle of Waterloo in 1815 and an important member of virtually every Tory government from 1819 to 1846. He was prime minister from 1828–30. He was instinctively conservative but did change his mind on Catholic Emancipation.

Liverpool, 2nd Earl of Pittite politician. He was prime minister from 1812 to 1827. He favoured modest, cautious administrative change and reducing tariffs to boost trade and enhance national prosperity. His government always opposed parliamentary reform, suppressing radicalism in the years 1815–20. A stroke ended his career.

Tory Political party, at this time sometimes also called Pittite. Its main policies included: support for existing authority; using the monarchy as a symbol of national unity; resistance to reform; support for the Church of England and, for many, opposition to religious toleration.

Coalition government A government in which power is shared and the ministers forming the government come from more than one party. In our period, the governments formed by Canning (1827), Goderich (1827) and Grey (1830) were all coalitions.

Pittite Literally a supporter of William Pitt the Younger, prime minister from 1783–1801 and 1804–6. It can be used almost interchangeably with the term 'Tory'. The main features of Pittite policy were resistance to extra-parliamentary agitation, the maintenance of public order and trade liberalisation via reduced tariffs and tolls.

attention now than it used to do and, arguably, than it should. If the emphasis is placed more on social, cultural, industrial and domestic political developments, it is true that 1815 is an altogether less significant date. No new government took office in Britain then, and the end of the French wars marked no important change in Britain's domestic political affairs. When Wellington won the battle of Waterloo, Robert Banks Jenkinson, second **Earl of Liverpool**, had been prime minister for exactly three years. He led a Tory government, most of whose important members had come to political maturity during the earlier phase of the French Wars, and whose guiding principle had become opposition to reform for fear of opening the way to a British revolution.

THE POLITICAL LANDSCAPE

The new **Tory** party had effectively been created as a **coalition** of anti-reforming land and other property owners under the prime ministership of William Pitt the Younger in 1794, although Liverpool was the first prime minister of the period to acknowledge the description 'Tory'. Some historians prefer to use the adjective '**Pittite**' to describe Liverpool's **government**. Whichever name is used, the prime minister held a secure majority in the **House of Commons**. The only non-Tory **ministry** to be formed between 1794 and 1830 – the so-called but hopelessly misnamed 'Ministry of all the Talents' headed by Pitt's cousin **William Grenville** – lasted for 13 months, from February 1806 to March 1807. Two brief Pittite ministries succeeded it, headed by the Duke of Portland (1807–9) and Spencer Perceval (1809–12). Liverpool had become Prime Minister after the assassination of Perceval. Although his ministry had endured several early crises, he proved to be a great political survivor and it was ill-health in the form of a debilitating stroke, rather than political defeat, which removed him from office early in 1827. Liverpool is far from being the best-known or most distinguished of British prime ministers, but he had many modest virtues. He was both dully competent and completely trustworthy. More talented but fractious colleagues would work with him when they would not cooperate with others. By 1827, he seemed not only irremovable but irreplaceable. As we shall see (see below, pp. 69–87), the Tory party could not replace him without breaking up. Liverpool's proved to be by some distance the longest prime ministership in the nineteenth and twentieth centuries.

The monarchy, which still possessed separate and distinctive powers in Britain in the early nineteenth century, did not change hands in 1815. The King had in 1801 dismissed William Pitt the Younger (a popular, even revered, prime minister with a strong parliamentary majority) because he disagreed with him on an important issue of policy. Yet he did not create a constitutional crisis in so doing. The monarch remained the most important influence in the choice of every prime minister between the 1720s and the 1820s. The wishes of the House of Commons and the **House of Lords** were the only factors the monarch was wise to take into account; those of the electorate mattered not at all. Yet as the right of the King to appoint his favourites to sensitive or influential positions by a system of 'patronage' was whittled away at the end of the eighteenth century, so royal power began to decline (Evans, 1985).

King **George III** had been on the throne since 1760 but his dull, unimaginative, inflexible but dutiful reign ended in a long coda framed by progressive mental instability. 'Farmer George' began talking to the trees at Windsor Castle and, after various bouts of intellectual collapse, he was declared permanently unfit to govern in February 1811. His eldest son, also George, took on the duties of monarchy under the title of Prince **Regent**. The Prince, who became King as **George IV** in 1820, was a superficially pleasant man of some aesthetic sensibility, but he was also vain, gross, profligate and, when thwarted, spiteful. He was also politically incompetent, never understanding the distinction between a petulant outburst (of which he made many) and a firm statement (of which, though he thought differently, he made very few). While he was regent or monarch from 1811 to 1830, the remaining powers of the monarchy ebbed even more rapidly. It is probably true that George III mad had greater respect from his subjects than George IV sane. Rarely, in the chequered history of the British monarchy, has a king been so vilified.

BRITISH SOCIETY IN 1815

There is a more fundamental reason why 1815 needs to be placed in a broader context. At the time, parts of Britain were being rapidly industrialized. Historians are now much more cautious than they were in the 1960s about suggesting that an '**industrial revolution**' took place within such a narrow time frame as the half-century between 1780 and 1830 (Crafts, 1985; Mokyr, 1998). Growth in productivity is now calculated to be much slower than once thought, while many industries made relatively little use of technological change until well into the nineteenth century. Although some areas of Britain did undergo fierce and radical change as a result of mechanization in this period, the pace of technological change now seems relatively slow over the country as a whole and labour productivity and economic growth not specially remarkable. Not surprisingly, some historians doubt whether the

---

Government The collective group responsible for devising policies at national level. Members of the government are called 'Ministers'. However, only the more senior ones, who met regularly to discuss business, formed the Cabinet. Ministers sat in both the House of Commons and the House of Lords.

House of Commons Collectively, the men elected, or selected, as Members of Parliament to represent constituencies in each of the four countries of the United Kingdom. The House of Commons from 1801–32 had 658 members: 489 from England, 100 from Ireland, 45 from Scotland and 30 from Wales.

Ministry Name given to a group of ministers, who had roles in government as officers under the crown. Thus, when we refer to 'Liverpool's ministry', we mean the ministers who served in the government of Lord Liverpool, whether they were in the Cabinet or not.

Grenville, William Wyndham Pittite and Whig politician. He was, in effect, leader of the Whig party from 1807–17 but opposed most parliamentary and economic reforms favoured by the Foxite Whigs who comprised the majority of the party. He resigned in 1817; most of his followers joined Liverpool's Tory government in 1822.

House of Lords Collectively, male members of the aristocracy, and the twenty-six bishops of the Church of England. Their duties were similar to those of members of the Commons but they either inherited their titles or were, as senior Anglican clerics, appointed. Many new peerages were created in the late 18th and early 19th centuries.

George III Monarch from 1760 to 1820. Aware that the Hanoverian monarchy had never been popular, he emphasized his Britishness. He was a dutiful, conscientious monarch if lacking in imagination and insight. He opposed emancipation for Roman Catholics. He was mentally incapacitated for the last ten years of his reign.

Regent In monarchical terms, someone performing the role and duties on behalf of another. Regencies were common when the monarch was an infant or child. In our period, the 'Prince Regent' assumed the role of a monarch from 1811–20 because of his father's mental incapacity.

use of the phrase 'industrial revolution' is appropriate. They still agree, however, on two basic points. First, the cumulative transformation associated with the process of industrialization – though it takes place over a longer time scale than once assumed – changes societies much more fundamentally than any political or diplomatic 'revolution'. Secondly, these changes occurred first in Great Britain. Many of the crises with which this book is concerned were part of the early consequences of the discontinuity we might still call the Industrial Revolution. Any study which begins its detailed treatment in 1815 must show awareness of the transformations which affected Britain at least from the second half of the eighteenth century onwards. No one date marks the beginning of the Industrial Revolution but 1815 cannot be considered important in any wider industrial and social context.

British society was under great strain between 1815 and 1832 largely because of the speed of change. At the most basic level, it was getting bigger all the time. After a period of stagnation in the early eighteenth century, the population began to grow steadily from the 1730s and with extraordinary rapidity from the 1780s. At the time of the first official census in 1801, the population of Britain was about 10.6 million, almost double its level a century earlier. Britain's population was also growing faster than that of Western Europe as a whole. According to latest estimates, in 1680 Britain contained 7.6 per cent of Western Europe's population. By 1840, that had increased to 10.5 per cent (Floud and Johnson, 2004: 57–8). In the mere 17 years covered by this book it increased by almost 29 per cent from an estimated 12.9 million to 16.6 million. British population never grew faster than in the 20 years after 1811.

As those who study developing countries in our own time are well aware, rapid population increase is almost invariably accompanied by social dislocation. Britain in the early nineteenth century was indebted to an efficient domestic agricultural system and a rapidly developing pattern of international trade for the simple fact that very few of her population starved. But dislocation manifested itself in other ways. Rapid fluctuations in food prices lay behind much of the unrest of the period 1815–20. The average price of wheat, and wheaten bread formed the English population's staple diet, was never higher in the whole of the nineteenth century than in the decade 1810–19, and prices rarely fluctuated as bewilderingly.

Two other aspects of population change in this period have received less attention but are at least equally important. Britain's was a young population and it was mobile. Birth rates were extremely high, largely because more women were marrying earlier. This they were able to do because of increased job opportunities, although not necessarily for women, in a rapidly expanding economy. On average, in the first two decades of the eighteenth century, women in England got married for the first time at the age of 26.2 years. By the 1830s, this had fallen to 23.1 years (Tranter, 1985; Floud and Johnson, 2004: 73). These raw figures mask substantial regional and social variations. Where work for women was limited but wage levels for men relatively high, as in mining communities, women married earlier. Where traditional agricultural smallholdings survived the substantial rural changes of the eighteenth and early nineteenth centuries and where living-in farm service predominated, they married later. Nevertheless, the overall trend is clear and it reflects substantial changes in the economy. Given the limited number of years in which women are highly fertile, relatively small changes in the age of first marriage can have dramatic consequences on population distribution. It has been estimated that no less than 48 per cent of the population of England and Wales in 1821 was less than 15 years of age. Such a skewed distribution towards the very young placed enormous burdens on income earners and contributed to the desperation of much of the 'hunger politics' of this period.

Migration, in the early stages predominantly of the young and unmarried, to cities offering the prospect of at least casual work was also a factor in the growing instability of life. Joanna Innes has recently drawn attention to the ways in which charitable provision to meet short-term crises expanded in the war years before 1815 (Cunningham and Innes, 1998: 73–4). This development increased concerns that much charity was being given in wasteful or inefficient ways. It is also worth considering to what extent protest movements are dependent upon the active participation of teenagers and young adults for their mass appeal. A population containing an unusually large proportion of young folk is inherently less stable than one in which the distribution is more even.

The dominant picture of social change in early industrial Britain concentrates on urban growth, factory production and on working conditions dominated allegedly by William Blake's 'dark, satanic mills'. No one doubts that the Industrial Revolution involved factories and the emergence of more specialized patterns of work in which human labour might be subordinated to the arbitrary rhythms of the machine. Nor is it to be denied that most factories (though not the earliest, which were water powered and necessarily located in rural valleys with fast-flowing streams and rivers) were found in towns. The Industrial Revolution and urban growth went hand in hand. It is important to remember four points about this development, however.

First, the Industrial Revolution took place over a much longer time than is frequently assumed. In our period, factory production was almost exclusively concentrated on the manufacture of cheap textile goods, first cottons, then woollens. This took place in three areas of Britain: south-east Lancashire and north-east Cheshire; the central valley of Scotland; and Yorkshire's West Riding. Here grew up the great factory towns of early industrial Britain:

George IV Prince Regent from 1811–20 (when his father was mentally incapable) and monarch from 1820–30. He frequently disagreed with his Prime Minister, Lord Liverpool. He meddled in politics but was increasingly unable to influence affairs. The powers of the monarchy declined during his reign.

Industrial Revolution Name given to the development whereby the process of manufacturing was greatly accelerated by more efficient means of production, especially by mechanisation in new factories. Britain underwent such a process in the eighteenth and nineteenth centuries.

Manchester, Bolton, Salford, Stockport, Glasgow, Paisley, Leeds, Bradford and the rest. Secondly, these factory towns were by no means dominated by monster factories employing thousands of workers in vast, impersonal surroundings. In 1841, only 3 per cent of cotton firms in Lancashire, the county of greatest factory concentration, employed more than 1,000 workers; 43 per cent employed fewer than 100 (Gatrell, 1977). The scale of industrial production before 1850 has been widely over-estimated.

Thirdly, much urban growth in the first half of the nineteenth century resulted from an expansion and consolidation of traditional methods, rather than from factory production. Birmingham, the centre of the West Midlands metal trades, and Sheffield, its counterpart in south Yorkshire, both doubled their populations in the first 30 years of the nineteenth century, a faster rate of growth than many textile towns. Yet both towns teemed with workshops owned by small **master-manufacturers** who employed skilled craftsmen, journeymen and apprentices as in the eighteenth century. The scale, but not the nature, of such towns had changed. Urban growth did not depend upon factory production, and it is worth noting that one of the fastest urban growth rates in the decade 1821–31 was recorded on the Sussex coast by Brighton, a leisure town made spectacularly fashionable by the patronage of George IV.

The fourth point to bear in mind, and one particularly and poignantly relevant to the protests of rural workers, is that urban growth in this period did not result from wholesale migration from countryside to town the moment the spinning mills of Lancashire began to turn out cotton undergarments. The wildly misleading image of a rural peasantry, 'proletarianized' and dispossessed by the parliamentary enclosure movement between 1760 and 1820, and rushing to the new towns in consequence, should be expunged from our textbooks for ever.

Long-distance migration from countryside to town was very much the exception, relating only to the growth of London, which remained by a huge margin Britain's biggest city (and whose population of 1.7 million in 1831 accounted for one-eighth of England's inhabitants) despite more obvious developments further north; and to emigration from Ireland, which was well under way before the potato famine of 1845–7. The main reason for the enormously rapid growth of the Glasgows, Manchesters and Boltons was short-distance migration from surrounding countryside and, more important still, a high rate of natural increase in these towns because of the extremely high birth rate. In the rural south, with few alternative job opportunities away from agriculture, population continued obstinately and redundantly to rise until the 1850s, bringing desperation and misery in its wake.

The social context of Britain's early Industrial Revolution is, therefore, complex but important for an understanding of the political struggles after

Master-manufacturers Term applied usually to skilled men who set themselves up in business on their own account rather than being employed by an owner. Most manufacturers had served an apprenticeship in a given skill. Most employed only a small number of workmen and relied more on handcraft than on machinery.

1815. One point, however, is crystal clear. The economic power base of the country was shifting dramatically. With every year that passed, the case for increasing the political representation of the urban and industrial counties from Warwickshire northwards became more difficult to resist. Yet political change is rarely effected in consequence of genteel, rational calculation and debate; grievance and distress are the more usual stimuli. Neither was in short supply in the hectic years which followed Wellington's victory at Waterloo.

2

Britain in Crisis? 1815–20

LORD LIVERPOOL, HIS MINISTRY AND ITS PARLIAMENTARY OPPONENTS

At the time of the battle of Waterloo, Lord Liverpool's government seemed securely established. Few, however, called it a 'Tory government', as modern historians generally do. In essence, it was Pittite, both since key members owed their loyalty and their political education to the former prime minister and because of continued support for Pitt's staunch anti-reformist policies during the French wars, which were still raging when Liverpool took office. Liverpool's personal position, however, was initially precarious. He had not been the Prince Regent's first or second choice when Spencer Perceval was assassinated and he did not cut much of a dash in Parliament. He was helped by the fortunes of war. Victories in the Spanish Peninsula in 1813–14 and the collapse of Napoleon's armies in eastern and central Europe after the Russian campaign of 1812 increased the new prime minister's standing and reputation. By 1815 Liverpool had about 80 more regular supporters than his Whig opponents led by **Earl Grey** and **Lord Grenville** and this advantage increased somewhat over the next five years (Evans, 2001; Derry, 2001).

Even a secure government in the early nineteenth century, however, could not guarantee an overall majority in the House of Commons, for two reasons. First, in contrast to the situation in the twentieth century, a substantial, though dwindling, minority of members of parliament (MPs) were independent of party and saw their duty as representing their constituents in a disinterested manner. Second, among those who were usually disposed to support the government no regular system of '**whips**' existed to anchor party discipline. Thus, support might be given on an *ad hoc* or conditional basis. It has been argued by leading authorities that party allegiance in the Liverpool period was not strong and may even have been weakening (Gash, 1979; Cookson, 1975; Fraser, 1983). Recent research by the History of Parliament

Trust has demonstrated the fallibility of this view (Thorne, 1986), but spasmodic attendance at debates and the lack of tight party control made the calculation of majorities an uncertain business.

The ability of the Commons to act independently of government policy was most embarrassingly demonstrated in March 1816 when, to reduce the crippling burden of debt run up during the war, the administration proposed to retain income tax, though at half the rate at which it had been levied during the Napoleonic wars. The Chancellor of the Exchequer, Nicholas **Vansittart**, introduced a proposal to this effect. As the government well knew, income tax was the most efficient way yet devised for raising money from the reasonably well-off. MPs needed no reminding, however, that it had been first introduced by Pitt the Younger in 1799 only as a wartime expedient [**Doc. 2, p. 106**]. Opponents of income tax argued that its continuance in peacetime was both an infringement of individual liberties and a breach of faith given the circumstances in which it had first been levied. The **City of London** presented a petition against the tax which contained 22,000 signatures of merchants, bankers and shopkeepers (Hilton, 2006; Evans, 2001). About 400 anti-tax petitions were received in similar vein.

The government's parliamentary managers had anticipated a comfortable majority, yet they lost the income tax in the House of Commons by 37 votes. As the *Annual Register* reported, the announcement of the result was attended by 'a long and loud cheering across the House which was re-echoed by the crowd that filled the lobbies and avenues, and the event was felt in general throughout the nation as a relief from an oppressive burden'. Viscount **Castlereagh** shamefacedly informed the Prince Regent that several had voted against 'whose support had been calculated upon'. He also believed that the public was demonstrating an 'ignorant impatience of taxation'. It is significant that twice as many MPs representing **county constituencies**, generally regarded before 1832 as among the more independent-minded members, voted against the government as for it. *The Times* spoke for most property owners when it pronounced in the wake of the defeat that the Commons 'felt with the feelings of the country' (Cookson, 1975). Thoroughly discomfited, the government immediately agreed not to renew the malt tax, another substantial revenue provider. These two taxes would have brought in £17.5 million in a year, about a fifth of the government's anticipated revenue. The Chancellor was forced instead to raise money by loans, which pleased the London bankers but stored up longer-term problems (Evans, 2001; Hilton, 1977).

With greater debating talent at his disposal in the House of Commons, Liverpool's taxation policy might have survived. However, as Norman Gash has pointed out, Liverpool was one of nine cabinet ministers in the House of Lords. Of the four who sat in the Commons, only Castlereagh was even a

Vansittart, Nicholas Tory politician. He is best known as Liverpool's Chancellor of the Exchequer from 1812 to 1823. His attempts to deal with the burden of debt national finances were ham-fisted and he lost the support both of the Bank of England and of many in his own party.

City of London The small area, towards the east of the modern capital city, around the old city walls. It housed the main financial and commercial structures not just of London but England. The city's population was much smaller than that of London as a whole, though it generated a disproportionate amount of the capital's wealth.

Castlereagh, Viscount Tory politician. He was Foreign Secretary from 1812 to his suicide in 1822. He was the leading figure in 'Congress' diplomacy. His main purpose was to achieve a balance of power between European states to preserve European peace and support Britain's commercial development.

County constituencies Every English county, irrespective of its size or population, sent two members to the House of Commons. All owners of land worth at least 40s (£2) were entitled to vote. County MPs were usually accorded higher status, largely because they had more voters than most boroughs.

passably effective speaker. Vansittart was poor, and Bragge-Bathurst and Wellesley-Pole (Wellington's brother), patronage appointments hidden away in minor offices, disastrous (Gash, 1979). Liverpool's government was by no means unusual in having both more and abler cabinet ministers in the Lords. Especially before 1832, government was controlled by the great landowners of the country, many of whom had inherited their titles and the political influence which went with them. However, in the seventeenth century the Commons had won control over financial matters. A government concerned overwhelmingly between 1815 and 1820 with economic crises, and the political discontents to which they gave rise, should have been more strongly represented in the lower house.

In a broader chronological context, the government's taxation reverses of 1816 can be seen as inaugurating a new phase of public policy, characterized by financial **retrenchment** and administrative reform (see pp. 44–6). In this, however reluctantly, Liverpool's government was responding to pressure particularly from propertied public opinion. One historian has described Britain in the eighteenth and early nineteenth centuries as a 'fiscal-military state': geared for frequent war and financed by ever higher levels of taxation and extensive loans. After 1815, it was being rolled back, eventually ushering in a regime characterized by very limited state intervention (*laissez-faire*) and low taxation. It was both a substantial, and a profoundly important, shift (Harling and Mandler, 1993).

Government control of the lower house improved somewhat when the Earl of Buckinghamshire died in 1816 and was replaced by George **Canning** as President of the Board of Control. Canning was one of the best speakers in the Commons but his very debating virtues made him an unpopular colleague. His quickness and self-confidence were allied to a waspish wit which was not invariably directed at political opponents. Canning was the source of much ill-feeling in an increasingly cantankerous Cabinet throughout the rest of Liverpool's long ministry. A less controversial promotion in 1818 brought another effective recruit in Frederick **Robinson**, who was to be one of the main instigators of government economic policy in the 1820s (see pp. 44–9).

Much the most celebrated recruit to Liverpool's government sat in the Lords. The Duke of Wellington returned home from France at the end of 1818 after duty as both British ambassador there and as supreme commander of the allied army of occupation (Thompson, 1986). After some reluctance, and an insistence to Liverpool that he was not a 'party man', he accepted an appropriately military cabinet office as Master General of the Ordnance. In 1818, Liverpool felt that Wellington's immense prestige would add necessary weight to a government beset with problems. There is no reason to think that it was in danger of collapse, but Wellington's presence provided reassurance to independent country gentlemen and waverers that

---

Retrenchment Originally a military term, this refers to government policy designed to reduce expenditure and produce better-balanced budgets. It was a policy advocated by political economists, especially after the massive expenditure incurred by the French wars, and it greatly influenced the policies of Huskisson and Robinson in the 1820s.

Laissez-faire Meaning literally to leave alone, the phrase became attached to an economic policy based on free trade, low taxation and limited role for the state as compared with private enterprise.

Canning, George Tory politician and journalist. He served as Liverpool's Foreign Secretary from 1822–27 supporting nationalists seeking to break free from continental European empires. He succeeded Liverpool as prime minister early in 1827 but died in office four months later.

Robinson, Frederick John (also Goderich) Tory politician. He piloted the new Corn Law through the Commons in 1815 and became Chancellor of the Exchequer from 1823, developing reformist economic policies alongside Huskisson. He succeeded Canning as prime minister in 1827, but briefly and unsuccessfully.

Liverpool's was a ministry to be trusted in difficult times. His acceptance of office inaugurated the second, lengthier and far less distinguished course of his career which saw Wellington as a cabinet minister in various Tory administrations between 1818 and 1846, one of which he led, and which established him very clearly, and at times controversially, as a 'party man'.

Whatever the preferred contemporary nomenclature, Liverpool's administration can now be seen as a thoroughly and uncompromisingly 'Tory' administration in its opposition to 'French principles' of **representative government**, based on the rights of citizenship; in its defence of property as the essential guarantor of stability; in its belief that if order and unrestrained liberty were in conflict then the former must take precedence over the latter; in its zealous, if not intolerant, defence of the privileges of the **Church of England**; in its belief that attacks on the church were *ipso facto* attacks on the state; and in its conviction that landed property should be pre-eminent over commercial or moneyed interests. Though a large majority of MPs of all persuasions were landowners, the **Whigs** had in their ranks roughly twice as many MPs from commercial or urban backgrounds as had the Tories. The Tories had an equivalently dominant representation among retired army or navy officers. Events during the wars had enabled the Tory party profitably to stress its patriotic, as well as its ideological, credentials.

Liverpool's government also emphasized, though it rarely practised, deference to the monarchy. Liverpool was wont to contrast this with an ingrained Whig tradition which saw monarchy as prone to authoritarianism and threatening of the people's liberties. The Whig leadership, controlled as it was by the greatest and bluest-blooded of aristocratic families, claimed the right to speak for propertied Englishmen, against the interests or prerogatives of the Crown if necessary. Tory attitudes were usually different, however difficult the personality of an individual monarch. In a sense Liverpool himself symbolized the difference. Though himself an earl, his father, Charles Jenkinson, had earned his advancement from relatively humble origins by efficient and unswervingly loyal service to George III which had been rewarded with a peerage. Two of Liverpool's most reactionary **ministers**, **Viscount Sidmouth** at the Home Office, and Lord **Eldon**, his Lord Chancellor, were – at least in the rarified world of aristocratic politics – *parvenus* from the professional and trading classes. Sidmouth's father had been personal physician to the Pitt the Elder, Earl of Chatham, in the 1770s. Eldon, whose reputation during 20 years as Lord Chancellor was one of opposition to virtually every legal reform which was proposed, was the son of a prosperous Newcastle coal merchant. Viscount Castlereagh came from a landed background, but it was an Irish one, and he came to the attention of British politicians as the Chief Secretary who cleaned up the mess left by the Irish rebellion of 1798.

Representative government Government based on the idea that those in authority need to show their legitimacy by representing the interests and needs of the community as a whole. Many political radicals argued that representative government required a legislative assembly directly elected by all, or at least all male, citizens.

Church of England The official, or state, church of England, sometimes known as 'the Anglican church' or 'the Established Church'. It came into being during the Reformation of the 16th century. The monarch was head of the church. Senior clergy were appointed by the government and bishops were members of the House of Lords.

Whig Political party, politically dominant for much of the eighteenth century but mostly out of office in the early nineteenth. Its main policies included: limiting the powers of the monarchy; religious toleration; support for a range of reforms, including parliamentary reform. It was the forerunner of the modern Liberal party.

Government ministers Collective name given to those who served in central government and who received seals of office from the monarch. A small number of more senior ministers served in the Cabinet.

The leaders of the Whig opposition were more homogeneously aristocratic but they could rarely mount an effective challenge to Liverpool. Since they had not anticipated his defeat over income tax in 1816, they were not properly prepared to exploit the short-term opportunities which a perplexed, if not humiliated, government afforded. More important, however, were divisions within the opposition. The bulk of the 150 or so who voted regularly and consistently against the government were inheritors of the tradition of eighteenth-century Whiggery, held together by the **patronage** and pull of the great landed families (Jupp, 2006; Hay, 2005; Hill, 1985). They saw themselves as the solid, responsible ballast of the country, supremely equipped alike by their breeding and their broad education to keep it safe from the dangerous, polarized extremes of autocracy and republicanism. They believed that the so-called 'Glorious Revolution' of 1688 represented the ultimate triumph of propertied moderation and compromise and they saw themselves as inheritors of the tradition of **limited monarchy** which it established. This tradition encompassed support for liberty and, especially, toleration for Roman Catholics and **Dissenters**.

More recently, the Whig tradition had been diverted (perverted, conservative Whig critics who followed Pitt in 1794 believed) by support for parliamentary reform as the best guarantor of continued broadly based consent for aristocratic government and by scepticism about, or downright hostility towards, the wars with France. This was the legacy of Charles James Fox, who had died in 1806. His mantle had fallen upon Earl Grey, who as a young **radical** Whig in the 1790s had been instrumental in persuading Fox to support parliamentary reform.

The titular leader of the Whigs, however, came from a different political tradition. Lord Grenville had been a leading minister in Pitt's governments in the 1790s, but had refused to serve Henry Addington, his replacement, because of the new prime minister's peace policy after 1801. He also broke with his former Pittite allies over their subservience to the King's continuing anti-Catholic prejudices. Grenville had led the brief 'Talents' ministry (see above, p. 4) and, after its dismissal, retained leadership of the opposition (Jupp, 1985). Grenville was increasingly uncomfortable leading the Whigs after 1815: first because he believed in retrenchment and cheap government even more than did the prime minister and thus ran into conflict with many of the Whigs' more radical allies, and secondly because he was totally hostile to parliamentary reform. In 1817, he finally ceased to work with Grey and other prominent Whigs such as Holland, Lansdowne, Whitbread and **Brougham** after announcing his support for the government's policies designed to secure law and property against extra-parliamentary agitation (see below, p. 21). Parliamentary reform was becoming an increasing embarrassment to mainstream Whigs and in 1816 Holland declared roundly: 'The nearer I look to parliamentary reform the less I own I like it' (Evans, 1985). Yet its supporters could not be left in the lurch by the opposition and the Whigs would have to carry their reform cross on into the 1820s, though without the **Grenvillites**.

Whig performances in the Commons could, on occasion, be very effective. The Whigs had in Samuel **Romilly** and Henry Brougham two very fine debaters and they could make the more halting Tories look foolish (Hay, 2005). Increasingly, however, their energies were channelled into specific-issue campaigns, like educational and legal reform, which brought few party rewards. The Whigs were also afflicted by the consequences of personal tragedy. Both Whitbread (in 1815) and Romilly (in 1818) committed suicide and their departure made the prospect of effective collaboration between mainstream Whigs and radical politicians of more democratic temper like Sir Francis **Burdett** and Henry Brougham less likely. For many reasons, therefore, the Whigs rarely punched their full weight. They offered Liverpool a less serious challenge than their strength of numbers in the Commons might suggest. As time went on, and helped by fears about extra-parliamentary agitation and disturbance, the Tories under Liverpool, despite their divisions on the Catholic and other questions, appeared to be the more cohesive party.

THE REVIVAL OF RADICAL POLITICS, 1815–17

The leading historian of the English working class has called the years which immediately followed Waterloo 'the heroic age of popular Radicalism' (Thompson, 1963: 603). Individual heroisms there were a-plenty. Many leading radicals served terms of imprisonment for opposition to the government in these years; some were convicted of treason and executed. The 'heroic age' implies much more than this, however. Between 1815 and 1820, the government faced a challenge, not only to its specific policies, but to its very authority, which was broader in its base and more significant in its long-term implications than any of those confronting its predecessors.

This is not to say that Liverpool's government was more vulnerable to overthrow than those which went before. Such a claim would be patently absurd. Liverpool, after all, survived when Harold in 1066, Richard III in 1485 and Charles I in 1649 did not. The true significance of the years 1815–20 is that they witnessed increasingly confident attacks on the notion that government should be directed and controlled by a small number of wealthy, and mostly unelected, folk. Legitimate government, it was contended,

Dissenters Those Christians who were not members of the state church – the Church of England – and who 'dissented' from its doctrines. In our period, Dissent was growing in both numbers and influence. The largest dissenting churches were the Methodist, Baptist and Congregationalist.

Radicalism The term covering belief in, usually extensive, reforms. Radical politicians called mostly for political and religious reform. The term 'philosophical radical' was used to describe those who wanted major reforms in the role and functions of government.

Brougham, Baron Whig politician, lawyer and writer. He helped found the intellectual journal *Edinburgh Review* in 1802 and took up a range of reformist causes, including Catholic emancipation and the abolition of slavery in British colonies. He joined Grey's cabinet as Lord Chancellor in 1830.

Grenvillites Political grouping headed by William Wyndham Grenville. In our period the Grenvillites were closely linked to the Whigs until 1816; thereafter they veered increasingly towards the Tories. Grenvillites appeared in Liverpool's administration during the 1820s.

Romilly, Samuel Whig politician. He promoted a number of important law reforms not least on debt and against excessive punishments for criminal offences. He also supported the abolition of the slave trade. He committed suicide in 1818.

Burdett, Sir Francis Wealthy radical politician committed to a range of political and religious reforms. After 1815, though distrusted by more extreme radicals he introduced a Bill calling for manhood suffrage and annual parliaments. He also attacked those he called 'demagogues' who led the people astray.

Economic warfare The strategy adopted by Napoleon to defeat Britain after 1805. He tried to prevent British imports reaching the Continent or continental raw materials and manufactured goods coming into Britain. Britain retaliated and trade hostilities leading to depression and unemployment resulted.

Country banks Local banks, often containing only a single branch, which sprang up in the eighteenth century. In 1815, more than 300 were in existence. Some expanded and were very secure; others were vulnerable to insolvency during adverse trading conditions. The local banking system was virtually destroyed by a crisis in 1825–6.

should be about *representation* rather than the unearned reward of inheritance. This principle was far from new. It had been raised by numerous radical sects during the 'English Revolution' of the 1640s and 1650s. In Europe, it was the common political discourse of the eighteenth-century Enlightenment. This discourse, popularized and widely disseminated by Thomas Paine and his followers in the 1790s, had challenged the authority of William Pitt during the French Wars, when it had provoked a remarkably solid alliance of property owners against the pretensions of skilled workers and a few writers and intellectuals (Perkin, 1969; Thompson, 1963; Harling, 1996; Wood, 1994; Royle, 2000).

After 1815, however, that patriotic alliance broke up. In the last years of the war, cotton manufacturers in Lancashire felt the pinch as the **economic warfare** between Britain and the French destroyed many of their markets. Depression and bankruptcy tested their loyalty to the old order beyond breaking point. The expansion of wartime credit came back to haunt both government and investors alike. Almost 800 **country banks** were in operation during the later stages of the war, many of them not properly capitalized. The issuing of banknotes added to pressures of inflation. Bad harvests and the choking off of much foreign trade by Napoleon's 'Continental System' brought a spate of bank failures in the last years of the war. The largely unsuccessful **Anglo-American War** of 1812–15 exacerbated the problem. Deflation occurred in 1814–15 and many more banks failed during a major crisis in 1816 (Floud and Johnson, 2004: I, 162–3).

Factory and other industrial workers were laid off in large numbers when the mills lost orders. They were also forced to pay high **indirect taxes** on basic items of consumption like bread, sugar, soap, tea and malt to pay for the war, and were hit in 1812 by wheat prices which rose to the stratospheric level of 126s (£6.30) a quarter (against a late eighteenth-century average of around 50s (£2.50) (Evans, 2001: 510). It is not surprising that they proved susceptible to the reformist arguments of the veteran radical John Cartwright as he toured the industrial districts of the midlands and northern England in that year and again in 1813 and 1815. By the end of the war, parts of England which had either ignored or been lukewarm towards parliamentary reform in the 1790s were now not only receptive but beginning to generate their own leaders and their own political consciousness.

Liverpool's government after 1815, therefore, faced dual challenges which threatened to coalesce in a mighty engine of agitation which a landowners' Parliament would be powerless to resist. On the one hand, it was losing the support of the manufacturing interest, particularly in the north of England. On the other, working people, whose disaffection had previously been concentrated in places like London, Norwich and Sheffield – older urban craft towns occupied by literate and politically aware skilled men – were showing an increasing tendency to challenge the government in the new industrial centres of Manchester, Stockport, Bolton and Leeds (Glen, 1984; Thompson, 1963). Industrialization was making its first serious impact on the political life of the nation.

In this context, Lord Liverpool's decision to introduce a new protective tariff against the importation of foreign corn in 1815 was particularly significant. **Corn laws** were not new. As recently as 1804 a law had been enacted imposing punitive duties on the import of corn when the domestic price fell below 63s (£3.15) a quarter (Hilton, 1977: 6). The 1815 corn law prohibited the importation of any foreign corn until domestic prices reached 80s (£4). Its political impact was dramatic. Liverpool soberly told the House of Lords **[Doc. 1, p. 106]** that the purpose of the new law was to guarantee continued domestic production at a time of falling prices. This would not only stave off famine – a constant government worry at a time of population growth – but also help to stabilize prices.

Outside Parliament, and particularly in the urban areas of the country, an entirely different interpretation was put on Liverpool's motives. *The London Chronicle* pointed out that 'the landed interest want to have a law for raising the price of corn to double the amount of what it was before the war began' (Stevenson, 1979: 190). Henry **Hunt**, rapidly making a name for himself as an effective platform orator with an instinct for the political jugular, wrote a pamphlet in which he insisted that, though a landowner himself, the only interpretation that could be put upon the bill was that it was for 'the benefit and aggrandizement of a few rapacious landholders . . . at the cruel expense of the hitherto greatly oppressed community' (Belchem, 1985: 48–9).

The 'greatly oppressed community' had direct ways of showing its displeasure. The passage of the 1815 corn law was attended by riots in London during which troops had to defend Parliament. Elsewhere, the political temperature was raised several notches. Unproductive landowners were depicted in entrenched positions against productive workers. This was to prove the more important response since it changed the focus of disturbance. Rioting was endemic in eighteenth-century society and, when it had a political rather than an economic basis, its motivation was likely to be conservative rather than progressive. The anti-Catholic Gordon riots of 1780 and the anti-Dissenting and anti-reformist Priestley riots of 1791 are prime examples.

By the early nineteenth century, however, the legitimacy of laws passed by unrepresentative parliaments was being challenged. The new corn law was seen as the work of landowners keen to line their own pockets. No amount of argument by Liverpool in the Lords or Vansittart in the Commons could convince the inhabitants of northern industrial towns otherwise. The corn law concentrated minds on the issue of parliamentary reform as the only effective means of redress. It is hardly surprising that the reform movement in this period was so anti-aristocratic. At the same time, pro-establishment rioting all but disappeared.

Anglo-American War, 1812–15 A conflict which is now little remembered in Britain, but which significantly added to the economic difficulties the country experienced towards the end of the Napoleonic Wars. Neither country could establish a decisive advantage before The Treaty of Ghent brought the war to a close.

Indirect taxes Taxes which are levied not 'directly' on a person's land, other property or income but on the goods which they buy. Such taxes could be a particular burden on those with limited incomes because the proportion of those incomes subject to a given indirect tax was much greater than for someone who was wealthy.

Corn laws Legislation protecting British landowners and farmers against foreign competition. A new corn law was passed in 1815. It prohibited foreign corn being imported until the domestic price reached a very high level of 80s (£4) a quarter. It was widely condemned by political radicals as biased towards landowners.

Hunt, Henry Radical politician known as 'Orator Hunt'. After 1815, he developed the peaceful mass meeting into a key feature of radical protest. He was the key speaker at the meeting in St Peter's Fields, Manchester, in August 1819 which developed into the 'Peterloo Massacre'. He was MP for Preston from 1830–2.

Poor law The system whereby local parishes were required to provide for those unable to look after themselves. It came under increasing attack from the end of the eighteenth century as costs grew. Many proposals were made to reform it. A new poor law, based on proposals by a Royal Commission, was approved in 1834.

Poor Law Overseers Those responsible for the day-to-day administration of the poor law at parish level. They were unpaid but their expenses were defrayed by local ratepayers. Overseers was strongly criticised by the Royal Commission on the Poor Laws because many were inefficient and had little incentive to do a good job.

Bamford, Samuel Lancashire weaver, writer and radical politician. He became a radical during the trade depression at the end of the Napoleonic wars. He was a strong supporter of 'Orator Hunt'. He became less active after 1820, devoting more of his attention to journalism and other writing.

Radicalism The term covering belief in, usually extensive, reforms. Radical politicians called mostly for political and religious reform. The term 'philosophical radical' was used to describe those who wanted major reforms in the role and functions of government.

The great political catalyst was economic distress. With the coming of peace, the government no longer needed armaments or so many uniforms. It was also forced into deflationary policies by the defeat of its taxation proposals (see above, p. 11) while the demobilization of about 400,000 servicemen glutted an already depressed labour market. Wages in 1815–16 were squeezed downwards, especially in rural areas where unemployment was most acute and the cost of relieving the poor highest. By 1817, **poor law** relief, which had cost ratepayers only £2 million in the mid-1770s, had reached almost £8 million. In East Anglia, agricultural labourers, long considered inert and entirely unpolitical, rioted, burning ricks and demanding bread. Slogans such as 'Bread or Blood' circulated widely and figures associated with authority, such as harsh **poor law overseers** or grasping parsons and clerical magistrates, were singled out for abuse and attack (Peacock, 1965; Poynter, 1969; Evans, 1975).

The evidence of **Samuel Bamford**, a leading Lancashire radical working man and admittedly no impartial witness, nevertheless indicates the geographical extent of discontent in 1815 and 1816:

'At Bridport, there were riots on account of the high price of bread; at Bideford there were similar disturbances to prevent the exportation of grain; at Bury, by the unemployed, to destroy machinery; at Ely, not suppressed without bloodshed; at Newcastle-on-Tyne, by colliers and others; at Glasgow, where blood was shed; at Preston, by unemployed weavers; at Nottingham, by Luddites, who destroyed thirty frames; at Merthyr Tydville on a reduction of wages; at Birmingham, by the unemployed; and at Dundee, where, owing to the high price of meal, upwards of one hundred shops were plundered'.

(S. Bamford, *Passages in the Life of a Radical* Ch 1;
see also **Doc. 16, p. 114**)

In such a disturbed climate, the cause of parliamentary reform revived. Whereas in the 1790s it was uncertain whether leadership lay in the hands of aristocratic Whigs or of extra-parliamentary radicals, after 1815 no doubt remained. **Radicalism** focused on a reform of Parliament and that focus lay outside Parliament itself.

Following the lead given by Major John Cartwright, numerous Hampden Clubs (taking their name aptly from John Hampden who opposed **arbitrary government** in the form of Charles I's ship money in the 1630s) were formed in the last years of the war and immediately afterwards. All of them called for reform but many, especially in the Lancashire cotton towns, went against Cartwright's more modest proposals and called for governments to be elected by full manhood suffrage.

In this, they were encouraged by the emergence of a much more self-confident radical press. It is difficult to exaggerate the importance of the popular press as an educative and a cultural force. Journals like **William Cobbett**'s *Weekly Political Register*, T.J. Wooler's *Black Dwarf*, William Hone's *Reformists' Register* and Thomas Sherwin's *Political Register* were read aloud and discussed at meetings in public houses known to be sympathetic to radical and democratic causes. They thus spanned the otherwise broad gulf between the literate and the non-literate. All but the first of these newspapers were founded in the years immediately after the war.

Printing the editorials of his *Register*, first launched in 1802 but selling at a prohibitively expensive one shilling (5p), on a single sheet ironically called *Twopenny Trash*, enabled William Cobbett, a journalist of genius, to reach a mass audience. From November 1816, circulation spiralled. At a time when 5,000 was considered an excellent sale for a national newspaper, Cobbett claimed 'sixty or seventy thousand' for his cheap *Register*. Samuel Bamford asserted that Cobbett's works were read 'on nearly every cottage hearth in the manufacturing districts of South Lancashire, in those of Leicester, Derby and Nottingham; also in many of the Scottish manufacturing towns.' For this mass audience Cobbett had both a direct and an indirect message. First, he asserted plainly to his readers that 'misgovernment' was the cause of their distress and its 'proper corrective', as Bamford put it, 'parliamentary reform'. Cobbett's target, therefore, was what he called 'Old Corruption'. Here he was attacking that patronage system of appointments by which an unelected group of leading landowners decided who should have important jobs. This landed elite, in Cobbett's view, raised money by taxing ordinary people, not so much to pay for the legitimate functions of government, but to buttress an unrepresentative and unjustified system which suppressed the liberties of the people (Harling, 1996: 1). Secondly, he worked on the self-regard of his readers. Addressing 'Friends and Fellow Countrymen' in November 1816, he plainly told them that 'Whatever the Pride of rank, or riches or of scholarship may have induced some men to believe . . . the real strength and all the resources of a country, ever have sprung and ever must spring, from the *labour* of its people' (Thompson, 1963: 620–1) **[Doc. 17, p. 115]**. Never one to underestimate his own influence, Cobbett claimed that the effects of his work were 'prodigious; the people everywhere on the stir in the cause of parliamentary reform' (Green, 1983: 385).

Radical clubs and political newspapers were two means of advancing the democratic cause. The third, and most alarming to the government, was the monster demonstration backed by mass petitions to Parliament for redress of grievances and acknowledgement of rights. The presentation of petitions was a long-established, and perfectly constitutional practice, of course, but the campaigns of 1816–17 injected a coercive element. The strategy developed

Arbitrary government Government in which the exercise of authority is unrestrained. In some contexts, the phrase can also imply government which depends on particular prejudices or whims rather than on the outcome of rational deliberation between alternative policies.

Cobbett, William Radical journalist and parliamentary reformer. He published the weekly *Political Register* almost continuously from 1802–32, and *Rural Rides* (1830), the result of extensive tours through the agricultural areas of southern England from 1825. He became MP for the new borough of Oldham in 1832.

by the demagogic utterances of Henry Hunt at the three meetings held in Spa Fields, London, was to show the authorities the force of public opinion and its latent power if petitions for reform were denied. The largest such meeting was held in December 1816. It passed resolutions calling for annually elected Parliaments and universal suffrage. Provincial meetings were also held. One such, at Thrushgrove on the outskirts of Glasgow in October 1816, was reported to have been attended by 40,000 people. In Sheffield in December a splinter group broke off from the main reform demonstration, and carried a blood-stained loaf – symbolizing 'Bread or Blood' – around the town. Some windows were smashed and the leader of the group was arrested (Stevenson, 1979: 207–8).

In January 1817, at Cartwright's instigation, a meeting of delegates from radical societies throughout the country met at the Crown and Anchor tavern in London. In the manner of many such radical gatherings between the 1790s and the 1840s, there was much disagreement over tactics and much opportunity for radical spokesmen to demonstrate that their commitment to reform was at least equalled by their commitment to self-advertisement and aggrandisement. The radical MPs for Westminster, Francis Burdett and Lord Cochrane, were both alienated by Hunt's determination immediately to present a petition for annual Parliaments and universal suffrage. The reformers' case was not so strongly represented in Parliament that the radicals could afford to jeopardize any kind of sympathetic hearing there and, outside Parliament, both Cartwright and Cobbett had severe disagreements with Hunt and the mainly northern delegates who supported him.

As in the 1790s, reformers divided into camps which might be broadly distinguished as 'constitutionalist' (those who wished to proceed by argument and rational persuasion), and 'coercionist' (those who either advocated violent overthrow of the existing constitution or, like Hunt himself, were prepared to use the threat of violence to put pressure on the authorities). As in the 1790s, also, it suited the government's book to believe that the radical cause had been hijacked by violent revolutionaries and it embarked on policies of selective represssion. Like Pitt, Liverpool set up a '**Committee of Secrecy**' which heard much evidence, some of it accurate, some of it the exaggeration or pure fabrication of spies and *agents provocateurs*, of revolutionary preparations **[Doc. 21, p. 118]**.

The main blame was laid on the followers of **Thomas Spence**, a Newcastle bookseller who had died in 1814, but who had converted many to his plan for radical reform based upon the expropriation of private estates and the nationalization of land. These 'Spencean Philanthropists', who included Thomas Evans, James Watson, **Arthur Thistlewood** and Thomas Preston, made no secret of their republicanism and some of them were engaged in revolutionary preparations late in 1816. Watson and Thistlewood were

Committee of secrecy A committee consisting of members of parliament in effect appointed by the government to hear evidence about possible conspiracies and treasonable activity. After hearing the evidence, the committee reported its findings to Parliament.

Spence, Thomas Bookseller and author. He died in 1814 but his ideas were influential after 1815. He believed in land nationalization or a form of agrarian communism. From 1815–20, some of the most violent radicals, such as Arthur Thistlewood and the Cato Street conspirators, were attracted by his ideas.

Thistlewood, Arthur Revolutionary. Involved with Spencean land reformers, he helped organise the Spa Fields demonstration in 1816. He is best known for his involvement in the Cato Street conspiracy, which led to his arrest on a charge of high treason. He was convicted and suffered both hanging and decapitation.

alleged to be involved in looting gunsmiths' shops and attempting an attack on the Tower after the December Spa Fields Meeting **[Docs. 19 and 20, pp. 117–18]**. They were tried for high treason but acquitted later in 1817. The House of Lords had reached a different conclusion. In February 1817, the Report of its 'Secret Committee . . . respecting certain dangerous meetings and combinations' had 'no doubt . . . that a traitorous conspiracy has been formed in the metropolis for the purpose of overthrowing, by means of a general insurrection, the established government, laws and constitution of this kingdom, and of effecting a general plunder and division of property' (Hansard, 1st ser., vol xxxv, 1817, col 412).

The government's legislative response also bore an uncanny resemblance to Pitt's in 1795. In February and March 1817, too, **habeas corpus** was temporarily suspended, allowing suspected persons to be held indefinitely without charges being brought against them. A new Seditious Meetings Act prevented societies and clubs holding meetings without the approval of magistrates. Sidmouth, the Home Secretary, sent out circulars to magistrates reminding them of the wide powers they could use to suppress disturbances; he further urged their use as needed. As in the 1790s, also, these measures had at least temporary success. Reform meetings became far less frequent. William Cobbett hastily left the country for the United States, though not before angrily denouncing an offer of £10,000 allegedly made to him by Sidmouth on condition that he stopped publication of the *Register* and retired to his Hampshire farm (Green, 1983: 391).

The government was probably not as alarmed about revolutionary preparations as it liked to pretend. Its spies kept it very well informed; a good intelligence system and pre-emptive force against those small, and disparate, minorities prepared to challenge its new legislation was amply sufficient. Some historians have made arduous endeavours both to unearth widespread revolutionary conspiracy and to lionize the conspirators. Although the Commons had contemptuously rejected a reform bill in January 1817, the evidence points more to the desperation of hunger as a motivating force for disturbance than to careful, concerted revolutionary planning. Fearing humiliation and unnecessary bloodshed, indeed, Samuel Bamford and other well-informed radicals tried to dissuade handloom weavers gathered in Manchester in March 1817 from marching to London to present a petition to the Prince Regent. About 300 of the 4,000 who had assembled ignored the advice and set out with blankets strapped to their backs for bedding – hence the grandiose title 'The March of the Blanketeers'. They got no further than Stockport, seven miles away, where they were turned back by the local yeomanry. A brief scuffle ensued in which one man was killed. A localized attempt at a rising in Manchester was easily thwarted three weeks later.

Habeas corpus A writ requiring a person accused of a crime to be brought before a Court to determine guilt or innocence. Without it, suspected criminals could be kept in gaol indefinitely without the authorities having to produce evidence against a suspect. The government suspended Habeas Corpus during periods of disturbance.

Plots for a more general rising in the spring of 1817, hatched mainly in those areas of Yorkshire and the east Midlands which had seen Luddite disturbances five years earlier, were expertly infiltrated by a government agent known as 'Oliver the Spy', in reality a discharged debtor, W. J. Richards. The planned 'rising' became in June a sad, doomed march on Nottingham by about 200 men led from the Derbyshire Peak District of Pentrich by **Jeremiah Brandreth**, a skilled worker in his late twenties. Forty-five men were arrested and charged with high treason. Three, including Brandreth, were executed and the majority of the rest joined the ever-swelling number of politically undesirable convicts in the new colonies of Australia.

Brandreth, Jeremiah Nottinghamshire hosiery worker He led the Pentrich Rising in 1817. When the Rising failed, he was arrested, charged with treason and hanged.

On one level, the events of the first half of 1817 were a major success for the government. Public reaction to its vigorous response, however, was far from uniformly favourable. One lesson the radicals learned from these half-cocked disturbances was that they needed to mobilize mass support more effectively. If they could bring the masses on to the crowded streets of the rapidly growing commercial and industrial towns chanting reformist verses and slogans, displaying symbolic Caps of Liberty and waving pro-Reform, anti-Corruption banners, they could demonstrate that their cause was not to be thwarted by either spies or anti-libertarian legislation.

The radical press was also much more effective than its establishment counterparts. It continued its campaign of vilification, arguing – with some Whig support – that the government had misjudged the public mood and had over-reacted. With characteristic restraint, the editor of *Gorgon*, John Wade, accused the government of 'the most abominable practices recorded in history' (Thompson, 1963: 663). Liverpool's ministers were soon to discover that, with no war to rally the loyalty of propertied opinion, and with an ever more self-conscious and self-confident industrial sector of the economy unsympathetic to Tory politics, reform would be far less easily controlled after 1817 than it had been in the 1790s.

PETERLOO AND THE CATO STREET CONSPIRACY

After the March of the Blanketeers, the government enjoyed a brief respite from radical activity. The 1817 harvest was good. Trade revived in Lancashire where literate and politically aware weavers had been giving much strength to radical protest since 1812. Unemployment fell. In consequence, 'hunger politics' were less apparent. The government remained chronically short of cash but its position at Westminster was strengthened by the defection of the Grenvillites from the Whigs in 1817 (see above, p. 14). It could trust the political nation with a general election in 1818 from which it emerged, as in the previous election of 1812, with more than twice as many seats as the Whigs and a slightly strengthened position overall (Thorne, 1986: i, 235, 263). The repeal of the Seditious Meetings Act and the reinstatement of the Habeas Corpus Amendment Act in 1818 were tangible evidence of declining alarm.

Some political protest continued in 1818, of course. The radical press still published vigorous condemnations of government policy. Wooler's *Black Dwarf* took over from the *Political Register* as the leading organ of protest during William Cobbett's sojourn in the United States **[Doc. 22, p. 119]**. The *Manchester Observer* began publication in January 1818; it advocated immediate parliamentary reform. Its circulation between 1818 and 1821 was substantial, although its impact was regional and short-term. Political clubs still met in public houses. Parliamentary reform petitions bombarded Westminster. It has been estimated that 1,500 were received in the course of 1818 (Stevenson, 1979: 211).

Luddism had been a marked feature of labour disturbances in the last years of the Napoleonic Wars. Now, the improvement of trade brought a revival of trade union activity with the Lancashire weavers much to the fore. Trade unions, or 'combinations' as they were called, were all formally banned between 1799 and 1824 but, thinly disguised as sickness and benefit insurance clubs, they continued to exist. Between 1812 and 1814 textile weavers' unions had led campaigns against reduced wages and against the introduction of unskilled workers into their trade, thus 'diluting' it. They had also sought, unavailingly, to preserve apprenticeship as a necessary condition of entry to trades. Both power-loom and handloom weavers sought wage increases during the spring and summer of 1818. Their strategy was to use a period of good trade, and thus relative labour scarcity, to coerce employers into diverting some of their profits into weavers' pockets. Radical political societies supported the weavers' claims and, after one demonstration in 1818, the Stockport **yeomanry**, which included manufacturers, shopkeepers and a few conservative skilled workers, used force to disperse rioters. It was to prove an unhappy precedent.

The failure of the weavers' agitation, combined with a worsening economic climate from the late summer of 1818, led to renewed concentration on politics and the formation of a 'Union for the Promotion of Human Happiness'. This union, which provided a lead for many others in the north of England in 1818–19, was organized on the basis of cooperation between skilled workers and the lower **middle classes**. Its objective was parliamentary reform. The unions emphasized the close links between radical politics and religious **nonconformity**, and they also placed an emphasis on education. If working men were to vote, they must know the issues upon which

Luddism The term originated from the name of the mythical figure 'Ned Ludd' who was supposed to have led workers to break machinery in the years 1811–16. Luddites were very specific in their targets, attacking only those machines which threatened the livelihoods of skilled workers in the textile trades.

Yeomanry Mounted troops who supported the regular soldiery. Their main purpose was national defence and they were organised into county regiments during the French wars. The local yeomanry mounted the attack on the massed crowd at St Peter's Fields, Manchester, in August 1819, precipitating the 'Peterloo Massacre'.

Middle classes A rather vague term covering a wide variety of occupations and wealth. Broadly, the middle classes divide into two categories. The industrial/commercial middle classes were in business and the professional middle classes were people with expert skills, such as lawyers, doctors or academics.

Nonconformists Literally, those who did not 'conform' to the doctrines of the Established Church, which was in England and Ireland the Church of England. See also Dissenters.

Sunday schools Schools which provided religious instruction, especially for the poor. They are associated with the Evangelical revival from the 1770s and 1780s onwards. Sunday schools took children out of church during adult worship and provided them with separate instruction in literacy and numeracy as well as religion.

Evangelical A Protestant Christian who believed that the Bible offers direct lessons in moral behaviour and that a Christian should undergo a process of 'conversion' (or rebirth) to a heightened spiritual awareness. Evangelical Christians concentrated attention on moral and social issues, including slavery and prison conditions.

their choices would turn. Many **Sunday schools** now became political as well as religious agencies – much to the annoyance of **evangelicals** who had supported the Sunday schools of the late eighteenth century as bastions of order and conservatism, where young minds could be trained up to industry, virtue and a dutiful acceptance of the existing social hierarchy.

The participation of women in radical politics was also a feature of these years. Some separate 'Female Unions' were formed early in 1819, apparently more alarming to the authorities than were their male counterparts. Stockport women reformers were accused of 'demoralizing the rising generation' and training 'their infants to the hatred of every thing that is orderly and decent, and to rear up rebels against God and State' (Glen, 1984: 232).

With the return of want to the industrial north, radical leaders were once again able to organize mass meetings. Increasingly, under the urging of John Cartwright, discussion began to turn on presenting reform petitions en masse, rather than through one of the few MPs favourable to the cause. A series of mass meetings was organized in Birmingham, Leeds, London and Manchester in the first half of 1819. In January, Henry Hunt addressed a large crowd at St Peter's Fields, Manchester. He argued that a hostile Parliament should be ignored and a petition presented directly to the Prince Regent demanding universal suffrage and annually elected Parliaments. Meetings in Birmingham and Leeds elected delegates from towns currently unrepresented in Parliament who were to meet in London and consider further action. Such meetings could be interpreted as a direct challenge to the authority of Parliament. Reports from spies and *agents provocateurs* reached the Home Secretary, Sidmouth, claiming that arming and drilling were taking place among radical groups. It is clear from Home Office evidence that the government was prepared to face down any challenge. In response to spies' reports early in 1819 that an insurrection in Lancashire might be imminent, Sidmouth's under-secretary Henry Hobhouse replied that 'your Country will not be tranquillized, until Blood shall have been shed either by Law or the sword. Lord Sidmouth will not fail to be prepared for either alternative' (Poole, 2006: 264).

Fears of a breakdown of public order, which government spies at least constructed as preparation for full-scale rebellion, were therefore rife when Hunt accepted an invitation to address yet another open-air meeting in Manchester in August 1819, organized by the Patriotic Union Society. Hunt's appeal for a peaceable assembly cut little ice with Lancashire magistrates who had seen previous meetings end in violence and who knew that the political temperature in the summer of 1819 was higher than ever. An interchange of correspondence between the Home Office and Lancashire magistrates indicates the authorities' perception that a mass Reform meeting might be a mere pretext for treason and revolution. By the time Sidmouth and his colleagues were prepared to acknowledge that the Hunt meeting might not, after all, be seditious it was too late. When about 60,000 men, women and children assembled in St Peter's Fields on 16 August, the local authorities, with at least tacit support from the government, were determined not to let the meeting take its course. On Home Office advice, Hunt was arrested. The meeting was forcibly broken up by the local yeomanry and, when they got into difficulties, by hussars using sabres. More than 600 people were injured in the dispersal and up to 17 died – sabred or trampled – either on the day or shortly afterwards. The event was speedily dubbed 'The Peterloo Massacre' in bitingly ironic reference to Wellington's most famous military victory.

Peterloo provided the radical cause with martyrs and the press exploited the situation to maximum effect. Liverpool's government felt obliged to defend the Manchester and Salford authorities but the defence had a hollow ring, as the prime minister himself privately admitted. In the growing public clamour for reform, the Whigs were forced to take up the question again. Their enthusiasm was warmed when the government dismissed Earl Fitzwilliam from his post as Lord Lieutenant of Yorkshire for supporting an enquiry into the causes and course of the events in Manchester. Nothing rallied Whig opinion so effectively as a Tory humiliation of one of the great landowning families, and Fitzwilliam was a mainstay of Whig support in the north of England.

Peterloo also confirmed reform as a truly national cause. Political unions were formed in parts of the country, such as Newcastle-on-Tyne and the Black Country area of south Staffordshire, where radicalism had previously been weak. By the autumn of 1819, even the formation of 'armed associations' of property owners could not quieten the reformers, and threats of violence increased. Rioting was commonplace; attempts at armed rebellion were mounted in Huddersfield and Burnley. Rumours of arming and drilling were pervasive. Liverpool's old colleague, Lord Grenville (see above p. 14), urged him to pass stern legislation to stave off a British revolution on the French model.

Peterloo also provided radical satirists with both an easy target and an opportunity to make money. The visual medium was pre-eminent here. Cartoons, etchings and engravings appeared in large numbers. All carried the message that what was already being called 'the Massacre' had created martyrs for the radical cause. George Cruikshank fashioned an ironic 'Peterloo Medal' showing a member of the Yeomanry attacking a thin, unarmed man with an axe. The border was decorated with skulls. Perhaps the most innovative of the satirists, William Hone, published *The Political House that Jack Built* in December 1819 in collaboration with Cruikshank. It parodied the authorities using the form of one of the most famous nursery rhymes. The frontispiece conveys an especially withering image in the form of a wood engraving bearing the title 'The Pen and the Sword'. The Duke of Wellington, the victor of Waterloo, had recently been brought into the government. He is seen placing his own sword on scales which show various aspects of government response to the outcry provoked by Peterloo on the one side and simply a quill pen on the other. The balance, of course, is tipped in favour of the pen. Hone's *Political House* sold over 100,000 copies in less than a year (Wood, 1994). Visual imagery proved particularly potent in a society which was still, among ordinary working folk, no more than semi-literate.

For the last time during the pre-1832 period, the government responded to the call for reform with repression. The Six Acts (or 'Gagging Acts' as they were not inappropriately dubbed) were rushed through Parliament in December 1819. These Acts prohibited any gatherings for arming or drilling; gave magistrates in the disturbed areas powers to search for arms; prevented defendants from gaining delays by postponing their answers to specific charges; prohibited meetings of more than 50 persons without magistrates' consent, and indemnified magistrates against the consequences of casualties suffered in dispersing illegal assemblies; increased the penalties for writing seditious or blasphemous libels; and imposed punitive stamp duties on pamphlets and papers which had been fomenting discontent. The Acts were a commentary on recent disturbances and, by regulating both meetings and the press, indicated clearly enough where the Tories laid the blame.

Carlile, Richard Radical journalist strongly influenced by Thomas Paine. Much of his writing was irreligious, bringing him into conflict with other radicals. He was arrested for making blasphemous statements in 1819 and imprisoned for six years. From prison, he published the weekly journal *Republican*.

The Acts were used selectively to remove radicals from the scene. Hunt, Wooler, **Richard Carlile** and even the aristocratic radical MP Sir Francis Burdett were all locked up by the summer of 1820. The efficiency of Sidmouth and his intelligence-gathering activities perhaps deserve greater emphasis than they have received. Historians out of sympathy with the Liverpool government lay articulate, sympathetic and not inaccurate stress on the extent of radical activity. Yet it was contained. The crisis of 1819 was met decisively but – Peterloo and local excesses apart – central government avoided unselective brutality. The situation was one which could easily have been mishandled by a Tory government and, left to the prejudices of Eldon, a Lord Chancellor of little political sensitivity, it would have been. Eldon railed against the decision to prosecute Hunt and his colleagues for mere sedition and not treason: 'Can any man doubt . . . that these meetings are overt acts of conspirators, to instigate to such specific acts of treason? . . . I cannot doubt it.' (Melikan, 1999: 266).

Utilitarianism Philosophy which holds that the purpose of government should be to secure the maximum happiness and benefit for the largest number of citizens. It was developed in its modern form by Jeremy Bentham and, later, John Stuart Mill. It guided the formulation of much social policy from the 1830s.

The firmness of Liverpool and Sidmouth has earned them few accolades but political judgements are more often made on the basis of **utilitarian** than philosophical criteria. It is not necessary to sympathise with the government's objectives to appreciate its competence in a crisis. As E.P. Thompson remarked on Pitt's similar policies in the 1790s, the government's bark proved much worse than its bite. Political acumen was needed to understand that a loud bark was what the government guard-dog needed. Wholesale biting might indeed have led to shooting the dog.

In 1819, as in 1795 and 1817, legislative action proved sufficient to contain the radical challenge. In reality this challenge was less concerted and less effectively led than might appear from the noise it made and the alarm it induced in some quarters. Very different views about tactics and even ultimate ends were held by radical sympathisers. It was one thing to accept that the unreformed House of Commons was increasingly at variance with early nineteenth-century British society, quite another to agree on a specific reform programme. The preponderant weight of radical opinion between 1815 and 1820 was indeed democratic, but influential middle-class reformers, like old John Cartwright, continued to favour a household suffrage. Whig pro-reformers tended to be even more cautious. They preferred to disfranchise rotten or **pocket boroughs**, give seats to leading industrial towns and then soberly debate what qualifications for the vote best fitted an emerging industrial age. Such a gradualist approach invited the contempt of radical populists such as Hunt, Cobbett or Carlile.

Disagreements on means were even more debilitating. Richard Carlile was a disciple of Tom Paine who extended Paine's **republican** sentiments into an almost pathological hatred for the Church of England as an agency of conservatism, mystification and superstition. His reaction to the Peterloo Massacre was unequivocal: 'The People have now no recourse left but to arm themselves, immediately, for the recovery of their rights' (Dinwiddy, 1986: 34). Democratic radicals divided broadly into 'moral force' and 'physical force' camps. Moral-force leaders, many of them religious nonconformists and trade unionists, continued to believe, as Paine had done, that the concentrated power of reason trained on the ramparts of hereditary privilege and vested interest would bring about a peaceful transition of power. Physical-force leaders, citing Peterloo, drew the less sanguine conclusion that vested interests cannot be argued into renouncing their privileges. Force must be met with force. Many advocates of physical force, however, of whom Henry Hunt was the pre-eminent example, were prepared to threaten violence as a coercive tactic while in practice were reluctant to put their threats into practice.

It might be argued that hungry handloom weavers and factory operatives were badly let down by their leaders in 1819–20. Hunt and Cobbett, certainly, had self-regarding, vainglorious streaks which got in the way of realistic planning. Too many radical leaders were windbags, carried away by their rhetoric and heedless of the effects their intoxicating language had on empty stomachs and unprepared minds. More important, however, was the evanescence of radicalism. Though Peterloo had excited massive national hostility, long-term support for radicalism remained largely concentrated in

Pocket borough Term used to indicate that a borough was, in effect, owned ('in the pocket of') usually by a member of the aristocracy or the crown. Elections in such boroughs were rare because the outcome was so often a foregone conclusion. Pocket boroughs could even be bought and sold.

Republican Someone who does not believe in the principle of monarchy. Following Tom Paine, most republicans reject the idea of hereditary succession.

London and the textile districts. Its mass appeal was critically determined by bread prices, wage and unemployment levels.

Liverpool and Sidmouth were also shrewd enough to realize that every threat of violence alienated middle-class support. The middle classes had no particular love for Liverpool's protectionist agricultural policies which, indirectly, threatened industrial markets, but fear for their property was a much more potent factor in 1819. It should be remembered that it was representatives of an alarmed Lancashire bourgeoisie who, as members of the Manchester Yeomanry, cut swathes through a reform crowd at St Peter's Fields. Even in the autumn of 1819, the threat of revolution was not so great as radical activity made it seem and the best hope of constitutional reform, which lay in alliance between the middle and working classes against the landowners, was actually reduced by the alarm which reports of arming and drilling generated. The Six Acts were welcomed by the bourgeoisie, and those with little or no property to lose had insufficient unity of purpose or decisive leadership to compensate.

Genuine revolutionaries are not deterred by adverse legislation and a few of these existed both in England and Scotland in 1819–20. The Spencean (see pp. 20–1) Arthur Thistlewood was already familiar to the authorities by 1820. He had instigated the riots which followed the London Spa Fields meeting in November 1816 and had embarrassed the authorities several times since then. For challenging Sidmouth to a duel, he had been imprisoned without trial for over a year in 1818–19. On his release, which coincided with Peterloo, he began to lay revolutionary plans in London with a fellow Spencean, Dr James Watson, and members of the recently formed London 'Committee of Two Hundred'. Rumours began to circulate that Thistlewood and Watson were planning a nationwide rebellion with the help of revolutionaries in Lancashire and Yorkshire. A simultaneous rising early in 1820 was planned to coincide with the assassination of the entire cabinet as they attended a dinner at the home of the Earl of Harrowby, the career politician from a legal family who was Lord President of the Council throughout the Liverpool administration. As usual, the conspiracy was infiltrated by a government agent, in this case George Edwards. The authorities were able to apprehend the conspirators as they assembled in Cato Street in February. Thistlewood and four accomplices were speedily tried for high treason and executed three months later. Five others were transported.

Sidmouth, not given to hasty or alarmist utterances, nevertheless believed the Cato Street conspiracy to have been part of a wider plot. The theory is supported by a number of outbreaks both in Scotland and Yorkshire immediately after the conspiracy's failure became apparent. An attempt by weavers to seize Glasgow predictably failed but about 20 men decamped to Bonnymuir in Stirlingshire, led by Andrew Hardie and John Baird. There they offered battle to the yeomanry and hussars who came in search of them. A similar number from Strathaven, some 20 miles south of Glasgow, under the leadership of a veteran radical from the 1790s, marched north to occupy the city at the same time but fled when the hopelessness of their position became clear, as it rapidly did. These three leaders suffered the same fate as Thistlewood, while the lesser lights were transported (Royle, 2000). Within a week, Yorkshire weavers had attempted to take control of Huddersfield. More than 300 assembled on the moors outside Barnsley carrying flags and weapons. John Blackwell, a journeyman tailor who had organized a post-Peterloo reform meeting in Sheffield, tried to seize the Attercliffe barracks in that city (Stevenson, 1979).

The doomed and desperate efforts in the spring of 1820 deserve mention not because they offered any real threat to the government – though it is worth noting that assassination attempts only need to succeed once – but because each drew on a much broader base of pro-reform sympathy. London, industrial Lancashire, south and west Yorkshire and central Scotland were all substantially disturbed at this time. The government was well-positioned to anticipate trouble from revolutionaries but it did not make the mistake of assuming that only small bands of desperadoes were disenchanted. One of the Tories' rising stars, Sir **Robert Peel**, perhaps put it best in a private letter to the Secretary for the Admiralty and writer, John Wilson Croker:

> 'Do not you think that the tone of England – of that great compound of folly, weakness, prejudice, wrong feeling, right feeling, obstinacy and newspaper paragraphs, which is called public opinion – is more liberal, to use an odious but intelligible phrase, than the policy of the government?'
> (Gash, 1985: 250–1)

No one could mistake Peel for a political reformer, but by the middle of 1820 some anti-reformers were beginning to consider how best 'respectable opinion' might be assuaged and whether recent events had given greater credence to hotheads and revolutionaries. Peel, for one, did not believe that the reform question would disappear with the return of prosperity.

THE CURIOUS AFFAIR OF QUEEN CAROLINE

Only against a background of disturbance does the tragi-comedy of the **Queen Caroline** affair make sense. Yet in 1820–1 it severely embarrassed Lord Liverpool, lost him the confidence of George IV, and almost brought

Peel, Sir Robert Tory politician. From an industrial family, he was a reforming Home Secretary under Liverpool from 1822. He persuaded Wellington to pass Catholic emancipation in 1829, provoking deep divisions within the Tory party and much hostility towards him personally. He was prime minister in 1834–5 and 1841–6.

Caroline of Brunswick-Wolfenbüttel Queen 1820–1. Married to George, Prince of Wales, in 1795, the couple were never compatible. On becoming King, George IV tried to divorce her. The scandal made both parties a laughing stock. Caroline avoided divorce but was prohibited from attending the Coronation. She died soon after.

about his dismissal from office. The affair also gave rise to the last great wave of public demonstrations before the Reform crisis.

The background details are quickly told. Prince George had married his cousin Princess Caroline of Brunswick-Wolfenbüttel in 1795, an earlier marriage – unapproved by the Prince's father George III – to the Roman Catholic Maria Fitzherbert in 1785 having been quietly ignored. The new union was never close and both partners quickly sought alternative outlets for their not inconsiderable energies. Once Regent, and freed from his father's claustrophobic orthodoxy on the subject, George hastened to put his unloved wife to one side. She was bribed with a yearly annuity to leave the country in 1814, moving to Italy where she soon settled to an existence of insouciant promiscuity. Some of the more salacious details were revealed to the Regent in 1819 in a report which he intended to make the grounds of a divorce action. Other than via her yearly *douceur* of £3,000, Caroline had no contact with the Regent. She was not even informed of the death of their only child, Princess Charlotte, in childbirth in 1817 – an event of substantial dynastic significance since it left George with no direct heir, and eventually paved the way for the reign of Queen **Victoria**.

Victoria Monarch from 1837 to 1901. She came to the throne only as the result of fortuitous deaths during our period. She was the daughter of George III's fourth son. Her father died in 1820 and all three of her father's elder brothers died before her without leaving any living legitimate children.

George III died on 29 January 1820 and George IV wasted no time in informing his ministers that, outweighing all other considerations of state, his urgent priority was a divorce. Caroline's name was not to appear in the Anglican prayer book. Above all, Caroline was not to be crowned as his Queen. Liverpool and his ministers urged caution. The country was still in a disturbed condition, and such action against the Queen would provoke national hostility which, given the inevitable delays attending any contested divorce, would be indefinitely prolonged.

Much turned on the new King's personal unpopularity. The Hanoverians had not inspired affection since they had saved the nation for Protestantism in the unedifying shape of George I in 1714. The fourth George, however, plumbed new depths, embodying all the worst failings of the German dynasty: inflexibility; petulance; fierce, unpredictable and uncontrollable rages; promiscuity; and an incorrigible lack of political sense. George's numerous sexual indiscretions had received wide, and mocking, publicity both written and, via engravings and cartoons, visual. During the recent disturbances the Regent's personal habits had been lampooned by radical cartoonists. Their representation of George as a fat, flatulent, dissolute slob, indeed, served as an effective allegorical indictment of aristocratic government as a whole. The fact that he was also a man of considerable aesthetic sensibility was either ignored, or used as a further stick to beat him with on grounds of cost and waste. As Liverpool knew all too well, the King's suing for divorce could only mobilize the nation on behalf of the Queen, whatever her own shortcomings.

Furthermore, the new Queen was determined to play a fully theatrical part in the unfolding drama. She signified her intention to return to England where she would contest divorce proceedings with vigour, and would accept support from any quarter. In the early months of 1820, indeed, she was relying on the advice of the radical master draper and former Lord Mayor of London, Matthew Wood. He informed her that the people of London would prove stout champions. Thus fortified, Caroline published an open letter in leading newspapers in which she lambasted her husband for his despicable actions and for using his influence to close all European courts to her. She asserted her constitutional rights as the King's wife and proclaimed, 'England is my real home to which I shall immediately fly' (Halevy, 1926: 90).

In the circumstances, the failure of Liverpool's hastily devised plan to pre vent the Queen's arrival is hardly surprising. He employed Henry Brougham, the prominent Whig lawyer who had, in effect, been the legal adviser to Caroline since 1812, to negotiate with her and to offer her £50,000 if she remained outside Britain (Stewart, 1985). By the time Brougham, whose personal political ambitions complicated matters, made the offer, the Queen was already deaf to any financial entreaty, being firmly committed to her English escapade. Her much-publicised arrival in London in June 1820 brought huge crowds on to the streets in her support (Stevenson, 1977).

Frustrated in its main objective, the government was forced to do the King's bidding. It introduced a Bill of 'Pains and Penalties' and began a trial of the Queen before the House of Lords on a charge of maintaining 'an adulterous connection with a foreigner', in fact her Italian butler Bartolomeo Pergami. Between August, when the trial began, and November, when the Bill was ignominiously withdrawn in the face of dangerously dwindling majorities in the Lords, the press had a series of circulation-boosting field days (Robins, 2006). The King was held up to ridicule as a licentious hypocrite accusing his wife of the very vices he had so long and so assiduously practised. *The Times* took the Queen's part along with the rest. William Cobbett, who could see no other issue in the autumn of 1820, acted as the Queen's unofficial cheer-leader and filled his *Political Register* with passionate articles in her defence (Burton, 1997). Cartoonists of genius, like George Cruikshank and William Hone, depicted the King of England in ever more ridiculous, degrading and humiliating postures. Never has the British monarchy been held in greater contempt (Wood, 1994).

Tumultuous crowds thronged the capital at Queen Caroline's every appearance; the city was illuminated in triumph on the day the Bill was withdrawn. The Caroline affair is often described as an episode in London radicalism, but it was in fact a national event. The Whigs organized county protest meetings against the Bill in Yorkshire, Northumberland, Durham, Buckinghamshire and Sussex. Newcastle-under-Lyme, in Staffordshire, was only one of many towns to send petitions in favour of the Queen. More than half its adult male population signed it. A congratulatory address followed when the Bill was withdrawn.

So soon after the Peterloo furore, the government could well have done without a further *cause célèbre*, especially one which it had tried hard to avoid. His peevishness reinforced by his mauling, the King blamed his troubles on his ministers and prepared in November to rid himself of Lord Liverpool. Had the Whigs not been split, as ever, on whether they would make a measure of parliamentary reform a condition of accepting office, it is probable that the King's bluster would for once have been translated into decisive action. He had, after all, offered the prime ministership to Lord Grenville, who had briefly been prime minister in 1806–7, but who refused it (Hay, 2005: 120). In the autumn of 1820, the Whigs came closer to a return to government than at any time between 1807 and 1827 **[Doc. 3, p. 107]**.

The affair did produce one ministerial casualty whom Liverpool could ill-afford to lose. George Canning, though increasingly frustrated by what he considered junior office as President of the Board of Control, and ostentatiously aware that his talents exceeded those of most of his colleagues, was the government's most incisive debater in the Commons. His relationship with Caroline had been close, and some informed gossip suggested that it exceeded the bounds of propriety. Canning opposed the prosecution of the Queen, absented himself on a convenient European tour during its course, and eventually sent his resignation to the prime minister in December 1820. At the time, it seemed a devastating blow, adding weight to the impression that the Queen Caroline affair represented the biggest crisis of the long Liverpool premiership.

Nevertheless, the arrival of Christmas afforded a breathing space during which propertied Englishmen could reflect. The Caroline affair was of no more permanent significance in the political constellation than the appearance of a comet. It dazzled its watchers while it lit up the late summer and autumn skies, but it was only a squalid squabble between a couple of coarse, graceless and obstinate, though highly privileged, individuals. This marital strife, whatever its publicity value, was not worthy of a ministerial crisis. Nor, as more reflective or high-minded radical writers like Wade and Wooler came to conclude, did the affair afford a proper springboard from which to launch a new reform campaign. So, while country gentlemen continued to conclude, as they had at least since 1816, that the Tories were a sounder bet than the Whigs, radicals outside Parliament continued their quest for a higher plane of political argument and a more elevated cause with which to mobilize the masses.

In any case, as the new year dawned, the redundantly vindicated Queen had nowhere to go. She would not be divorced but neither would she be permitted to exercise the duties of a Queen. When she accepted a pension of £50,000, a sum on offer to her several months previously, she lost whatever residual support she had for a renewal of the constitutional battle. The King would not let her attend his coronation in July 1821. Yet Caroline demonstrated her lack of both judgement and style by turning up uninvited at Westminster Abbey and banging on every door in turn in a vain attempt at admittance. As many in the large, and still sympathetic, London crowd must have realized, it was a characteristically public, yet futile, gesture.

Outside the capital, public opinion, especially among the propertied classes, moved steadily against the Queen. A spate of loyal addresses reached the King and government from 'independent **freeholders**' and others concerned to note that many of Caroline's supporters were men and women of the working classes, concerned more to challenge established authority than to champion the Queen's cause (Fulcher, 1995; Hunt, 1991). For some loyalists, the very entry of women into the political sphere was seen as a dangerous impertinence which was against the natural order of things.

The end was in any case near. Caroline, probably weakened by the strident exertions of the past year, succumbed with unexpected speed and decisiveness to a fever in August 1821. The King rejoiced. The prime minister, a naturally more magnanimous and reflective figure, could afford genuine condolence. His government had already drawn strength from falling prices and a return of prosperity (see pp. 22–3). The Whigs' dream of office had evaporated. Even before her final illness, Caroline had become a political irrelevance. The London crowds forced a diversion of her funeral *cortège* through the City from the planned anonymity of its route to Harwich and thence to a final resting place in Brunswick. This proved to be the last even vaguely menacing public assembly of the lower orders which Liverpool would have to face, although his government would survive for another five and a half years. As Boyd Hilton has put it, the Caroline affair proved only to be 'the storm before the calm' (Hilton, 2006: 269). The comet had burned itself out.

Freeholders Literally, people who own land free of any restrictions, such as leases or covenants. In our period, it was an important term since the possession of freehold land was one of the key qualifications for the vote in parliamentary elections, especially in county constituencies.

3

The Achievement of Stability? 1821–27

THE RETURN OF PROSPERITY

'Never in our memory was this part of the country in a state equally flourishing: our manufacturers are employed, our artisans happy and industrious, and loyalty and content have given place to jacobinism and sedition, which distress had mainly contributed to foster.'

(Glen, 1984: 254)

The *Stockport Advertiser* was reflecting in June 1823 on the buoyancy of the cotton trade rather than on the economy as a whole. Nevertheless, it has been generally accepted that for most of the 1820s the British economy was flourishing. After the dislocations of the immediate post-war period, which were accompanied by high levels of unemployment and high food prices, trade revived and distress ebbed.

As the *Stockport Advertiser* also implied, trade revival reduced the levels of working-class discontent. Mass protest movements were very rare between the Queen Caroline affair and the end of Liverpool's government in 1827. Radical leaders locked away in 1819–20 were generally released in 1821 and 1822. The most charismatic of them, Henry Hunt, was let out of Ilchester gaol in October 1822 – whence, typically, he had launched a series of stinging, if self-absorbed, diatribes on the state of British prisons. His release was joyously celebrated in many places but by a relatively small number of convinced political radicals; they did not occasion mass agitation or the threatening postures of 1819–20 (Belchem, 1985).

For much of the 1820s, radical energies were absorbed in longer-term strategy and ideology. As ever with the reform movement, squabbles broke out, most notably between Richard Carlile, who wished to see radicalism follow both a **republican** and an **atheistic** course **[Doc. 23, p. 119]** and Hunt, who knew how few radicals were atheists and how strong were the links between reform and religious nonconformity. In this decade both

Republican Someone who does not believe in the principle of monarchy. Following Tom Paine, most republicans reject the idea of hereditary succession.

Atheist A person who denies the existence of God. In this period, atheists could not become members of parliament or hold government office.

Thomas Hodgskin, a journalist who had served as a naval officer during the Napoleonic Wars, and William Thompson, an Irish landowner converted to the utopian socialism of Robert **Owen**, advanced theories postulating that labour was the source of all value. These had obvious implications for later socialist movements (Thompson, 1963; Thompson, 1984). Developments in these years contributed to the maturity of later protests but they did not immediately threaten the government.

Prosperity was the keynote of the 1820s, but it was neither universal nor continuous. Remarkably little is known about key indicators such as unemployment, for which no official records were kept until the 1890s. Thus, historians are reliant on impressionistic contemporary accounts of the 'state of trade'. The statistics which do survive are far less sophisticated than those available in our own day and they anyway assume the existence of a *national* economy which, even in the early stages of the Industrial Revolution, hardly existed. Movements within different sectors of the economy often contrast markedly and regional differences may be much more significant than national trends. Nevertheless, some obvious statements may be made with confidence. The economy grew much more rapidly in the 1820s than in the 1810s. The gross national product is estimated to have fallen by 3.5 per cent in the 1810s before rising by 16.8 per cent in the 1820s. All the conventional indicators used by economists to demonstrate growth are firmly in place. During the 1820s, earnings from foreign investment increased by 60 per cent and the amount of money deposited in private savings banks increased from £3.5 million in 1820 to £14.6 million in 1830 (Floud and McCloskey, 1994: i, 131) **[Doc. 7, p. 109]**.

The picture on the land, however, was less healthy. While manufactures, mining, building, trade and transport grew at an overall rate of about 26 per cent in the 1820s, agriculture, having declined sharply as food prices plummeted at the end of the French wars, increased by only 4.6 per cent (Deane and Cole, 1969: 166). Agriculture remained depressed from the end of the French wars until prices began to pick up in the middle of the 1830s. Only the presence of the Corn Laws (see above, p. 17) prevented even greater falls. Landowners and tenants, especially arable farmers, who had invested heavily and, as it turned out, unwisely when prices were high and credit cheap in the 1790s and 1800s, were put under severe pressure during the allegedly 'prosperous' 1820s, as the pages of the frequent parliamentary committees on agricultural distress made woefully clear.

It is worth noting that a 'landowners' Parliament' tolerated the fact that the agricultural sector of the economy fared much worse than any other in the decades before the first Reform Act. The irony was not lost on many backbenchers, concerned that the government was too sympathetic to the needs of commerce and to the theories of a new generation of political economists

Owen, Robert Manufacturer, philanthropist and socialist thinker. He set up a model cotton factory at New Lanark, with good quality housing and education for factory children. His ideas about cooperation between masters and workmen formed the basis of the nineteenth-century Co-Operative movement.

who preached free trade as the surest route to prosperity (Evans, 2001; Hilton, 1977) **[Docs. 4 and 6, p. 107 and p. 108]**. Agricultural labourers, whose numbers continued to increase while job opportunities dwindled, did worst of all. Even the normal means of relief, the Poor Law, became more stringently administered and more difficult to obtain during the 1820s. Protests by rural labourers, in the form of rick-burning and attacks on Poor Law overseers, were common in East Anglia, especially in 1822 (Prest, 1972).

For townsfolk, the main factors in the prosperity of the 1820s were the general buoyancy of economic activity which increased employment oppor-tunities, and the fall in food prices. A long-running and, on the whole, not very enlightening argument has raged on the implications of industrial growth for the living standards of working people between about 1780 and 1850 (Evans, 2001; Hunt, 1981; Taylor, 1975; Floud and McCloskey, 1994; Floud and Johnson, 2004: i, 268–94; Flinn, 1974; Lindert and Williamson, 1983). The main facets of that debate do not concern us here, but it is worth noting that both 'optimists' and 'pessimists' agree that during the 1820s real wages (which are calculated by comparing movements in money wages with those of prices) rose. This was largely because the cost of bread, still the staple diet of most British people, fell sharply. The average price of wheat (from which most bread was made) was more than one-third lower in the 1820s than in the 1810s. Even in the peak price year of 1825, wheat at 68s 6d (£3.42) a quarter was 25 per cent lower than the average price for the 1810s (Evans, 2001: 510). The very cause of agricultural distress, therefore, was the main factor in increased prosperity in the towns **[Doc. 5, p. 108]**.

In addition to agricultural labourers, the other large group of workers whose living standards almost certainly fell in the 1820s was the weavers. Handloom weavers were the most obvious casualties of technological advance. Their numbers had expanded rapidly in the late eighteenth century because the process of spinning was mechanized before weaving. This situation had created a substantial but short-term demand for weavers, whose wages had risen substantially during the French Wars. From the 1820s, however, the introduction of the new power loom reduced their earning power and in the most industrialized areas of the country first their wages and then their numbers began to drop sharply. In Stockport, for example, 5,000 handloom workers were employed in 1818. Over the next four years, the number declined to fewer than 3,000 and by 1832 to about 800 (Glen, 1984: 255). In London's East End, the Spitalfields silk weavers, whose numbers had likewise grown in the early years of the century, endured both wage cuts and unemployment from the mid-1820s partly as a result of the reduction of protection and a growing market for imported manufactured silks (Prothero, 1979).

During the years of prosperity, therefore, while most social groups benefited, more from lower prices than from higher wages, those who were threatened by the quickening pace of technological change faced crisis. The long-term outlook was also bleak for skilled workers whose bargaining power was threatened by competition from the unskilled who worked long hours in 'sweat shops' or 'slop shops' where products of inferior quality were made for a developing mass market. Tailors and shoemakers in London, for example, long considered among the aristocrats of labour, found it ever more difficult to maintain **wage differentials**. Rapid population growth, of course, increased labour supply (see above, pp. 6–8). In most periods of economic boom, higher general levels of prosperity disproportionately benefit the better-off. Although living standards almost certainly rose for most people in the 1820s, therefore, the gap widened between the middle classes, whose income came mainly from profit and investment, and the working classes, dependent more or less exclusively on wages.

It is characteristic of rapidly industrializing societies that their economic progress, remarkable in the longer term, is subject to short-term fluctuations. Even during the boom of the 1820s, one sharp slump was experienced, caused by excessive speculation in the money markets. The banking crisis of 1825–26 involved the outright failure of about 50 country banks while far more suspended cash payments. Share prices plummeted and panic spread through many London finance houses (Floud and Johnson, 2004: i, 162–3; Gordon, 1979). The government only narrowly avoided having to instruct the Bank of England to suspend payments to creditors in cash, which would have shattered already very fragile investor confidence. Peel was sure that the cause of the crisis was excessive speculative investment and consequent over-production. He told a colleague, almost with relish, that 'we have been working too fast'. He looked to the restoration of confidence in banks but only those 'which ought to be confided in' (Hilton, 2006: 327). His own **Liberal Toryism** was grounded in a moral belief in free-trade and **trade liberalization** (see pp. 47–9). Bankers who over-committed were morally wrong and investors foolish to trust their savings with them. A shakeout would see a healthier economy. He anticipated 'ultimate good after some severe suffering'. The government responded to the crisis by imposing strict controls on the issuing of bank notes in England, although Scotland (where the banking system was different) continued to issue large numbers of small-value notes for another 20 years (Daunton, 1995: 345).

In the real world of labour and employment, the crisis had important effects too. Unemployment temporarily rose in the cotton and woollen districts of Lancashire and Yorkshire and among the building and other skilled trades of London. Some rioting and machine breaking was experienced in the spring and summer of 1826. At Chadderton, near Manchester, in April,

Wage differentials Differences in the wages paid. The term is mostly used to describe how wage levels differ between one occupation and another or by how much they differ between skilled, semi-skilled and unskilled workers in the same trade.

Liberal Tories Name rather loosely applied to members of the Tory party who supported reformist policies, especially in the 1820s. The leading members of this group were Huskisson, Canning, Robinson and Peel. They were involved in administrative and legal reforms and the lowering of tariffs.

Trade liberalization The process whereby tariffs on trade were reduced with the purpose of increasing trade volumes and, thereby, the wealth of the nation. Liberalization was a reaction to policies which depended on protecting the trade of a nation by imposing protective duties.

indeed, seven rioters were killed by troops during attacks on mills which had introduced the new power looms (Stevenson, 1979: 233). The prosperity of the 1820s, therefore, was real but it stood on brittle foundations.

'LIBERAL TORYISM'? THE ACHIEVEMENT OF LORD LIVERPOOL

'Liberal Toryism' is the description which used to be given to the second, and shorter, period of Liverpool's administration. It is usually dated from the major ministerial changes made between August 1822 and January 1823. In this brief period, which begins with Castlereagh's suicide, six of the 13 portfolio cabinet posts changed hands: Canning took over the Foreign Office, and his old position of President of the Board of Control (with special responsibility for Indian affairs) went first to Bragge-Bathurst and then to Grenville's friend Charles Wynn. The old Chancellor of the Exchequer, Nicholas Vansittart (ennobled as Baron Bexley), became Chancellor of the Duchy of Lancaster, and was succeeded by Frederick Robinson. Robinson's successor as President of the Board of Trade, and thus responsible for commercial policy, was **William Huskisson**. Viscount Sidmouth, indelibly associated as Home Secretary with the Peterloo Crisis and the 'Six Acts' (see above pp. 24–6), was in his mid-sixties by 1822 and quite keen to retire. He remained in the Cabinet for two more years largely because the King wished it, but only as Minister without Portfolio. His postponed retirement nevertheless turned out to be very lengthy. He died in his late eighties in 1844. Sidmouth's successor at the Home Office was Sir Robert Peel, not yet in his mid-thirties, but with substantial ministerial experience in Ireland behind him; more recently he had been chairman of an important parliamentary committee on financial management (see p. 45). He was widely regarded as the ablest politician of his generation. Of the senior ministers, only Liverpool himself and Wellington retained their old posts.

It is understandable that these major changes should have been considered to mark a genuine transition in Liverpool's government from a '**reactionary**' phase, with the suppression of widespread popular unrest, to a 'liberal' one associated with a wide range of reforms in domestic and commercial affairs and a new stance in diplomacy. The impression is reinforced by an influential monograph on the 1820s published in 1967 by W.R. Brock entitled *Lord Liverpool and Liberal Toryism*. Nevertheless, the description is misleading. 'Liberal Toryism' should not imply a conscious governmental conversion from one policy to another. Liverpool's notion of Toryism has been indicated above (p. 13) and he embraced it no less warmly in 1827 than in 1815. It also incorporated from the very beginning a strong preference,

Huskisson, William Pittite Tory politician. He became President of the Board of Trade in 1823 and promoted trade liberalization policies. He also served in Canning and Goderich's governments but resigned from Wellington's government, with other 'liberal' colleagues in 1828. He was killed in a railway accident in 1830.

Reactionary The term is normally used to describe those who are resistant to change or who wish to re-establish an older policy or form of government. It derives from 'reaction'. The 'Ultra Tories' of the late 1820s and 1830s might properly be described as reactionaries.

implanted by Pitt, for the freeing up of trade regulations. Trade liberalization in the 1820s, as this process might be called, was not a new policy. Its
origins can be traced back to the younger Pitt in the 1780s, and the case
for viewing Liverpool's government in either its allegedly 'reactionary' or
its 'liberal' phases as predominantly Pittite, rather than Tory, has perhaps
been too readily dismissed by tidy-minded historians keen to use termino-
logy which would resonate more readily for students of nineteenth-century
British history.

Circumstances mainly, and personalities to a lesser degree, determined
that the last five years of Liverpool's government would be more concerned
with commerce than with public order and with cautious experiment rather
than with fearful retrenchment. Liverpool's governments present close paral-
lels between Pitt's peacetime policies of 1784–93 and Liverpool's between
1822 and 1827. Similarities also exist between Pitt's stress on public order
between 1793 and 1801 and Liverpool's between 1815 and 1820.

Liverpool lacked the intellectual independence and vision to strike out in
new directions. He was a consolidator rather than an innovator and he was
happy to follow the policy guidelines set out by his great predecessor. This is
why Disraeli described him a little later as the 'arch-mediocrity'. Before we
take too much notice of this famous put-down, however, we should remember, first, that Disraeli was no historian and, secondly, that he was barely
eight years old when Liverpool took office and in his early twenties when he
left it. It might therefore be worth asking what Disraeli knew about it.
Certainly, however, Liverpool's fussy, detail-ridden caution could infuriate
bright subordinates, notably George Canning. Contemporaries also referred
to his irritability and short temper. Such character traits do not necessarily
make for ineffective government, however, particularly when they are combined, as in Liverpool's case, with shrewd judgement about character and a
willingness to let able ministers take the lead in matters on which they were
expert.

The Prime Minister was keen to 'bring on' young men and to strengthen
the government team in the Commons. He could see political advantages
both in having able politicians like Peel and Huskisson carrying the burden
of debate against the Whigs and in having possible rivals to his own position
(and both had already shown ample evidence of their brilliance, in contrast
to Liverpool) neutralized by high office in his government. The so-called
'new men' had all served loyally enough in junior posts in the 1810s. They
did not regard their promotion as an opportunity to change the direction of
government policy, not least because that direction had already begun to shift
in a 'liberal' direction before 1822. As we shall see (pp. 44–50), much of the
groundwork for the reforms, adjustments and improvements of the 1820s
had been put in train both by their allegedly 'reactionary' predecessors and

by themselves in subordinate office. The real distinction is not philosophical but practical. Huskisson and Peel proved much more effective both in debate and in administration than their predecessors.

For three main reasons, therefore, the term Liberal Toryism should be used with care and not merely to contrast the later stages of Liverpool's government with the former. First, there was no ideological 'conversion' in 1822. Secondly, the new men were 'new' only in seniority within the government. For the most part, they were developing policy when holding ministerial posts below cabinet rank. Thirdly, the 'liberalism' (itself an ambiguous word) of the 1820s was more 'improving' than reformist and operated against a background of prosperity rather than, as for most of the period 1815-21, economic crisis. None of Liverpool's cabinet looked more favourably on parliamentary reform in, say, 1824 than in 1815. The Whig leader **Lord John Russell** introduced a Bill in 1822 to disfranchise a hundred of the smallest, and most corrupt, parliamentary boroughs. The seats thus released would have been redistributed to larger industrial and commercial towns and to the bigger counties. The Bill received no government encouragement and failed by a large majority in the Commons (Evans, 2001: 480).

The idea of enacting reform because of extra-parliamentary pressure remained anathema. It is tempting to see the route to the passage of the Great Reform Act in 1832 in linear terms: a Tory government, fearful of reform, cracks down in the 1810s, then becomes 'liberalized' during the prosperity of the 1820s. Liberalization makes the reforming task of the Whigs much easier when they finally achieve office in 1830. This simple model, still cherished by many students, is wholly wrong. Such Tory 'liberalization' as there was remained within the old, closed political world. It was radical enough on its own terms and the harbinger of a critical shift in the ethos of government (see pp. 100-1) but it was concerned with taxation, tariffs, law and administration. No sympathy was shown for the franchise demands of extra-parliamentary radicals be they from the middle or the working classes. Not until the Pittite Toryism which Liverpool knew, nurtured and practised was shattered after his death (see pp. 69-75) did parliamentary reform become a practical possibility.

Although the ministerial changes of 1822-23 did not signal any changes of principle, they did have a political purpose. The Caroline affair (see above pp. 29-33) and the antipathy towards his ministers which it had produced in George IV had weakened Liverpool's government. Vansittart's inadequacies showed up embarrassingly when the government was on the defensive and Sidmouth had lost what little command he had in the Commons in the aftermath of Peterloo. The Whigs were able to win some minor, but cumulatively significant, victories in the Commons by obtaining backbench support. In

Russell, Lord John Whig politician. He was one of the keenest parliamentary reformers in his party. He introduced an unsuccessful reform bill in 1822 and was one of the four members of a Committee selected by Earl Grey which drafted the Reform Bill in 1831. He was prime minister from 1846-52.

March 1822 they carried a motion to cut the navy estimates and consider reductions in taxation to landowners hit hard by the fall in agricultural prices (see pp. 48–9). Only threats of resignation by Liverpool pulled independent-minded but Tory-inclined backbenchers back into line. A rejuvenation of the government front bench in the Commons now had high priority for the prime minister.

The long process of estrangement between the Grenvillites and the Whigs was completed by Liverpool's Cabinet reshuffle. A Dukedom was sufficient to cement the loyalty of the Marquis of Buckingham, Grenville's successor as leader of his parliamentary faction. Charles Wynn also obtained minor Cabinet office. Of greater long-term significance was the appointment of Marquis Wellesley (Wellington's brother) as Lord Lieutenant of Ireland. Like most of the Grenvillites, Wellesley favoured Catholic emancipation and his appointment worried Liverpool's many anti-Catholic supporters. It served its immediate purpose, however. Whig hopes of bringing Liverpool's government down had probably been pitched too high even during the Caroline affair and they took a knock with the Queen's death in 1821. Bereft already of some of their ablest figures (see pp. 14–15), the Whigs lost heart when the ministerial reshuffle tilted the political arithmetic still further against them. Grey indulged in one of his huffy and periodic withdrawals from active political involvement. Whig party discipline slackened from 1823. The Whigs after 1822 were rarely able to raise more than 100 supporters in any **parliamentary division**. The party battle in Parliament was less keenly fought in the mid-1820s than at any time since 1815.

Parliamentary division Name given to the procedure for taking votes. The House is formally said to 'divide', so that members can vote for or against a proposal.

As so often happens in politics, however, the absence of keen rivalry between parties contending for power encouraged squabbles within them. Liverpool's ministers jockeyed both for immediate influence and, eventually, the succession. Wellington, Westmorland and Eldon – in modern parlance on the right of their party – all had doubts about British commercial policy both at home and abroad. These surfaced from time to time, notably in the winter of 1824–25 when the King criticised what he called the unwise 'Liberalism' of his government (Gash, 1984: 233). More serious was the growing split between the 'Protestants' and 'Catholics'. The Protestants comprised the group above plus Peel; they opposed any political concessions to Catholics, especially in Ireland. In this they had the full support of George IV. The 'Catholics' were led by Canning, as ambitious as he was tactless, and also anticipating political life after Liverpool. This group, which also included Huskisson and the old Grenvillites, might be considered on the left of the party. They favoured giving propertied Catholics the right both to vote in parliamentary elections and to sit in Parliament.

Liverpool tried to keep Catholic emancipation on the political back-burner. The issue had ended the younger Pitt's ministry in 1801 when George III had dug in his anti-Catholic heels with that obstinacy for which he was famous, and Liverpool knew what passions it still aroused in the country. He also believed it to be the only issue on which George IV could not be budged, bribed or cajoled. The emergence of **Daniel O'Connell**'s Catholic Association raised the political temperature in Ireland after 1823 and frustrated Liverpool's hopes. Its aims were to increase the representation and influence of Catholics in Ireland and also to repeal the 1800 Act of Union which had got rid of the separate Irish Parliament. The radical MP Francis Burdett took up the Catholic Association's cause at Westminster. Only a strong 'Protestant' majority in the House of Lords prevented both a measure of emancipation and also state salaries for Irish Catholic clergy being accepted in the spring of 1825, when both Liverpool and Peel contemplated resignation. The Catholic question was the major issue in the general election of 1826 and it brought Pittite/Tory disagreements consistently into the public eye for the first time since the end of the French Wars.

In the months before February 1827, when Liverpool suffered the cerebral haemorrhage which caused his resignation, therefore, his government was as divided as at any time in the previous 15 years. To the contentious issues of general commercial policy and **Catholic emancipation** was added in 1826 further disagreement over corn duties (see pp. 49–50). A poor harvest in 1825 had brought a sharp rise in wheat prices and the hot summer of 1826 threatened supplies of other foodstuffs. This, against a background of renewed distress in the north of England, caused ministers to scrutinise afresh the policy of protection for domestic corn producers. Huskisson and Wellington inevitably disagreed on the issue and the by now customary battle lines within the **Cabinet** were ready to be drawn again. Unkind critics asserted that Liverpool's concern to balance opposite forces within his government only created an atmosphere of vacillation and weakness. Some even believed that real power had passed to Canning already.

In fact, Liverpool's authority remained largely unchallenged by Cabinet colleagues to the end. He may have lacked vision and originality but he possessed a gift which sustains many balanced, decent and considerate folk – and Liverpool, for all his fussiness, was all three. He inspired trust. That trust he used to his political advantage, since he was able to persuade intrinsically abler colleagues to work under him when they would have been reluctant to accept the authority of anyone else. Where the younger Pitt collected acolytes, Liverpool sought loyalty. It is doubtful if he even considered himself a leader, although his ability to retain the support of brilliant, but quarrelsome, subordinates in the last years of his prime ministership certainly required leadership qualities. In his last years, he used wisely the experience gained through a lifetime in politics.

O'Connell, Daniel Irish nationalist. He founded the Catholic Association in 1823, which called for Catholic Emancipation, Repeal of the Act of Union, an end to tithe payments to the Anglican church and wider Catholic land-ownership. His election for County Clare in 1828 led directly to the Bill for Catholic Emancipation.

Catholic emancipation By legislation passed in 1829, Roman Catholics in the United Kingdom were entitled to vote in parliamentary elections and to be elected or appointed to most local or national positions of responsibility.

Cabinet The group of senior ministers who determine government policy. In our period, Cabinet members were beginning to accept collective responsibility for decisions, whether or not individual members disagreed about specific policies. Also, the Cabinet could present to Parliament policies with which the monarch disagreed.

Why Liverpool survived as prime minister for so long has perplexed many. Harsh critics have asserted that he survived precisely because survival, rather than leadership, was the height of his ambition. Long tenure of power was anyway easier when general elections were infrequent and most parliamentary seats not actually contested. In such circumstances public opinion, however hostile, was far less important than it was later to become. Before Liverpool, Walpole, Pitt and the formidably mediocre Lord North had all been prime minister continuously for more than ten years and all had successfully faced public hostility at least as great as anything encountered by Liverpool. Perhaps Liverpool's longevity seems remarkable in a twentieth-century, rather than a contemporary, context. Liverpool's political world, after all, was destroyed between 1828 and 1832 and survival in the highest office became much more difficult under the new rules. Only by the end of the twentieth century would a combination of **parliaments** dominated by genuinely mediocre careerists and the development of the black, and barely constitutional, arts of government whips and the 'spinning' of news contrive to keep three prime ministers (two of them pretty mediocre) in power for a combined, unbroken total of 28 years.

In a society dominated by conservative-minded property owners who had seen the chaotic consequences of ill considered change in revolutionary and Napoleonic France, a prime minister who fully shared their fears and who at least kept the lid on the kettle in Britain could survive. Liverpool relied on sufficient support from the landowners who were the dominant social group in both houses of parliament. The 'Six Acts' of 1819 had massive parliamentary support. In addition, Liverpool was fortunate that his uncertain early years as prime minister coincided with the years of victory over Napoleon.

These factors help to explain Liverpool's long tenure of power but they do not tell the whole story. They ignore generally secure Cabinet support. They ignore the immense variety of political experience which Liverpool had acquired before he became prime minister in 1812. His unrivalled knowledge of the workings of government and administration he put to effective use as prime minister. He was much more than a mere chairman of cabinet meetings, as his frequent, knowledgeable letters to colleagues reveal. They ignore the skill with which he conciliated awkward and prickly ministers, especially after 1822.

Perhaps most of all, they ignore the speed with which Britain was changing and the variety of problems that the pace of change engendered. No 'arch-mediocrity' could have kept abreast of developments and reacted to different circumstances as Liverpool was able to do. So, while Liverpool survived, in part because he did not attempt too much, he was shrewd enough to see that he could not proceed, as many of his backbenchers would have preferred, by venturing nothing, hoping vainly to stand upright and

Parliament The legislative body of a nation. Britain's parliament comprises the House of Commons and the House of Lords. Before 1832, the former was elected, on a very restricted franchise; the latter comprised members of the hereditary aristocracy, who served for life once they inherited their titles, and bishops of the Church of England.

unbending against the ever-increasing velocity of gales of social and industrial change. In appreciating when, and by how much, to defend existing institutions and when, and by how much, to seek to change them, he showed considerable tactical skill. Of course, those skills were deployed for a conservative purpose. His aim was to preserve an old order where property (particularly landed property) and hereditary succession determined the distribution of power. More than most of his contemporaries, however, he knew how to apply Edmund Burke's famous dictum that 'A state without the means of some change is without the means of its conservation'. It is important that Liverpool be judged by the criteria of his own time and by what he was attempting to achieve. The true measure of his political abilities is perhaps best demonstrated by the speed with which the Tory party destroyed both itself, and much of the old order it aimed to preserve, once Liverpool's experienced guidance was removed.

TRADE, TAXATION AND FINANCE

For several years after the end of the French Wars, British finances were in a mess. To pay for the wars, Britain had borrowed heavily and the burden of interest and loan repayments distorted government finance. In 1815, government expenditure exceeded income by 45 per cent and almost 80 per cent of that expenditure went on servicing a grotesquely swollen national debt (Hilton, 2006; Evans, 2001; Gash, 1979). Since country gentlemen would not permit the retention of income tax **[Doc. 2, p. 106]**, Liverpool embarked on a policy of savage retrenchment and cost-cutting to balance the books. Government expenditure was reduced by 50 per cent between 1815 and 1818, largely because of demobilizations in the armed forces. Even so, expenditure on the **national debt** remained almost 60 per cent of government expenditure in the years 1822–31 (Harling and Mandler, 1993: 49).

National debt Collective borrowing by government, both from individuals and from institutions at home or abroad. Its size tended to increase hugely during wartime and a key aim of government financial policy after 1815 was to spend less and rely less on loans, thus reducing the size of the debt.

The sailors and soldiers released on to the labour market did not readily find jobs (see above, pp. 16–17). High levels of unemployment contributed substantially to the rapidly growing cost of poor relief which reached a peak of £7.8 million in 1818. Since rates to finance this relief were being paid by property owners already complaining about excessive taxation, it is not surprising that the government ran the risk of alienating not only the poor, among whom radical politics made substantial headway between 1815 and 1820, but also their own natural constituency.

Matters were not helped by the manifest inadequacy of Nicholas Vansittart as Chancellor of the Exchequer. He dealt with mounting debt by raising new loans, mostly from the City of London. This strategy kept interest rates higher than a depressed economy could bear. Landowners, already heavily in debt thanks to wartime investments made on the assumption that agricultural prices would remain high, protested mightily at the unsustainable level of their debts when prices fell.

Government economic policy between 1815 and 1819 was one of drift, in anticipation of some natural process of adjustment to conditions of peace. Cash payments by the Bank had been suspended since Pitt's actions to stave off financial collapse in 1797, perhaps the most dangerous year for Britain during the whole of the French Wars. Although peace returned in 1815, the resumption of payments of bills in cash set against a clear standard of value was postponed year after year. Finally, in 1819, harried by an opposition Whig party growing in confidence after some modest gains in the general election the previous year and also by some Tory and independent backbenchers and influential junior ministers – notably William Huskisson – Liverpool took an initiative. He believed that business confidence would be restored only when the British currency returned to valuation on a **gold standard**, and when the Bank of England redeemed all notes on demand with gold or coin. Two **select committees** were set up, one to consider the state of the currency and the other to examine public finance more generally. They became important policy makers. Although the government was strongly represented on both, it would be an exaggeration to say that their deliberations always reflected government initiatives. In any case, the government was split on financial policy. In one sense, therefore, it was Parliament which drove Liverpool towards trade regulation.

Peel, who chaired the Currency Committee, rapidly concluded that Britain's system of paper currency fuelled inflation and reduced the value of the pound in foreign markets (Gash, 1985: 242). To deal with this, the Committee recommended a staged restitution of cash payments until payments in gold coin at the previous gold standard value of 1797 would be fully established by May 1823. This represented a victory for the increasingly influential political economists, led by **David Ricardo**, who argued that permanent prosperity could only be achieved in an economy based on a sound currency which could hold its value.

The return to 'sound currency' was perhaps even more of a victory for Huskisson, since he was closer to policy-making. A protégé of Canning, Huskisson was tucked away in the obscurity of the Department of Woods and Forests before 1823 but his influence on economic policy had grown steadily after 1816. He believed that peace had brought only stagnation of trade and that productive investment had been discouraged (Hilton, 1977: 31). Huskisson, perhaps the ablest of Liverpool's 'men of business', was instrumental in smoothing the transition from what had become – in the famous phrase of the historian John Brewer – a 'fiscal-military state' during

Gold standard Setting the value of paper money and gold against an agreed rate. Its purpose was to tie a nation's currency to the price of gold with the aim of preventing unpredictable fluctuations in the value of money. Britain was 'off the gold standard' from 1797–1821, when the Bank of England issued notes not tied to any external value.

Select committees Committees appointed by either House of Parliament to investigate an issue and to make recommendations which might lead to proposals for legislation. Parliament determines the composition and terms of reference of these committees.

Ricardo, David Political economist. Influenced by Adam Smith's views about free trade, he became one of his most influential disciples. He attacked the passing of a protective Corn Law in 1815 and argued that the unreformed poor laws increased, rather than relieving, poverty. He published *Principles of Political Economy* in 1817.

Tariffs The collective name for duties (taxes) paid on imports or exports. Tariffs were one of the main sources of revenue for government. In the 1820s, many tariffs were reduced in order to stimulate trade and national prosperity.

Customs Duties levied on goods produced or sold, particularly on goods or commodities coming into, or being exported from, a country. In our period, customs were a major source of revenue for the government.

Excise A tax or 'duty' levied on goods produced or sold *within* a country. In our period, excise duties were specially resented by ordinary people because they represented a tax which made food, drink and many other necessities more expensive than they would otherwise have been.

Paper currency Issuing bank notes is cheaper and easier than using large, heavy volumes of coin or metal as currency. Governments or banks often issued their own notes which were not linked to an external source of value such as gold. Relying on paper currency could lead to depreciation of its value.

the eighteenth and early nineteenth centuries to one committed to 'retrenchment'. Lower taxation would also provide greater incentives for traders and businessmen to invest and to expand their operations. The trade boom of the 1820s enabled the government to reduce **tariffs** (see below, pp. 47–8). Lowered **customs** and **excise** duties were more than compensated by the increased volume of trade.

Country gentlemen generally favoured the resumption of cash payments, despite the fact that easier credit in the era of 'paper money' (or **paper currency**) during the wars had increased the value of their land. For many, however, the return of cash payments and an agreed gold standard symbolized plain dealing. It also represented a rebuff for those City fund holders who had profited from speculation. Most of the **gentry** farmers had little direct involvement with the City of London and were highly suspicious of what went on there. They believed in honest, open and 'manly' dealings and distrusted murky financial stratagems which they barely understood but which they were sure characterized the City of London money markets. City traders were assumed to be involved in widespread deceit, chicanery – and easy, unearned profit. In fact, the return to the gold standard was completed by 1821, in advance of the Currency Committee's timetable.

Not surprisingly, the Committee on Finance recommended that the size of the national debt be reduced. Vansittart, with some reluctance, responded. His 1819 budget reduced the **Sinking Fund** and raised £3 million in indirect taxes, including a new duty on malt which increased the price of beer. The objective was a better balance of income and expenditure. To Liverpool, this represented the long-postponed return to post-war normality. He told Huskisson in September 1820 that only now, with the prospect of a fixed currency and the disappearance of 'annual loans' to bale the government out, was the nation 'settling itself into a state of peace' (Hilton, 1977: 66).

Britain's budgets did indeed mostly balance between 1819 and 1827. The budgeting strategy generally associated with 'Prosperity Robinson' was begun in the last years of Vansittart's stewardship, though 'Old Mouldy' or 'Poor Van', as he was variously known, only followed a policy set by others. Small surpluses and the return of 'normality' persuaded Liverpool that lowering tariff barriers would be the best long-term guarantee of national prosperity. In this, as in much else, he returned to the road down which Pitt had begun to travel during his peacetime administration of the 1780s with its emphasis on low tariffs and commercial expansion. This policy swam with an ever more powerful intellectual tide. Free trade was urged by political economists like David Ricardo and **J.R. McCulloch** with all the fervour of a moral crusade.

A famous speech delivered by Liverpool in May 1820 anticipated tariff reductions but carefully avoided specific commitments. The spadework was done by parliamentary select committees on which government supporters were in a majority. The most influential was the Foreign Trade Committee chaired by Thomas Wallace, one of the unsung but substantial influences in the free trade movement. His Committee recommended in 1820 a relaxation of the **Navigation Laws**, whose purpose had been the aggressive protection of British shipping, and also a reduction in the charges imposed on foreigners using British warehouses. In 1821 Wallace shepherded first through his Committee and then the Commons a reduction in the differential duty paid on Baltic as against Canadian timber. This modest change has been described as 'the first practical step towards implementation of the principle of *laissez-faire* in the post-war period' (Gordon, 1976: 116), and it was followed by five similar reductions in 1822 designed to extend opportunities for British traders, especially those working in northern Europe.

Wallace began a process of rationalizing and simplifying the complex legislation which weighed down trade with some 2,000 separate statutes. These restricted not only the movement of goods and raw materials but also the emigration of skilled workers and the export of machinery. Such protection for a nation whose industrial output greatly exceeded that of all her competitors made no sense; it merely invited retaliatory tariff walls and a general restriction of trade worldwide. Between 1822 and 1825 first Wallace and then Huskisson reduced the number of monopolies and relaxed the tight restrictions of the Navigation Laws. The most important measure was Huskisson's Reciprocity of Duties Act of 1823. Under it, any nation which agreed to equivalent (or 'reciprocal') reductions could transport goods to Britain on the same terms as British ships. Huskisson's aim was to reduce the cost of imports to British manufacturers. He also wished to resume the previously enormously profitable trading patterns between the United States, Britain and the British West Indian colonies. The overall objective was clear. As Huskisson put it, 'The means which lead to increased consumption, and which are the foundation . . . of our prosperity, will be most effectually promoted by an unrestrained competition not only between capital and industry of different classes in the same country, but also by extending that competition, as much as possible to all other countries' (Daunton, 1995: 551–2).

The complement of this policy was the lowering of domestic duties. Robinson's first annual budget, in 1823, concentrated on direct taxation. The removal of some £2 million was designed to mollify landowners who had suffered substantial reductions in prices and rents as soon as the availability of a surplus permitted. The focus of the budgets of 1824 and 1825, however, was on customs and excise duties. Duties on rum, coal, wool and silk were reduced in 1824. In 1825, while the trade boom provided increased government income despite reductions in duty, a thorough revision of the tariff system was begun. Robinson aimed to stimulate domestic demand by lower

Gentry Collective term covering smaller landowners. The amount of land owned varied widely but gentry families were usually comfortably off. Heads of gentry families usually exercised local influence as Justices of the Peace.

Sinking fund A sum set aside by government to reduce the size of the National Debt. By 1815, the huge costs of war meant that the sums set aside were inadequate to bring about any reduction. In 1819, the government decided that government revenue should exceed expenditure by £5 million a year.

McCulloch, John Ramsay Political economist. He tried to apply general ideas about economics to solving practical problems, such as the size of the national debt and the cost of the English poor law system before 1834. He influenced Peel's thinking on economic issues.

Navigation Laws Legislation designed to advantage British trade over foreign competition by imposing duties on imports. The laws came under increasing attack in the early part of the nineteenth century. Levels of duty were steadily reduced from the 1820s and the Navigation Laws were finally repealed in 1849.

prices and (like Pitt in the 1780s) to undercut the big business which smuggling had become, especially in the peninsular counties of Devon and Cornwall, where remote rocky coves and poor overland communications gave inbuilt advantages to nefarious locals who knew the difficult terrain. Some in the far south-west, indeed, saw smuggling as a practice validated by custom and usage which benefited local communities. Duties on a range of manufactured goods were reduced from 50 per cent to 20 per cent and on raw materials from 20 per cent to 10 per cent. The recovery of the British economy overall was sufficiently strong for the short slump in the winter of 1825–6 to be absorbed without undue strain. Robinson was able to budget for further government surpluses in 1827. Between 1821 and 1827, despite lower duties, customs revenue increased by 64 per cent (Gash, 1984; Evans, 2001: 193).

Such changes did not make Britain a free-trade nation. Modest protection remained, with a trading system now much more efficiently administered. The commercial interests government policy was designed to benefit responded pragmatically. As expounded by men like Ricardo, Wallace and Huskisson, the new economic policy was not always linked to specific interests and markets. Thus, while older trades and businesses saw reductions of duty as a possible threat to their markets, newer ventures tended to respond more enthusiastically to the opportunity to find new markets for their products.

The 1820 petition by London merchants in favour of free trade, sometimes cited as evidence of commercial unanimity, in fact reflected careful, and unrepresentative, lobbying by the overseas trader and political economist Thomas Tooke. Trading enterprises which had enjoyed extensive protection from government since the seventeenth century were not notably enthusiastic political economists or free traders. The East India Company and much of the shipping interest looked askance at measures to reduce the effectiveness of the Navigation Acts. Textile manufacturers, on the other hand, were anxious to increase still further the two-thirds share of Britain's export market they enjoyed in the 1820s (Evans, 2001: 500) and welcomed the new opportunities which trade liberalization brought.

Arable farming The farming of crops. In Britain, arable farming usually refers to the cultivation of corn, especially wheat, barley or oats. In England, the most corn is grown in the south and east of the country where the predominant weather is sunnier and drier.

Most controversy attended protection for agriculture. The logic of the political economists' case pointed to a revision of the strongly protectionist Corn Law of 1815 (see above, p. 17), yet the recent sharp fall in agricultural prices made it more difficult to follow a logical path. Wheat prices, which reached a post-war peak of 96s 11d (£4.84) a quarter in 1817, plummeted to 44s 7d (£2.23) by 1822. The talk was all of depression **[Docs. 5 and 6, p. 108]**. **Arable** land was not felt to be worth ploughing in parts of East Anglia in the early 1820s. Here, especially, tenant farmers fell into debt and labourers rioted. Huskisson, who as both an intellectual and, from 1823, MP for the commercial constituency of Liverpool, never had rural backbenchers' confidence, talked of cheaper bread benefiting the 'labouring parts of the community' (Hilton, 1977: 102). Sir John Sinclair spoke for the agricultural classes when he asserted that 'the cultivation of the soil . . . is the true basis of national prosperity' and that 'the interests of agriculture . . . ought never to be sacrificed for any considerations of distant commerce or of foreign policy' **[Doc. 4, p. 107]**.

A Central Agricultural Association, supported mainly by smaller land-owners and tenant farmers in the arable south of England, had been established in 1819 and flourished over the next few years of low agricultural prices and widespread hardship. Its moving spirit and chief propagandist was the Bristol solicitor and substantial Gloucestershire farmer, George Webb Hall. What has been called 'The Squires' Revolt' (Hilton, 2006: 268–74) of the early 1820s looked to more politically radical solutions. Its supporters found the populist, anti-City diatribes of William Cobbett much to their taste. Huskisson warned about 'the infection of radicalism . . . gradually making its way into the villages'.

In Parliament, larger landowners bridled at the assertions of the small-holders and tenants. This played into the hands of those urging trade liberalization, rather than higher protection, as the solution to the woes of the landed interest. The strength of the free-trade case within the parliamentary select committees was sufficient to negate calls for still higher protection. A bill to stiffen the Corn Laws was heavily defeated in the Commons in 1822. In the same year, a very cautious reduction in duty was approved when the 1815 Corn Law was amended to allow foreign corn into the country at graduated rates of duty when prices were between 70s (£3.50) and 85s (£4.25), and freely thereafter. It had no practical effect, however, since prices did not reach these levels while the law was in force. The Squires' Revolt subsided as quickly as it had arisen, most of its remaining supporters now calling, not for higher protection, but for the suspension of recently introduced cash payments and for devaluation of the currency. Their pleas fell on deaf ears.

A small circle of Liverpool's advisers, Huskisson, Canning, Peel and Robinson, all known to be sympathetic to the case for trade liberalization, worked towards more far-reaching solutions. The case for reform was strengthened when wheat prices rose sharply in 1826, following a poor harvest the previous year. The attractive political solution was a sliding scale of protective duties which would allow corn imports when domestic supplies were low and prices rising sharply, while keeping them out when the domestic harvest was adequate or better. Such a solution was less persuasive to the political economists. They argued that the removal of protection would stimulate rationalization of agriculture and promote more market-conscious farming. Political considerations suggested caution. The revised Corn Bill on which Huskisson and Liverpool had been working was not carried until 1828 – after the deaths of both Liverpool and his successor, George Canning.

The 1828 Corn Law was passed by the Wellington government. It repealed the 1815 and 1822 statutes and substituted a sliding scale operating when the domestic price was between 60s (£3) and 72s (£3.60) a quarter. Corn could be imported freely when the price reached 73s (£3.65). Wellington, more sympathetic to the interests of backbench squires than Huskisson had been, increased the duty payable when the sliding scale operated above the rate proposed in earlier drafts on the Bill in 1826 and 1827.

Trade policy moved on a broad front, but rather cautiously, in the years 1819–28. The direction of travel, however, was plain. It was towards liberalization, lower duties and more freedom for market forces to work their miracles. Though it is difficult to demonstrate cause and effect, the period was generally a prosperous one. Government-inclined journals, such as the *Annual Register*, were keen to link the improvement to the commercial initiatives **[Doc. 7, p. 109]** begun in the early 1820s. The wisdom, liberality and moderation of government to which the *Register* referred, however, would not have been recognized by substantial sectors of the population. Moreover, tensions within the government ranks were very close to the surface in 1826–27. Among those tensions, as the years after 1827 would reveal, trade policy cut across social as well as political divisions. Despite its increasing intellectual dominance between 1820 and about 1860, free trade remained a deeply divisive issue.

LAW REFORM

English law in the early nineteenth century was ripe for reform. The legal code, in theory extremely severe but in practice enforced haphazardly if not chaotically, attracted increasingly stringent criticism. More than 200 offences carried the death penalty, though this much-quoted statistic is misleading. The list of capital offences contained many duplications. Some identical crimes were stated to be capital offences in statutes enacted at different times and relating to different places. By our period the death penalty was rarely invoked except for those crimes considered to be the most serious, but these included both forgery and horse-stealing. Almost a third of all executions in London and Middlesex in the early years of the nineteenth century were for forgery (Emsley, 1987: 211).

The severity of punishments was almost certainly counter-productive. Juries were frequently reluctant to convict even when the evidence was unassailable. This was generally true of cases brought against food rioters. Food rioting, common when wheat or bread prices rose sharply, aimed at reducing

Plate 1 The New Custom House, Liverpool, c.1830 (engraving) (b&w photo) by English School, (19th century). XJF107828, Private Collection/The Bridgeman Art Library Nationality/English/out of copyright.

Plate 2 Robert Stewart, 2nd Marquess of Londonderry (Lord Castlereagh), by Sir Thomas Lawrence, 1809–1810 © National Portrait Gallery, London.

Plate 3 The Peterloo Massacre, 16th August 1819, pub. 1st October 1819 by Richard Carlile (coloured etching) by Cruikshank, George (1792–1878). MAN63034 © Manchester Art Gallery, UK/The Bridgeman Art Library, Nationality/English/out of copyright (PLEASE NOTE: The Bridgeman Art Library works with the owner of this image to clear permission. If you wish to reproduce this image, please inform us so that we can clear permission for you.)

Plate 4 The Execution of the Cato Street Conspirators on 1st May 1820 (engraving) (b/w photo)
by English School, (19th century) MOL226480 © Museum of London, UK/The Bridgeman Art
Library, Nationality/English/out of copyright.

Plate 5 How to get Un-married, – Ay, there's the Rub! by J.L. Marks, 1820 © National Portrait Gallery, London.

Plate 6 Robert Jenkinson, 2nd Earl of Liverpool, by Sir George Hayter, 1823 © National Portrait Gallery, London.

Plate 7 The King Commander in Chief; or, the Upset of the Waterloo-man, Bags & Baggage, by John Phillips, 1827 © National Portrait Gallery, London.

Plate 8 *Bristol seen from Pile Hill on the night of October 30th, 1831*, by Thomas Leeson Rowbotham. M4620 © Bristol Museums and Art Galleries.

Plate 9 Sir Robert Peel, 2nd Bt, by Henry William Pickersgill © National Portrait Gallery, London.

Plate 10 Grey's Monument, Newcastle-upon-Tyne. © Graeme Peacock Photographic Imagery, www.graeme-peacock.com

prices to 'natural' or 'customary' levels far below the temporary market price (Stevenson, 1979). Poaching, increasingly an organized crime carried out by disciplined local gangs, nevertheless attracted community sympathy in times of distress or high prices, since it ran foul of ferocious game laws. Convictions were less numerous than the authorities liked.

The draconian punishments which rioters and poachers might face emphasized the extent to which English law, enacted by a property-owning oligarchy, protected property first and foremost. This inherently inequitable situation became positively dangerous when linked to radical demands for political reform. Political thinkers of the eighteenth-century Enlightenment emphasized the importance of the principle of equality before the law. Few European states made any attempt to secure this. England's espousal of trial by jury and the usual requirement that those suspected of crimes had quickly to be brought before a court of law to answer charges rather than being detained indefinitely placed it among the more advanced of nations. English law, however, operated unequally, greatly favouring the rich and well-connected. The movement to reform the law and to improve conditions for convicts gained influential support, not only from humanitarians like the Bedfordshire philanthropist landowner John Howard or Whig intellectuals like Samuel Romilly and **Sir James Mackintosh**, but also from those who argued more pragmatically that a legal system which did not command popular consent could not, for all its casual and arbitrary savagery, protect property effectively.

Sir Robert Peel was the ideal figure to carry through a programme of law reform in a Tory government. He was not sentimental but was an exceptionally able and conscientious man whose talents were organizational and administrative rather than original and innovative. The English law required rationalization and codification; some argued that it should be scrapped and totally remodelled. The radical plans of zealots like the great English philosopher **Jeremy Bentham**, who corresponded copiously with Peel in the late 1820s, would not have been acceptable to backbench MPs. Backbenchers sought a more efficient system, particularly since crime statistics showed an alarming rise after the end of the Napoleonic Wars A parliamentary enquiry had unearthed an unwelcome development. Criminal commitments between 1809 and 1816 totalled 47,522 but had risen to 93,718 between 1818 and 1825, an increase of 97 per cent (Gash, 1985: 341). Criminologists and social historians tend to decry crime statistics, arguing that they are as likely to reflect fashions in prosecution or altered police attitudes as genuine changes in criminal behaviour. Maybe so. However, what contemporaries believed is more important and, whatever the truth lying behind the figures, rising crime statistics exerted a great visceral influence on contemporaries, as indeed they do to this day.

Mackintosh, Sir James Whig politician and writer. Became an MP in 1813. An influential figure among the Whig intellectuals and politicians who congregated at Holland House. He advocated moderate reform, the need for a free press, Catholic Emancipation and law reform.

Bentham, Jeremy Political philosopher best known for developing 'utilitarianism', a political philosophy which judged the appropriateness of systems according to their practical utility. He also influenced the development of classical economics and argued for radical political reform.

It is often noted that Peel's legal reforms were prompted by enquiries and reports made by the parliamentary committee of 1819 chaired by Mackintosh. It is less frequently observed that they took place during what contemporaries were convinced was a crime wave. Tory backbenchers and independent MPs hoped for more expeditious and effective justice to be meted out to wrongdoers. Peel concurred. He was no natural humanitarian. In rationalizing an outmoded and inefficient system, his main objective was to have more criminals convicted and, having been convicted, punished according to the rigour of the law. He wanted higher conviction rates as well as greater consistency in the meting out of punishments.

The Gaols Act of 1823 had been clearly presaged by early initiatives and would not have been possible but for the tireless propaganda work of John Howard, who had seen the wretchedness of local prisons when acting as county sheriff and who had written his influential *The State of the Prisons in England and Wales* as early as 1777. The Gaols Act represented the first articulation of national policy on prisons. Each county and large town must now maintain a common gaol or house of correction, paid for out of local rates. All such gaols were placed under a standard system of discipline with inspection by **Justices of the Peace**. The Act was extended in 1824 to include gaols in smaller towns. A system of classification of prisoners was also introduced (Gash, 1985; Henriques, 1979).

Justices of the Peace (JPs) People with authority in the local community who were expected to discharge a range of administrative duties. JPs had powers of arrest and could judge lesser crimes. In our period, they also supervised the poor law and levying of rates. Appointment was a mark of status.

While disappointing some Whig and humanitarian reformers with his caution, Peel nevertheless saw five statutes through Parliament in 1823 which greatly reduced the number of offences carrying the death penalty. As James Mackintosh had frequently noted, the British executed far more felons than did most European states. Larceny of property worth less than £2 was at last removed from the list of capital offences. These relaxations of the penal code were possibly partly because of thorough preparation within the Home Office. Peel relied here on the work of Henry Hobhouse, the diligent and experienced Under-Secretary he had inherited from Sidmouth. The political acceptability of this 'liberalization', however, owed much to MPs' realization that transportation was an ostensibly more humane but equally permanent way of ridding the state of its major transgressors. By the end of the 1820s, almost 5,000 convicts a year were being removed to the penal settlements in Australia. Almost a third of those convicted at assizes or quarter sessions, where the most serious cases were tried, were transported between 1810 and 1835 (Emsley, 1987).

Peel even had some success in reforming the fiercely – some English critics said notoriously – independent Scottish legal system with a consolidating statute of 1825 which, among other things, clarified the rights of defendants. In 1825, also, the Jury Act rationalized more than 80 statutes, making the law on jury selection and responsibilities much clearer. He had only minor success in unblocking the encrusted and overloaded channels of the Court of Chancery. Here the caustic high-Tory Lord Chancellor, Eldon, who held the office with one brief break from 1801 to 1827, set a precedent for some of his successors in preferring longevity to activity.

In administrative terms, the most ambitious of Peel's legal reforms were the great consolidating statutes of 1826 and 1827. That of 1826 improved the administration of criminal justice while five statutes passed in 1827 rationalized 92 ramshackle, and in many instances unworkable, pieces of legislation into a credible code dealing with theft and injury to property, offences which accounted for about 85 per cent of all committals. While Home Secretary in Wellington's administration in 1830, he also passed a statute which reduced the number of cases in which forgery might be considered a capital offence.

THE METROPOLITAN POLICE

In popular recollection, of course, Peel is the politician who 'created the police'. His names translate into the police's most common nicknames in the nineteenth century: 'Peelers' or 'Bobbies'. As so often, the truth is less dramatic and more subtle. The idea of a 'preventive police', whose functions would include not just catching offenders but deterring prospective criminals, had a long pedigree and as long a history of stern opposition. The parliamentary committee which Peel set up on becoming Home Secretary stated that 'It is difficult to reconcile an effective system of police with that perfect freedom of action and exemption from interference which are the great privileges and blessings of society in this country' (Halevy, 1926: 287). This vigorous defence of traditional liberties was buttressed during the French Wars by news of the distasteful centralism which Napoleon was visiting on the French. The English country gentleman, more vocal in Parliament on such questions than on any others except the price of corn, had both a xenophobic and a pragmatic dislike of bureaucracy, 'codes' and controls.

Peel, who had helped to create a Police Preservation Force in Ireland when Chief Secretary there, was better equipped than most politicians to see the advantages of professional policing but he did not envisage such forces outside London, whose population of 1.4 million in the 1820s was ten times as large as that of any other English city. It was also a city of migrants, transients and rootless persons. Though the statistics do not exist, it is a very strong probability that London housed a larger proportion of casual and unemployed labourers than any other. London was a special case, needing separate treatment. Elsewhere, until after the Municipal Corporations Act of 1835, the eighteenth-century system of local constables and watchmen survived. The onus of prosecution, if not necessarily arrest, was placed on the victim of a crime, not on the constable, so deterrence was very weak. London, however, had problems unique in scale if nothing else. They were highlighted by the rising crime figures. The historic City (with a mere 125,000 inhabitants) had a substantial force of watchmen and constables, as, by the 1820s, did some of the wealthy parishes in the metropolis. Elsewhere in the capital, population had massively outstripped the means of policing. Some administrative adjustments had been made immediately after the end of the war and by 1818 the Home Office had direct control over the Bow Street police force. This, however, was not considered large enough to cope with major outbreaks of crime or disorder.

Peel expanded the Bow Street force in 1822 by appointing 24 uniformed officers (known as 'redbreasts' because of the colour of their tunics) to patrol central London by day. More extensive solutions were required. As in other areas, Peel advocated controversial changes obliquely by appointing Select Committees dominated by government supporters. An initiative at the end of 1826 was frustrated when Liverpool's government came to an end, but Peel took the issue up again on returning to the Home Office in February 1828.

The Committee's recommendation that a uniformed, professional preventive police be established in London was, of course, Peel's preferred solution and the Metropolitan Police Act of 1829 acted upon it. Uniforms he deemed important because he wanted everyone to be aware of the presence of the new policemen. They were intended to be high-profile and thus to act as a deterrent to that casual and adventitious criminality against both property and person which so concerned 'respectable' citizens. The Act created an entirely new organization of five divisions under the control of two commissioners directly responsible to the home secretary. It was to be financed by a local rate. The police force of 3,000 recruited under this legislation became the first centralized force in the country. The City of London, which retained separate arrangements, was not included. It would be misleading to suggest that the Act produced overnight gains in policing efficiency or that the new constables were all models of incorruptible professionalism. Some of the wealthier London parishes complained that the new arrangements represented a backward step. They could give instructions to the old 'watch' but not to the new police, for whom, of course, they had to pay through the rates. Nevertheless, under the first commissioners, a retired army officer, Charles Rowan, and an Irish lawyer, Richard Mayne, impressive organizational progress was made in the 1830s. The administrative structure created in 1829 served as a significant model for the urban and rural police forces established between the mid-1830s and the late 1850s, and senior London officers became much in demand to run these provincial forces.

TRADE UNIONS

The right of working people to work together or, to use the word favoured at the time, 'combine', had been severely circumscribed by the passing of Combination Acts in 1799–1800, as part of the clampdown on political liberties during the French Revolutionary war of the 1790s. Although employers tended not to use this new legislation against workmen, preferring the more capacious possibilities afforded by the common law of conspiracy, there is no doubt that the balance of power between capital and labour was heavily tilted in favour of the former. The leading radical **Francis Place**, who was also a successful tailoring employer in London, reflected that cotton workers of Lancashire and Clydeside, in the vanguard of technological revolution in the early years of the nineteenth century, were especially vulnerable. 'The wonder is not that the men refrain from violence but that they not Burn all the factories and put the owners to death' (Miles, 1988: 161)

However, the legislation of 1824 and 1825 which repealed the Combination Acts and made trade unions legal did not result from massive protests by working people. Until the last quarter of the nineteenth century, unions, although numerous, were not national in scope. Individual unions were mostly formed by skilled workers of a particular town. They thus had restricted membership and many unionists were more keen to preserve job security and relatively privileged status of the skilled worker than they were to advance the interests of labour as a whole. Unions were therefore neither powerful nor specially important. Had they been so, it is doubtful whether Parliament would have consented to repeal. In fact, one argument used by **Joseph Hume**, the radical MP for Aberdeen, and by Place was that only their continued illegality persuaded workmen to form unions.

Place rested his case not on labour solidarity but on orthodox **political economy**. J.R. McCulloch was one of many who argued that wages would find their natural level in a competitive market; they could not be raised above it by combinations of workers. Combinations might, however, fulfil the useful function of persuading reluctant employers to increase wages to the 'proper' market level (Rule, 1986: 285) and should anyway be permitted in a free society. *The Edinburgh Review* and *The Scotsman* lent support to the cause and the Combination Acts were repealed in a thin and apathetic House of Commons. The free traders in the Cabinet were generally persuaded, though repeal was a backbench, not a government, initiative. Huskisson supported it because 'the laws against combinations have tended to multiply

Place, Francis Radical politician. Born into humble circumstances, he became a prosperous London master tailor but retained both his radical views and his talent for organization and lobbying. With Joseph Hume, he organized the campaign to repeal the Combination Acts. He was also active during the reform crisis.

Hume, Joseph Radical MP. He played a key role in persuading Parliament to repeal the Combination Acts, legalizing trade unions. He also supported both religious toleration and parliamentary reform. During the reform crisis, he was an intermediary between Whig politicians at Westminster and extra-parliamentary reformers.

Political economy The branch of economics which deals with issues relating to government including, for example, taxation policies and how government revenues are spent.

combinations . . . they had generally aggravated the evil they were intended to remove' (Evans, 2001: 206).

The economic boom of the mid-1820s, however, proved Huskisson wrong. Unions of skilled workers sprang up in Lancashire, the north-east, the Midlands and London as men attempted to capitalize on labour shortages. The hostile *Blackwood's Magazine* complained that these new unions (though, in reality, many were established **friendly societies** re-named unions) were 'filled with the worst spirit' and aimed 'to place the masters under the most grinding tyranny' (Rule, 1986: 286). Many did not survive the slump of late 1825 and 1826 but trade union activities sufficiently alarmed MPs to ensure the passage of an amending Act in 1825. Despite concern that the Combination Acts would be re-imposed, the new Act confirmed the legality of workmen's combinations 'solely for the purpose of consulting upon and determining the rate of wages or prices'. It did, however, spell out the illegality of any form of coercion or picketing. Prosecution under laws of conspiracy also remained a strong possibility (Price, 1986). Local magistrates often dealt severely with ordinary trade unionists brought before them charged with conspiracy offences.

Although trade union leaders and the key activists tended not to be prosecuted in the later 1820s and 1830s, the amending legislation of 1825, as later unionists would discover, gave workmen little effective protection. Peel believed the amended law to be 'founded upon just principles' (Halevy, 1926: 210). Workers should have the basic right to associate together. All of the stratagems which were likely to exert real pressure on employers, however, were anathema. Significantly, Peel anticipated that the 1825 Act would put an end to 'the worst of the evils of combination' – by which he meant strikes and any form of disorderly behaviour. The repeal of the Combination Acts was more effective in satisfying the consciences of free-trade politicians with certain abstract notions of 'liberty' than it was in establishing trade unionism as a viable collective activity.

Friendly Societies Organisations which collect funds and pay out benefits. They were established to enable ordinary folk to afford some larger outgoings. They enabled many poor people to have a respectable funeral, for example. Many also had an insurance function. Friendly Societies helped promote thrift and self-help.

4

Britain's Influence Abroad

FOREIGN POLICY UNDER VISCOUNT CASTLEREAGH

Brit016 foreign policy between the battle of Waterloo and the first Reform Act needs to be placed in the context of reaction to the major war which had disrupted Europe in the previous 20 years. As in the still greater world-wide conflagrations which ended in 1918 and 1945, the efforts of the victorious powers were bent towards creating conditions which would preserve the peace for future generations. The end of World War I brought the creation of the League of Nations; the last months of the Second World War witnessed the birth of the United Nations. In similar vein, the allies who had combined to bring about Napoleon's overthrow in 1815 created something called 'Congress Diplomacy'. This derived from an agreement, made by Britain, Austria, Prussia and Russia at the Congress of Vienna in 1815, to meet at regular intervals to monitor the workings of the peace settlement they had agreed to impose upon defeated France and to discuss matters of mutual concern (Evans, 2001: 522).

This Congress System was a major achievement of Viscount Castlereagh, Britain's foreign secretary from 1812 to 1822. Castlereagh was acknowledged by contemporaries to have been the prime mover of a settlement which would preserve the peace of Europe for 40 years. This was a major achievement in itself and especially in the light of the fact that eighteenth-century Europe had witnessed so much warfare between the major powers even before the French wars began in 1792.

The new 'system' associated Britain much more closely with peacetime diplomacy in Europe than had traditionally been the case. In a sense, this was inevitable. Britain had emerged from the wars not only as a great power but as the greatest power in Europe (see above, p. 3). Looked at from the Austrian or Prussian viewpoint, no European settlement in 1814–15 without Britain's assent and involvement would seem either secure or permanent.

The break with tradition, however, attracted criticism. In 1814–15 many argued that the French, as a defeated nation whose revolutionary ideology no less than its recently all-conquering armies, had wreaked such havoc in Europe that it should be made to pay a much heavier price than Castlereagh thought it wise to exact. Once the Congress System was in place, Castlereagh's enthusiastic diplomacy was attacked in Britain as the delusion of a man whose head had been turned by hob-nobbing with the great figures of Europe, like Tsar Alexander I of Russia or the Austrian foreign minister, Prince Klemens Metternich. Britain's interests, it was urged, would be better served by detachment from minor squabbles between European emperors and autocrats **[Doc. 10, p. 111]**. The country should rather follow those world-wide interests to which island status, maritime heritage and commercial considerations all seemed to point.

Castlereagh's diplomacy, however, was perfectly consistent. He had no greater desire than his critics to see Britain engaged in further European warfare, but he saw interventionist diplomacy as the best means to ensure this objective. Seeing Austria, Prussia and Russia – the other three powers who combined with Britain at the Treaty of Chaumont in 1814 in order to defeat France – all as potential disturbers of the European balance of power by becoming themselves too powerful, Castlereagh tried to hold each in check. In pursuit of this objective he sought to preserve the territorial integrity of smaller powers on which any of the other three might have designs (Hayes, 1975). His determination to offer France peace with honour derived from a hard-headed calculation that the humiliation of one of Europe's leading powers was no recipe for the long-term stability which Britain needed to pursue its commercial and colonial interests both in Europe and further afield.

Castlereagh's 'Congress strategy' owed much to the ideas of his old mentor, the Younger Pitt. When trying to stitch together a coalition against Napoleon in January 1805, Pitt suggested to the Russian ambassador that the eventual restoration of peace must be accompanied by 'a general Agreement and Guarantee for the mutual security and protection of the different Powers and for re-establishing a general System of Public Law in Europe' (Stevenson, 1979: 95).

Castlereagh's influence at the peace settlement was immense. The very presence of a British foreign secretary at a European conference table was unusual and Castlereagh capitalized upon it, winning golden opinions even from practised and devious diplomats for his hard work, his ability to gain the respect of the protagonists and his straightforwardness. He did not obtain all that he wanted, of course. A plan to strengthen Prussia, which he wished to see as a source of stability in northern-central Europe, by negotiating its take-over of neighbouring Saxony, came to nothing. Nor was he able to secure Poland from Russian control. These two reverses assumed greater significance later when it became clear that the main threat to Britain's European interests in the nineteenth century was to be Russia rather than France.

Nevertheless, on all the most crucial immediate issues for Britain, Castlereagh got his way. The sprawling empire of nepotism which Napoleon had created was dismantled. Yet, though France was forced to accept an army of occupation under the Duke of Wellington until 1818, all attempts to cut into its pre-1789 territories were blocked. The Bourbon monarchy was, of course, restored. Louis XVIII, younger brother of the executed Louis XVI, was confirmed after his long exile in Verona as the lawful King of France, though he ruled within certain constitutional constraints. The Austrian Netherlands and Holland, however, were merged into a single kingdom, thus acting as an effective buffer against French expansion to the north. Castlereagh, recalling the campaigns of Louis XIV in the 1670s, was convinced that it was France's fixed ambition 'to possess herself of the Low Countries and the territories on the left bank of the Rhine' (Chambertain, 1980: 101).

The reorganization of the German lands into a confederation of only 39 states also afforded prospects of greater stability, particularly since Prussia gained substantial territory in the Rhineland, including a crucial border with north-eastern France. Castlereagh hoped to see Prussia develop as the north German counterbalance to the Austrian Habsburg Empire in the south. The Spanish monarchy was restored in the unprepossessing person of Ferdinand VII in 1814 while the Italian peninsula, always an area of potential unrest in view of its numerous states, was substantially reorganized. The Habsburg Empire took over the economically prosperous northern states of Lombardy and Venetia, while Savoy and Genoa were annexed to Piedmont-Sardinia. The Papal States were restored and in southern Italy Naples saw the return of a Bourbon monarch. As a result of these adjustments, the respective spheres of European monarchical influence were more sharply defined.

Castlereagh was not foolish enough to demand mainland European territory as the price of British victory over the French, though Hanover, whose Elector had been the reigning British monarch since 1714, gained some. Much more important was the expansion of Britain's overseas empire. It has been noted that the French wars witnessed the most substantial increase in territory since Ireland and much of the eastern seaboard of America was occupied in the first half of the seventeenth century (Bayly, 1989: 100). It was crucial to Britain's interests that its overseas commercial and strategic influence be substantially enhanced. Not surprisingly, the peace settlement confirmed Britain's wartime winnings. The island territories captured during the wars were retained. The most important were in the West Indies, where Britain retained control of St Lucia, Tobago and Trinidad. Guyana, on the north-eastern tip of South America, was taken from the Dutch. In Europe, the North Sea island of Heligoland was acquired from Denmark, while Malta soon became Britain's guard dog in the Mediterranean. The Ionian Islands, off the west coast of Greece, also became British in 1815. The world-wide extent of Britain's interests was underscored by the acquisition of the Cape of Good Hope, Ceylon, Mauritius and the Seychelles. Opportunities for British traders in the east were substantially increased by these acquisitions. Singapore was added in 1819, ending the previous Dutch trading monopolies in the East Indies.

With French and Spanish influence substantially reduced in the West Indies and the long-standing Dutch pre-eminence in the Far East at an end, Britain's supremacy as a world-wide trading nation was by 1820 unchallengeable. There was substantial expansion of British rule over India in the period of the French wars, where the East India Company exercised formal control. By 1815, the Company (and thus, in effect, Britain) controlled virtually the whole of southern India. With a large army in place, Britain was also poised for further expansion northwards. Virtually the whole of the Indian sub-continent could be presented as 'the jewel in Britain's imperial crown' by the middle of the century. What the historian Ronald Hyam called 'Britain's Imperial Century' was launched during and immediately after the French Wars, long before the major territorial acquisitions in Africa in the 1880s and 1890s.

Castlereagh's own concerns, however, rarely strayed outside Europe. From the earliest days of the peace settlement, important differences of interpretation separated Britain from its allies. Put simply, Britain sought to **balance** out territorial interests in Europe to prevent any one nation from becoming threateningly powerful. Forms of government were of secondary importance. Despite much contemporary criticism, in which the poet Byron was prominent, Castlereagh did not believe that the ideological forces of liberalism and **nationalism** which had been let loose during the eighteenth-century Enlightenment and the French Wars, either could or should be suppressed. No Irish politician in the nineteenth century – Castlereagh was an Ulsterman from the so-called 'Protestant Ascendancy' – could be unaware of the importance of nationalism. Since Britain already had a representative government of sorts, its politicians were less fearful of deviations from the autocratic norm than were most hereditary rulers.

It was not surprising that the European emperors saw the settlement of 1814–15 as a means of re-confirming the supremacy of the old order. In September 1815, Tsar Alexander I of Russia persuaded the Austrian emperor and the King of Prussia to agree to 'remain united by the bonds of a true and indissoluble fraternity' and to 'lend each other aid and assistance' when required. It rapidly became clear that Alexander intended this 'Holy Alliance', as it soon became known, to be the means whereby nationalist or liberal

Balance of power The situation when no one power, or group of allied powers, can exert undue pressure on other states on account of larger territory or greater resources. In our period, British politicians and diplomats were generally trying to ensure that no European power became too powerful.

Nationalism The doctrine which believes in the integrity of the nation state as a political entity. In our period, it usually applied to nations attempting to break free from colonial rule, particularly those of the Spanish and Portuguese empires in South America and of the Ottoman (Turkish) Empire in South-East Europe.

movements in any part of Europe could be crushed. Britain had refused to sign the Holy Alliance and soon needed to defend its own, very different, interpretation of 'Congress diplomacy'.

At only the first Congress held under the arrangements made in Vienna – that of Aix-la-Chapelle in 1818 – did the great powers demonstrate anything approaching unity. Here arrangements were completed for re-admitting France, now an apparently secure monarchy, into the small circle of the great powers. The Quadruple Alliance became the Quintuple Alliance and France agreed 'to concur in the maintenance and consolidation of a System which has given Peace to Europe'.

Even at Aix-la-Chapelle, however, differences had surfaced about how the system should develop. Tsar Alexander was making aggressive noises against nationalist forces threatening Spanish territories in Latin America, but his plans for collective action to force the nationalists to back down came to nothing. However, between 1818 and 1821 liberal and nationalist movements in Europe, which affected Spain, Portugal and Naples, brought the ideological issue to the forefront. When the Greeks rebelled against the Ottoman Turks in March 1821, demanding independence, all the major European powers were affected, either by considerations of strategy or sentiment or both. Greece, of course, was the cradle of European civilization and most British statesmen knew considerably more Greek literature than they did contemporary science or economics. 'Philhellenism' – the love of Greek culture – influenced the attitudes of many.

At the Congress of Troppau in 1820, called by Alexander to discuss recent events in Spain, Portugal and Naples, the powers agreed on a 'Protocol' which would refuse recognition to any regime established by rebellion and which reserved the right to 'exercise effective and beneficial action' to restore 'legitimate' government to countries where rebellions had been successful (Chamberlain, 1980: 105). Significantly, Britain was not a party to this Protocol. Indeed, Castlereagh refused to send a full representative to Troppau. His observations on the conduct of the members of the Holy Alliance were set out in a famous State Paper written in May 1820 **[Doc. 11, p. 111]**.

Study of this important document indicates not only Castlereagh's level headed pragmatism but how little of real substance separated him from domestic critics of his foreign policy. Castlereagh was no heedless interventionist and he was well aware of dangers involved in extending the principles of Vienna into a reactionary coalition. More than most conservative European statesmen, he understood that the ideas released by the French revolution would not be suppressed by force of arms. He was not prepared to see broader considerations of strategy sacrificed on the altar of dogma. The reference to 'the spirit of Treason and Disaffection' in Britain is particularly significant in this context.

As early as 1820, therefore, different interpretations of the European 'system' presaged its downfall. The Congress adjourned at Troppau re-convened at Laibach at the beginning of 1821. British support for action against liberals and nationalists was severely limited. Castlereagh briefed his half-brother, Lord Charles Stewart, representing the government, on the important distinction to be drawn between intervention on principle and intervention where a great power's 'immediate security, or essential interests are seriously endangered by the internal transactions of another state' (Derry, 1976: 208). Such an interpretation would justify Austrian intervention to suppress nationalism in Naples, since Austria was a major power in Italy, but it could not justify Tsar Alexander's sending troops to Spain or Portugal, because no direct Russian interest could conceivably be at risk. The distinction was also pragmatically convenient, since Britain's relations with Austria were much warmer than those with Russia. Over the Greek rebellion, also Austro-British interests were in close accord and opposed to those of Russia.

Castlereagh wryly noted that the principles which Tsar Alexander fiercely upheld in Spain and the Americas could be conveniently bent when Russian interests were at stake. The Greek rebellion offered an opportunity for Russia to establish itself in the eastern Mediterranean at the expense of the Turks; few were fooled by the assertion that Russia wished to intervene to support rebellious, but Christian, nationalists against 'legitimate', but infidel, Turkish authority. British trading interests were directly affected by events in the Mediterranean and Castlereagh would not permit Russian initiatives in this area to go without challenge.

The Laibach Congress agreed to defer consideration of these weighty matters and it was decided to hold a fresh Congress at Verona in October 1822. By the end of the Laibach meeting, however, it was clear that the respective, and increasingly conflicting, interests of the great powers were assuming much greater importance than were abstract declarations of conservative principle. To that extent, events proved Castlereagh's instincts sound.

By the summer of 1822, however, Castlereagh himself was far from sound. The Duke of Wellington wrote despairingly in early August that the Foreign Secretary, whose 'sober mind' had previously been his hallmark, was now 'in a state bordering upon Insanity' (Thompson, 1986: 38). Perhaps depressed by the overwork generated in combining conduct of foreign policy with domestic duties as Leader of the House of Commons, certainly alarmed by the prospect of a public accusation of homosexuality (for which allegation, incidentally, there is very little evidence), Castlereagh cut his throat on 12 August, dying almost immediately. His death provoked a ministerial crisis but, as we shall see (pp. 63–8), it produced no dramatic shifts in the directions taken by British foreign policy. The collapse of Congress Diplomacy, and Britain's renunciation of close European accords, for

which Canning is usually given the major credit, had not only been anticipated but accepted by his predecessor.

FOREIGN POLICY UNDER CANNING

There used to be a fashion for contrasting the foreign policy of Castlereagh
with that of his successor, George Canning. This fashion generally portrayed
Castlereagh as the friend of established, autocratic regimes who, in pursuit
of his anti-liberal objectives, involved Britain in close alliances with the
crowned heads of Europe. Canning, though a staunch parliamentary anti-
reformer, was a supporter of liberal and national movements abroad who
reverted to the normal peacetime tradition of keeping Europe, and its rival
powers, at arm's length.

The fallibility of this view of Castlereagh was suggested above (see p. 62)
and it will be argued here that the characterisation is of limited value on the
Canning side of the equation too. Nevertheless, it is true that Castlereagh's
'Congress diplomacy' attracted widespread criticism not only in the radical
press, which was to be expected, but also in the Cabinet, where none spoke
more sharply about it than Canning. Canning's aversion to Britain's participation in great-power meetings rested both on present needs and on Britain's
historical avoidance of European entanglement **[Doc. 10, p. 111]**.

Canning's reaction might be explained by envy of Castlereagh's success.
Only a year apart in age, they had been personal rivals since the days of their
political apprenticeships under the younger Pitt. Both were seen as rising
stars but Canning had made much the greater initial, but short-term, impact
and had been Foreign Secretary in Portland's brief Tory administration
in 1807. The two men had fought a well-publicised duel in 1809 after
Castlereagh accused Canning, not without justice, of trying to undermine his
cabinet position as Secretary for War when the conflict with Napoleon was
going badly. Liverpool as prime minister showed evident, and characteristic,
preference for Castlereagh's stolid dependability over Canning's mercurial
and abrasive talents. Canning was at first out of Liverpool's Cabinet and then,
from 1816–22, occupied, as President of the Board of Control, a post considerably more junior than Castlereagh's. It rankled.

However much politicians seek to deny it, opportunism and self-interest
greatly influence their actions, and the real enemies of self-advancement are
more often found within one's own party than in the ranks of the opposition.
So with Castlereagh and Canning. Canning's much greater fluency in debate
and his more assiduous concern about public opinion – he was perhaps the
first major British politician to concern himself with cultivating a distinctive

'image' – emphasized the presentational contrasts between the two men. Beneath the presentation, however, the two men did genuinely differ over the likely benefits of Congress diplomacy. Canning was always sceptical and the unravelling of the Congress system probably contributed to Castlereagh's mental instability at the end of his life.

The Duke of Wellington represented Britain at the last authentic Congress, which began in Verona in the autumn of 1822 a couple of months after Castlereagh's death. Wellington was the cabinet minister least in sympathy with Canning's approach to politics, though he recognized that his experience, his talent and his popularity outside Westminster made any attempt to block his promotion to the Foreign Office unwise. Wellington did important work in persuading a very reluctant George IV not to veto it, though he regretted his initiative a little later as relations with Canning soured yet further. Wellington and Canning were in no serious disagreement about policy at Verona, however. Indeed, the guidelines drawn up by Castlereagh were adopted. Wellington helped to forestall Tsar Alexander's plans for combined allied intervention on behalf of the beleaguered Ferdinand VII of Spain. He was also sufficiently wary of Russian intentions over the Greek rebellion (see above, pp. 60–2) to draw closer to Metternich and the Austrians, thus confirming that the great-power accord of 1815–18 was already obsolete. Canning after 1822 merely made manifest what was almost certainly clear to Castlereagh in 1821: that Britain must detach itself from general systems and seek alliances which best suited specific circumstances. 'Every nation for itself, and God for us all' is how Canning put it. Metternich harboured a personal detestation of Canning, calling him 'a world scourge' (Seton-Watson, 1937: 95), and he greatly exaggerated his 'liberal' instincts in foreign policy. However, the two men acted harmoniously enough to ensure that the Greek rebellion was not exploited by the Russians to increase their influence in the Mediterranean.

The Congress System was finally killed at St Petersburg in 1825 when the Austrians and Russians failed to agree on a joint response to the Greek problem. Britain, which was not represented at St Petersburg, had recognized an independent Greek government in 1823, although Canning was more anxious to safeguard Britain's trading and strategic interests in the Mediterranean than he was to assert any nationalist priorities.

When the new Russian Tsar, Nicholas I, showed a determination to exploit Turkish weakness in Greece, Canning sought an agreement with the Russians, his primary objective being to avoid a Russo-Turkish war and consequent instability in the Mediterranean. Wellington was despatched to St Petersburg and a protocol between Britain and Russia was signed in 1826. This recognized what was in effect an independent Greece though it was to remain under very limited Turkish sovereignty. This was confirmed, with the addition of French signatures, as the Treaty of London in July 1827 (Evans, 2001: 523).

The treaty represented the peak of British influence over the tortuous process of Greek independence. Less than a month after it was signed Canning died. The subsequent drift in foreign policy during the Goderich and Wellington administrations when the Earl of Dudley and the inexperienced Earl of Aberdeen were in charge allowed Russia to capitalize. An allied fleet under the command of Admiral Codrington soundly defeated the Turks at the Battle of Navarino in 1827, though the battle might well have been avoided, thus securing greater stability in southern Europe. A brief Russo-Turkish war followed and it had damaging consequences. It undermined the Anglo-Russian alliance and persuaded Wellington to believe that British interests lay rather in propping up the Turks. A pro-Turkish policy was both unrealistic and unpopular at home. It implied a lessening commitment to the Greeks at a time when public sympathy for their cause was at its height. By the time the Greeks obtained complete independence in 1832, Russia's influence in the Balkans was much extended. Britain's stock in the Mediterranean stood lower than in the Canning era and this for a time threatened imperial and commercial interests both in India and the Middle East.

Important though the Greek issue was, Canning believed that the most important areas of British interest in the 1820s lay in the western Mediterranean and Latin America. Britain's relations with Spain and Portugal had strong strategic and commercial implications. Unimpeded British access to Mediterranean trade required stability on the Iberian peninsula, and Britain had traditionally close links with Portugal. Spanish and Portuguese controls over the South American colonies they had ruled since the sixteenth century crumbled very rapidly early in the nineteenth. Canning made no secret of the fact that he intended to maximize the commercial opportunities thus presented.

Both Spain and Portugal were enfeebled states in the 1820s. The Spanish constitution of 1812, never supported by King Ferdinand, was overthrown with the aid of French troops in 1823, when Louis XVIII cited the agreements at the Congresses of Troppau and Laibach as warrant for intervention. Spain returned to **absolute government**. Canning, whose foreign policy came under constant challenge from Wellington, was not in a strong position in Cabinet and allowed himself to be persuaded not to intervene since the Spaniards were divided and Britain's interests not directly threatened.

Britain's involvement with Portugal was much more extensive. Indeed, British officers under Viscount Beresford had helped the Portuguese government to keep liberal forces at bay from 1816 to 1820 while the Portuguese monarch, King John VI, preferred for his own safety to remain in the

Absolute government
A form of government in which there is no limit or restraint on the power which can be exercised by one leader or by a governing group. Someone exercising such rule, or supporting it, is often called an 'absolutist'.

Portguese colony of Brazil. The liberals were successful in imposing a constitution on the King in the early 1820s although Portugal remained both economically weak and politically divided. After King John's death in 1826, Britain sent 4,000 troops to the Portuguese capital, Lisbon, to the support of a fleet of warships already in the River Tagus. The purpose was to guarantee the stability of the existing government and to prevent Portugal from domination by any other of the great powers, especially Spain. Canning wrote to the British ambassador in Lisbon that Britain had 'treaties of ancient obligation' which gave it 'a preponderance in the affairs of Portugal which . . . she has not the choice of abandoning' (Hinde, 1973: 412–13).

In reality, British intervention owed much more to concern with the balance of power than to any chivalrous considerations towards a long-standing ally. Spain threatening Portugal with the support of France threatened Britain's commercial interests. Canning was not slow to exploit public opinion which was much more liberal than most of his cabinet colleagues, and especially Wellington whose interventions and expostulations to George IV strongly implied that he himself deserved to be in charge of foreign affairs. Canning's speech of explanation to the Commons **[Doc. 14, p. 113]** was well received by the Whig opposition, while many Tories believed that Canning's real purpose was to weaken established authority and order.

Canning told Wellington soon after becoming Foreign Secretary that 'the American questions are out of all proportion more important to us than the European. . . . if we do not seize and turn them to our advantage in time, we shall rue the loss of an opportunity never, never to be recovered' (Hinde, 1973: 345). The 'opportunity' was primarily commercial. Buenos Aires, Colombia and Mexico, erstwhile Spanish possessions whose independence Britain recognized in 1824, and Brazil, recognized as independent from Portugal the following year, all became important in Britain's fast-developing 'informal empire' based on trade. Britain had no intention of annexing them as colonies but rapidly established itself as the leading supplier of manufactured goods to these newly independent states. It was this commercial hegemony which Canning meant when, in welcoming the independence of the Latin American states, he declared that 'Spanish America is free; and if we do not mismanage our affairs sadly, she is English' (Hyam, 1976: 169). Both the Manchester and the Birmingham Chambers of Commerce petitioned Parliament to recognize the independence of the Latin American states. It was a plea which Canning, who was for ten years an MP for Liverpool, Britain's largest commercial city outside London, was unlikely to ignore.

Canning's Latin American policy had a strategic dimension too. In 1823, he extracted from the French ambassador, Prince Polignac, an agreement known as the Polignac Memorandum. This pledged that France, because of its recent interventions there the dominant influence in Spain, had no territorial ambitions in the New World. Polignac expected this 'gentleman's agreement' to remain private, and thus deniable. He was outraged that Canning should seek to make public political capital from informal diplomatic discussions between statesmen of different nations. The Memorandum chimed in neatly with the famous Declaration of the US President James Monroe in December 1823 that 'the American continents . . . are henceforth not to be considered as future subjects for colonization by any European power'. Monroe's Declaration offered no threat to Britain, whose future designs in South American were commercial rather than colonial, and it unintentionally supported Canning's own strategy. In his own famous phrase **[Doc. 14, p. 113]**, Canning 'called the New World into existence, to redress the balance of the old . . . if France had Spain, it should not be Spain "with the Indies" '.

Canning's other key strategic consideration has received less notice from European historians, but is probably the more important. His Latin American policy was designed to put a brake on US colonialism. Britain's commercial interests were supported by the British navy and this fact was probably sufficient to ensure that the United States confined its territorial claims to the north of America. Canning laid great stress on the need to curb the 'ambition and ascendancy of the United States of America'. Two 'Great Powers' thus developed in the Americas. In the middle of the continent, the influence of the United States was unchallengeable and its economy grew rapidly because of both early industrial growth and its steady movement westwards towards California. The United States was nevertheless uneasily sandwiched between a British colonial presence in Canada in the North and a rapidly expanding British commercial and colonial influence in Latin America and the West Indies to the south.

Canning took great pride in his Latin American policy but it did nothing to strengthen his political position at home. Latin American nationalism was regarded as a strange, alien force by most of his cabinet colleagues. Wellington spluttered that Canning's policy had delivered the continent into the hands of 'revolutionary rascals and blackguards' (Thompson, 1986: 46). He especially resented, as did many diplomats in Europe, that Canning had acted unilaterally in recognizing the independence of Latin American countries and had refused to send a British delegate to the Conference of European powers in Paris in 1824 summoned to discuss the changing situation in the Americas. George IV's ancient prejudice against Canning was still further strengthened and he plotted to have him removed, a manoeuvre which Liverpool resisted.

By 1825, however, Canning himself felt secure enough to face the King down. He threatened to make public evidence concerning the King's encouragement of factions in the Tory party who wished to bring the Foreign

Secretary down. Well aware of which man would command the greater support both in the newspapers and at the court of public opinion more generally, the King hastily backed down. For the remaining two years of Canning's life George, much to Wellington's disgust, presented himself as a strong, if incongruous, supporter of his foreign secretary and turned immediately to him to replace the stricken Liverpool as prime minister in 1827.

Canning grossly exaggerated the extent of immediate commercial benefit Britain would derive from its support of newly independent nations in south America. Paradoxically, the biggest growth in Latin American trade occurred in the last decade *before* the spate of independence declarations, not in the first decade after. British exports to Latin America stood at £2.5 million in 1815 and £5 million in 1825. By 1835, they had hardly increased at all in real terms. As a proportion of British exports, indeed, they had fallen back from 13 per cent to 11 per cent (Evans, 2001: 501). The new states were under-populated and, until the advent of railways in the 1860s, most had only rudimentary communication networks. They were also developing their own basic domestic industries and so had less dependence on Britain's manufactured goods. The expectations of Birmingham and Manchester traders were frequently to be disappointed in Colombia, Mexico and Brazil.

5

Stability Shattered 1827–32

THE BREAK-UP OF THE TORY PARTY, 1827–30

Although it is easy to discover portents in the preceding years (see pp. 40–2), the suddenness with which the Tory party fell apart after Liverpool's stroke in February 1827 amazed contemporaries. The society hostess Lady Cowper remarked in May that 'there is such confusion and splitting among families and parties that it is quite . . . a danger to talk politics at all, and yet it is impossible to talk of anything else' (Hinde, 1973: 451). The protracted negotiations to form a new Cabinet involved disagreements within the Whig, as well as the Tory, party, though the Whigs survived them much better.

Some historians are reluctant to acknowledge parties as the central element in politics between 1815 and 1832 and they have cited the extraordinary confusion which followed Liverpool's resignation as evidence for their view (Gash, 1979; Cookson, 1975; Clark, 1980; Fraser, 1983). The actors in the drama, however, invariably made party disunity its central focus, which they would hardly have done if politics had been conducted in 'non-party' forms while Liverpool was prime minister. We must allow that party allegiance was by no means binding on a large number of backbench MPs. Fewer than half of them in the parliaments elected in the years 1802–30 voted consistently for one party or the other. We are a good half-century away from the development of tightly disciplined political parties whose writ ran through to the humblest or least 'party political' of **backbenchers**.

It is also true that some political insiders believed that tensions in the 1820s were weakening old bonds. The third Baron Holland, a leading Whig, believed in 1826 that 'party government' was dead, killed by deep divisions on a surprisingly wide variety of issues in both the main parties: religious, national, commercial and personal (Jupp, 1998: 242). There is no doubt that the period 1827–32 witnessed some surprising realignments from which

Backbench member of parliament A member of parliament who does not hold any government office or act as a senior figure in the opposition. Some backbenchers were independent of any political party and refused to accept party labels; others were happy to be known as 'Whigs' or 'Tories' but often voted against their party.

the old Tory, or Pittite, party held together till 1827 by Lord Liverpool was the main loser. However, 'party government' survived, albeit in a different configuration. Times of party fluidity are not uncommon in the longer run of British politics, as the years 1792–94, 1846–59, 1885–86, 1916–22 and, on the centre-left more recently, 1981–88, all demonstrate (O'Gorman, 1984). It is surely better to see the period 1827–30 as one in which major shifts in existing party loyalties took place, rather than as an indicator of the looseness of party ties.

Such periods, of course, alter existing assumptions and perceptions. The one discussed here brought radical parliamentary reform to the forefront of British politics in 1830 when five years earlier nothing seemed less likely. Nevertheless, the break-up of Liverpool's apparently unchallengeable hold on a Tory party with a very comfortable governing majority had nothing to do with the franchise and much to do with those personal antagonisms and vanities which are so often the harbingers of political change. It had even more to do with religion. Students in a predominantly secular age are prone to overlook the raw, emotional power of the Christian religion as a conventional political issue. Yet it was the Catholic question which had made Liverpool talk of resignation in 1826 and which precluded the formation of a stable Tory ministry after he had gone.

So dramatic are the changes which took place over the next five years that they have persuaded one historian that, until they blew the political structure apart in 1827–8, society and politics in England remained overwhelmingly Anglican, monarchical, authoritarian and deferential. Thereafter, hurricane-force winds, continuing unabated until 1832, destroyed the ancient edifice (Clark, 1985). Such an extreme view flies in the face of too much evidence, from the changes brought about by unprecedentedly rapid commercial expansion and industrial growth on the one hand to the contempt in which George IV was held on the other, to be persuasive as a whole. Yet it does indicate how much happened in this brief period.

For some years, Liverpool had regarded George Canning as his natural successor. Canning, however, though he had both experience and ability, lacked Liverpool's authority. He had two other disadvantages. His partisan nature and highly developed talent for browbeating did not compel either respect or deference in colleagues of similar seniority. As we have seen (p. 64), Wellington, in particular, loathed him. He was also the firmest supporter in Liverpool's Cabinet of Roman Catholic emancipation, a cause for which there was no marked public sympathy in Britain and much violent hostility within his own party. Although Canning had no intention of sponsoring an inevitably divisive Emancipation Bill, he would not guarantee to oppose any such Bill if introduced by others. That degree of equivocation was enough to lose him the support of convinced Tory 'Protestants'.

Canning's firmest supporter during the period of more than two months which it took to install him as prime minister was the King, once his most implacable enemy. As we have seen, George IV had grown closer to Canning in the last years of Liverpool's government (p. 68), both belatedly acknowledging the success of his foreign minister's policies and fearing the implications of his hold on public opinion. He therefore saw no reason to depart from Liverpool's preference. Half of Liverpool's Cabinet, however, did. The 'Protestants', led by Wellington, Peel, Westmorland, Melville, Eldon and Bathurst, all refused to serve under Canning **[Doc. 15, p. 113]**. Wellington even quit as commander-in-chief. In all, about 40 office holders resigned.

Canning did not have sufficient talent at his disposal among 'Catholic' Tories to fill the gaps, though he seized the opportunity to promote Viscount **Palmerston**, who had been secretary of war since 1809, to his first cabinet post. Palmerston, who was to become the great survivor of nineteenth-century politics, would spend 27 of the next 38 years until his death in 1865 as a cabinet minister. Since the Tories who departed would not commit themselves to supporting a Canningite ministry, parliamentary arithmetic dictated an approach to the Whigs who, having been out of office since 1807, might have been expected to jump at any offer. Some did but others preferred to maintain party divisions. The result was a split in both parties. Grey, whose personal hostility to Canning – at least as great as Wellington's – was mingled with snobbish disdain at a prime minister whose mother had been an actress, refused to have anything to do with an alliance. Many Whigs, Lord John Russell among them, took their lead from Grey. The Whigs who stayed out of Canning's government were among the most aristocratic members of the party.

Eventually, after hectoring from Brougham, who feared the return of a reactionary high-Tory ministry and who was prepared, as he put it, to do '*anything* to lock the door for ever on Eldon and Co' (Gash, 1986: 215), enough Whig support was pledged to allow Canning to anticipate parliamentary majorities. Three Whigs, Lansdowne, Tierney and the Earl of Carlisle, joined the Cabinet. One discontented Whig asserted that Canning's elevation had 'dissected both Whigs and Tories' (Evans, 1985: 218). This was only a mild exaggeration and during the spring of 1827 political opinion polarized on one large, and dangerous, issue – Catholic Emancipation – and on one controversial politician – Canning. Party labels became temporarily subordinate.

Canning, whose health had been poor for upwards of a year, declared himself 'quite knocked up' in July 1827 and died early the following month. Strain and the overwork involved in both heading an inexperienced government and acting as his own Chancellor of the Exchequer were contributory factors, though lung and liver inflammation was diagnosed. Given the difficulties which had attended the formation of Canning's government, George IV was reluctant to disturb its hard-won balance. He was also out of humour

Palmerston, 3rd Viscount Liberal Tory, then Whig, politician. He was Secretary at War from 1809–27. He entered the Cabinet under Goderich and resigned from Wellington's government with the Canningites in 1828. His break with the Tories proved to be permanent and he became Foreign Secretary under Grey.

with the 'ultra' Tories whom he believed had betrayed Canning. Thus, to preserve continuity, he turned to Frederick Robinson who had taken a peerage
as Viscount Goderich after accepting Canning's offer to lead for the government in the House of Lords a few months earlier.

Goderich had extensive ministerial experience, having been in office continuously since 1809 (Bourne, 1982). He had served Liverpool with quiet
efficiency and had been fortunate to serve as Chancellor of the Exchequer
during an economic boom (see above, pp. 46–8). What he had never shown,
however, was leadership. His only virtue as prime minister in 1827 was that
he permitted the delicate political balancing act which the Canning government represented to be briefly maintained. He had the additional, but
dubious, merit in George IV's eyes of allowing the King to exercise an influence over appointments which neither Liverpool nor, briefly, Canning had
allowed him. He seems to have dictated to Goderich who should be
chancellor of the exchequer – a self-defeating gesture since the new man,
J.C. Herries, was poles apart from the indispensable William Huskisson
politically. Huskisson was anyway less than delighted to be Secretary for
War and the Colonies. Herries and Huskisson were also personal enemies.
To have kept them in a Cabinet for any length of time would have required
strong leadership at the top when the opposite was the case.

The Goderich ministry was the last occasion in British history when the
monarch ruled as well as reigned. George IV's new prime minister lacked
all conviction. He was unable to rally Whig support. The Whigs, for once
rightly, feared inappropriate royal influence and also believed, wrongly,
that the return of Wellington as commander-in-chief indicated insidious
high-Tory influence backstage. Goderich's ministry collapsed inwards in the
autumn of 1827 when the Secretary for War (Huskisson), the Home Secretary
(Lansdowne) and the Chancellor of the Exchequer (Herries) all attempted to
resign. Woebegone and lacking anyone's confidence, Goderich submitted
a tearful resignation to the King early in January 1828, thus avoiding the
embarrassment of having to defend his record before Parliament. He remains
the only prime minister never to have faced a parliamentary session. The fact
that his ministry lasted for almost five months indicates how brief parliamentary sessions usually were before the first Reform Act. Huskisson suggested that
'never, surely, was there a man at the head of affairs so weak, undecided, and
utterly helpless' (Hilton, 2006: 63).

Events in January 1828 left the King with no alternative but to turn back
to the 'Protestant' Tories, and he could at least recognise the obvious. The day
after Goderich's resignation, George invited Wellington to form a 'strong government' (Jenkins, 1999: 71). Wellington, having a soldier's uncomplicated
view about the evils which had beset the nation since Liverpool's resignation,
accepted readily. He envisaged a strong and properly 'Tory' administration

with himself directing affairs in the Lords and Peel leading in the Commons. The Whigs were not considered for office and Wellington's instinct was to dismiss the Canningite 'pro-Catholics', led by Huskisson, along with them. Only Peel's insistence on strong debating talent in the Commons persuaded the new prime minister to keep them on.

The Tory ministry, therefore, initially looked similar to Liverpool's, but any hopes that it could establish an equivalent stability rapidly crumbled to dust. A broad-based Tory government lasted for only four months. From the beginning, there was a lack of trust. Wellington made no secret of the fact that he blamed Huskisson and the Canningites for the weaknesses of government in 1827 and, against Peel's advice, manoeuvred for any opportunity to be rid of them. He squabbled with them over levels of protection in the new Corn Bill (p. 50). They suspected him of trying to undo Canning's foreign policy (p. 64), although Wellington had kept one of their number, the Earl of Dudley, at the Foreign Office.

The eventual rift, in May 1828, occurred over a trivial disagreement about how to redistribute two parliamentary boroughs which had been disfranchised for corruption at the 1826 general election. When his preference for giving the new seats to large boroughs rather than to the counties was overruled, Huskisson made what he believed to be a merely formal offer of resignation. He was surprised at the alacrity with which Wellington accepted it. Dudley, Grant, William Lamb (soon to inherit the title of Viscount **Melbourne** by which he is much better known) and Palmerston left with Huskisson and the resulting Tory ministry became unequivocally 'Protestant' in complexion.

This ministerial reshuffle had more profound consequences than either side could have known at the time. The Canningites rapidly made common cause with their recent Whig allies while Grey, who had stood aloof from Canning's entreaties in 1827, increasingly saw the value of a united opposition against what the Whigs believed to be an 'ultra' Tory government. Once the Canningites had accepted the necessity for parliamentary reform, which during 1829 and 1830 they all did, the way was open for a permanent political realignment. The Whigs were the main beneficiaries. The departed Canningites would never take office in a Tory government again. The most durable of them, Palmerston, is almost invariably remembered as the greatest of the Whig foreign secretaries. His 'liberal Tory' origins are virtually forgotten.

In jumping from the Canningite frying pan, Wellington soon discovered that he had landed himself in that most intense of Tory fires – the one stoked by religious bigotry. In a sense, his problem was that he was never the unbending '**Ultra**' which the Whigs feared, and the real Tory 'Ultras' hoped, him to be. At the annual Tory Pitt dinner, Lord Eldon celebrated the departure of the Canningites as a victory for the Protestant Ascendancy. Wellington meanwhile tried to convince himself that 'this country was never governed

Melbourne, 2nd Viscount Whig and Canningite politician. He supported George Canning in the 1820s and, with other 'Liberal Tories' resigned from Wellington's government in 1828. He was Home Secretary in Grey's coalition government of 1830 but lukewarm on parliamentary reform. He succeeded Grey as prime minister in 1834.

Ultra-Tories ('Ultras') Name given to 'extreme' Tories who opposed almost all reforms. Most were especially antagonistic to the religious reforms of 1828–9 which gave greater civil liberties to Dissenters and Roman Catholics, although opposition to parliamentary reform was also widespread.

in practice according to the extreme principles of any party whatever; much less according to extremes which other opposing parties attribute to its adversaries' (Thompson, 1986: 80). The Ultras failed to heed the warning.

The reconstruction of Wellington's ministry itself led inexorably to a still more damaging Tory split. To replace Grant as president of the board of trade, Wellington chose an Irishman, Vesey Fitzgerald. According to the practice of the time, Fitzgerald had to resign his seat at County Clare and fight a by-election in his new guise as a Cabinet minister. Despite the fact that Fitzgerald was known to favour Catholic emancipation, Daniel O'Connell judged this to be an appropriate moment to bring his campaign to a climax. He stood against Fitzgerald in the County Clare by-election of July 1828 and won resoundingly. The victory brought the emancipation issue to crisis point, as O'Connell had hoped. As a Catholic, he was debarred from taking his seat at Westminster, but he made it quite clear that the Protestant Ascendancy might expect violence if the law were not amended to enable him to represent his constituents.

Peel, who knew as much about Ireland as anyone in Wellington's Cabinet, counselled his chief that O'Connell could not be defied without substantial civil commotion (Hilton, 2006: 392). He did, however, go on to suggest that any unrest could easily be put down. It seems that Peel had been converted – however reluctantly – to the desirability of Catholic Emancipation. Perhaps he had already realised that the security of Ireland within the United Kingdom depended upon the creation of loyal Catholics who could call themselves citizens in the full sense. Wellington certainly did not take this view. He had already raised the temperature in Ireland by dismissing a Chief Secretary, the Marquis of Anglesey, for advising concessions. He now deferred to Peel, drew back from confrontation and prepared a Catholic Emancipation Bill (pp. 78–9), although he had to brave the threat of dismissal by George IV in doing so.

Royal anger Wellington could discount. The King did indeed attempt to dismiss him in March 1829, and install a ministry perhaps headed by the staunchly anti-Catholic Eldon. This was never practical politics; any Eldon ministry would have been immediately voted down in the House of Commons. Wellington was right to calculate that no remotely palatable alternative parliamentary support was available to George IV. The Tory Ultras were another matter. Their fury was wondrous to behold. The Dowager Duchess of Richmond showed her contempt for Wellington's 'ratting' on his Protestant commitments by festooning her drawing room with stuffed rats labelled with the names of ministers (Brock, 1973: 54). Sir Robert Peel resigned his seat at Oxford University and was defeated by Tory 'Protestants' when he recontested it. He had to take a pocket borough to remain in Parliament. The Earl of Winchilsea charged Wellington in *The Standard* newspaper with hatching a cynical plan for the infringement of Englishmen's liberties and 'the introduction of Popery in every department of the State' (Gash, 1985: 581). Winchilsea and Wellington fought a duel over the accusation at Battersea Fields in March 1829.

Canningite and Whig votes meant that Wellington was in no danger of parliamentary defeat over Catholic emancipation, but the 173 Tory back-benchers in the Commons and the 109 peers who voted against him in the Lords in March 1829 were placing a time bomb under his ministry. The Ultras would not be mollified; a few were even converted to parliamentary reform in the misguided belief that only the government's rotten boroughs had thwarted popular anti-Catholic sentiment (Evans, 2001: 259). Between the spring of 1829 and the autumn of 1830 Wellington's government was on long notice of ejection. The Tory party was shattered into three feuding groups. The Canningites by mid-1830 were all but committed to the Whigs. Wellington and Peel were finding out how long the centre could hold. The Ultra-Tories fumed, fulminated and plotted against leaders by whom they felt betrayed. The cause of parliamentary reform was greatly advanced by these decisive splits in Liverpool's anti-reform party, but it was religion rather than wider representation which had brought them about.

Economic discontent added to the government's difficulties from late 1829 onwards. Rejuvenated and more broadly based extra-parliamentary pressure for reform surfaced (see below, pp. 81–4). The death of George IV in June 1830 necessitated a general election. Wellington hoped to use it, in the time-honoured way, to strengthen his position in Parliament by use of government patronage. His electoral fire was directed at Canningite MPs, whom he believed to be vulnerable. He was mistaken. The Canningite Charles Grant defeated a government challenger at Inverness. The Home Secretary's younger brother, Jonathan Peel, was beaten in the large, and relatively **democratic**, borough of Norwich **[Docs 26–28, pp. 121–2]** and Wellington also lost one of the government's more eloquent journalistic supporters, John Wilson Croker. The election did not produce overwhelming anti-government majorities. As was the norm before 1832, few seats were actually contested. The consensus was that the government made only a small net loss but its psychological effect was substantial.

The election, and the European revolutions which also took place in 1830 in France, Belgium and Poland, convinced more wavering MPs of the need for concessions on parliamentary reform. The Whigs were encouraged to raise the issue again. Wellington's own conviction remained anti-reformist but, after Catholic emancipation, Ultra backing was uncertain. His famous speech in early November 1830 **[Doc. 29, p. 123]**, asserting that the existing franchise and distribution of seats had the entire confidence of the country, was, therefore, foolhardy, even considered within a Westminster perspective.

Democratic government A government selected, usually in an election, by virtually all adults. In our period, very few considered extending the vote to women. Radical parliamentary reformers were divided between those who wanted 'one man, one vote' and those who wanted a large, but not democratic, expansion of voting rights.

In the country as a whole, the judgement was ludicrous. Wellington's error – he plaintively enquired of the Earl of Aberdeen on sitting down, 'I have not said too much, have I?' – was seized on by Whigs and Canningites. With Ultra support, they engineered a government defeat on a minor issue but one which Wellington had intimated he would consider one of confidence in his government. He resigned immediately.

Wellington had not enjoyed being prime minister. He frequently talked to friends about his desire to give up office (Jupp, 1998: 44). He hung on largely because of his belief in firm, stable government which he believed that, even in the autumn of 1830 and with Peel in support, he was better placed to provide than anyone else. He deserves somewhat more credit as prime minister than he has received. He could make good debating points in the Lords, although he was never flexible or light-footed in responding to criticism. He worked extremely hard. Ultimately, though, the bedrock soldier was not made for the more dextrous, and duplicitous, arts of politics. He continued to believe that the old political and social order was the best guarantee of security which the nation could have. He failed to appreciate how rapidly, and irreversibly, that nation was changing. He ignored public opinion at the very time when it was becoming a potent element in political life.

A Whig-led coalition government under Earl Grey took its place, pledged to parliamentary reform. The Whig backbencher, Sir Robert Heron, summed up the rapidity with which events had changed: 'Two years ago, I thought Reform of Parliament almost hopeless. I now believe it to be certain and approaching' (Brock, 1973: 100).

RELIGIOUS REFORMS, 1828–29

In February 1828, after concerted action by leading Nonconformists and some younger members of the Whig party, Lord John Russell sponsored a motion in the House of Commons calling on MPs to consider whether existing legislation, which barred Protestant dissenters from holding any office in local or central government, should be repealed. The Corporation and Test Acts had been passed in 1661 and 1673 respectively. Their intention was to demonstrate that the Church of England was regarded as an essential bastion of strength for the restored monarchy of Charles II after the dark days of Oliver Cromwell and the English republic. Many republicans had been inflexible and dogmatic dissenters, as much opposed to bishops as to kings. The Restoration of 1660 conveyed a double message. It would restore the monarchy, of course, but it also restored the Church of England 'as by law established' to its old position of dominance.

Nonconformists, or 'Dissenters' as they were sometimes known, had always been permitted to sit as MPs, though not to hold office. Since the Hanoverian succession of 1714, the practical disabilities imposed by the Test and Corporation Acts had gradually diminished; many blind eyes had been turned and many indemnities were issued by the authorities. Yet the Acts remained – a symbolic demonstration that Nonconformists were second-class citizens. Many eighteenth-century attempts at repeal had failed before the French Revolution postponed all libertarian reforms. Now Russell's motion was passed by more than 40 votes in the Commons and, when it reached the Lords, the Anglican bishops were not disposed to block it. Peel's role was critical. He was prepared to see the legislation repealed if the privileged legal and political status of the Church of England remained, with bishops sitting in the Lords and key church appointments continuing to be made by the monarch and government. He sounded out opinion in the Lords and secured the support of the two archbishops and four leading bishops (Clark, 1985). Charles Lloyd, the Bishop of Oxford and one of Peel's old University tutors, had tried to persuade him that the Acts might be defended as essential to the survival of the Church of England. Peel rejected this advice, arguing that the Church should not need the support of ancient statutes to protect it in the early nineteenth century. It would anyway retain its status as the established church but it should be confident enough to be able to stand on its own feet. 'I do not think . . . that the Church of England must fall if the Test and Corporation Acts are repealed', he stated [Hilton, 2006: 381]. A hasty amendment in the Lords by Edward Copleston, Bishop of Llandaff, inserting the words 'on the faith of a Christian' kept public office closed to Jews, atheists and **agnostics**. Anti-dissenting Ultra Tories, however, received little encouragement from the bishops in the House of Lords, where they might most have expected to find it. As frequently happened, Wellington's emotional aversion to compromise on religious issues was overborne by his respect for Peel's logic and political acumen. He supported his home secretary. Thus it was that the Test and Corporations Acts were repealed by an overwhelmingly 'Protestant' Tory government with much less parliamentary opposition than might have been expected.

When a **private member's bill** to permit Jews to sit in Parliament and to hold office was presented in 1830, however, it was rejected. Peel, following the line taken earlier by Bishop Copleston, was one of many to argue that the different outcome for religious dissenters and for Jews was entirely appropriate. In a Christian country, Parliament should remain closed to non-Christians.

As has been seen (pp. 74–5), the passage of Roman Catholic Emancipation was much more contentious than the repeal of the Test and Corporations Acts. It engendered vituperative and long-lasting bitterness within the

Agnostic One who feels that there is not enough evidence to determine whether God exists or not, or that nothing can be known about the existence of God. It follows that an agnostic would not (for other than cynical reasons) be a member of any orthodox church.

Private member's bill A proposal for legislation which is presented not by a political party but by an individual MP. Most legislation until the middle of the nineteenth century came about in this way.

Tory party. Nevertheless, Wellington's Tory government in February 1829 sponsored a bill to repeal all penal laws against any of His Majesty's Catholic subjects in Great Britain or Ireland **[Doc. 25, p. 120]**. Like the Test and Corporation Acts, most of the relevant anti-Catholic legislation had been passed towards the end of the seventeenth century: in 1678 during the so-called 'Popish Plot' and in 1689 when Protestant dominance was institutionalized by statute in the 'Glorious Revolution'. Most of the 'persecuting' legislation against Catholics in Britain – long a dead letter – had been repealed in 1791. From 1793, Catholics in Ireland were permitted to vote and to hold a range of civil offices in the country, if they met the stringent property qualifications. These voting rights were transferred to the United Kingdom Parliament, along with Ireland's 100 MPs, in 1801 under the Act of Union. However, in Britain Catholics were still debarred from voting, from holding public office and from sitting in Parliament.

Roman Catholic emancipation in Ireland had been hedged by two important qualifications. The arrival of Catholic MPs was accompanied by a sharp increase in the county voting qualification in Ireland from 40s (£2) to £10, thus removing the anyway remote possibility of a mass peasant vote in that country. The Catholic Association of Daniel O'Connell was also formally suppressed in order to appease those who thought it an affront to law and order. This was mostly window-dressing, however, since the Association had been established primarily to secure that which its Tory opponents now conceded. Given the virulence of anti-Catholicism in England, not least in the poorer areas of large towns where British working men frequently felt threatened by Irish immigration, the two-to-one vote by the Lords in favour of emancipation in April 1829 was surprising. It shocked the King who believed himself 'deserted by an aristocracy which had supported his father' (Clark, 1985: 398). That the King's trenchant and well-publicised opposition could so easily be overborne was a clear indication that the power of the monarchy had evaporated. Protestant Ultras, equally aghast at what they saw as a fundamental act of betrayal and a supine concession to the forces of 'revolution', were left to plot their revenge against Wellington and Peel (p. 79).

It is tempting to see both pieces of reformist legislation in 'Whiggish' terms. Those historians who see the unfolding of the past along broadly progressive lines have no difficulty in explaining these important religious changes as part of that conversion to principles of toleration and liberality which was the hallmark of a mature and successful people. Since religious bigotry, in their eyes, was essentially benighted, the changes of 1828 and 1829 represented progress.

Although the 1820s saw numerous examples of legislation which can be interpreted as broadly 'liberal', historians working in the last quarter of a century have seen sufficient examples in their own time of religious zealotry and bigotry alive and well and living almost all over the globe to be sceptical of what might be called the 'progressivist' model of religious change (Cannon, 1981; Clark, 1985; Machin, 1964; Davis, 1982; Machin, 1984; Machin, 1979). Accordingly, they have been critical of two assumptions about the religious legislation of 1828–9. The first is that these Acts are best seen as a tasty *hors d'oeuvre* to the more significant 'achievement' of parliamentary reform in 1832. The second is that the anti-reformist Ultra Tories were ignorant, bigoted, reactionary folk with no coherent philosophy, only a set of unpleasant 'gut assumptions' which were, quite rightly, challenged and defeated.

Catholic Emancipation was no *hors d'oeuvre*. Those who opposed the religious reforms of 1828–29 regarded them as a 'treason' greater than that which took place in 1832. Only in the context of later political reforms, which eventually culminated in a full, democratic franchise, can the importance of 1832 be properly gauged. Such a perspective was not available to the Marquis of Winchilsea, Lord Eldon or any of the Tory Ultras who felt so keenly betrayed by Wellington and Peel. Their historical perspective, naturally, derived from the seventeenth and eighteenth centuries when religion was the most important determinant of political attitudes. It was to remain so for most of the nineteenth century. While the changes of 1828 and 1829 weakened the case against political reform, therefore, this was far less important for defenders of the Anglican establishment (which, before 1832, meant defenders of the existing political as well as religious settlement) than the radical changes which the state was making on religion. As John Cannon has written, 'One of the most essential features of the old constitution was the identification of Church and State, dovetailed together under aristocratic supervision' (Cannon, 1981: 102).

Thus, for conservatives on the religious question, the legislation of 1828–9 weakened state as well as Church **[Doc. 24, p. 120]**. Eldon considered repeal of the Test and Corporation Acts 'a manoeuvre in favour of Popery, carried on under cover of liberality to the Dissenters'. When the Catholic Bill was considered the following year, he appeared in the unlikely guise of tribune of the people, playing expertly on the populist anti-Catholicism which made emancipation, even in England, a much livelier issue than repeal of the Test and Corporation Acts:

'The people were justly attached to the constitution of 1688 [the Glorious Revolution which installed Dutch Protestant William III in place of the English Catholic James II]; they looked to it as the foundation and bulwark of their freedom. If a part were changed, there might be a change in the whole; and that change they dreaded'

(Clark, 1985: 398).

In the context of the early nineteenth century, it is easy to demonstrate that the Ultras did indeed have a coherent position. It will not do to dismiss them as faintly absurd backwoodsmen vainly striving to hold back the inexorably reformist tide of history. Yet this is what has frequently been done. When society was urbanizing rapidly (see above, pp. 7–8) and the centre of economic gravity was shifting from south to north, they represented rural England in general and the arable south and east in particular. With both dissent and Catholicism making impressive strides (see below, pp. 80–1) in the urban north, they defended the supremacy of Anglicanism from communities in which the Church of England remained both overwhelmingly dominant and well-served by its clergymen. When political economists preached free trade and the supreme social and economic arbitration of the marketplace, most Ultras defended protection for land as the pre-eminent form of property. They also asserted the organic unity of a society founded on an established hierarchy that recognized paternalist values.

It is not necessary to agree with the Ultras in order to understand their philosophy. To deny its structural coherence is to accept that history is indeed the propaganda of the victors. In one sense, the alleged Tory 'backwoodsmen' of aristocratic England are in as much need of rescue from 'the enormous condescension of posterity' as were England's lower orders before Edward Thompson both rehabilitated and romanticized them (Thompson, 1963). A critical reading of the Tory house journals *The Quarterly Review* and *Blackwood's Edinburgh Magazine* does not show either of them to be the intellectual inferior of the Whig *Edinburgh Review* or the radical-Benthamite *Westminster Review*. Their real crime was to have lost the argument to superior economic forces in a rapidly industrializing society. History forgives such 'crimes' less readily than it should.

The preceding paragraphs are not an apologia for the Ultras, merely a plea for disinterested appraisal of their position. It is not necessary to resort to economic determinism to discover why, on the religious issue, they lost so decisively. Peel, particularly, and Wellington could see potential benefits in terms of social stability from granting Catholic emancipation in Ireland (see above, p. 74). Even in England, however, Catholicism was gaining strength. From a small base among the gentry of the north-west since the late sixteenth century, Roman Catholicism doubled in strength between 1800 and 1830. Almost half the Catholic community, furthermore, was located in the thriving Lancashire commercial and industrial towns of Liverpool, Manchester, Preston and Wigan (Evans, 2001; Cannon, 1981; Bossy, 1975). Catholicism was a more important force in English society than it had been since the Reformation.

Dissent, too, after many years in the doldrums in the first half of the eighteenth century, was picking up. The 'old dissent', represented by Presbyterianism, Congregationalists and Baptists, increased its combined membership by about 77 per cent to 743,000 between 1800 and 1830. The Methodists, more recently established, increased their membership by more than three times to about 300,000 in the same period, though they had divided into warring sects after John Wesley's death in 1791. Methodists, it is interesting to note, were much more anti-Catholic than most Nonconformists in this period. They did not campaign actively, as did the older dissenting groups, for repeal of the Test and Corporation Acts (Evans, 2001; Hempton, 1984; Machin, 1984).

Overall, it was difficult for Peel and Wellington to deny: first, that dissenters offered no evident threat to public order in Britain; secondly, that they were growing substantially in numbers; thirdly, that their contribution to trade, commerce and industry was disproportionately strong; and fourthly, that existing legislation was the more anomalous when religious plurality was an established fact in England, Scotland and Wales. Continued Anglican hegemony required more special pleading than either thought it prudent to attempt. Only in the hectic years between 1829 and 1832 did the force of the anti-reforming case become more apparent. Looked at through Tory eyes, it seemed that the government was not making judicious concessions over marginal issues: it was destroying the ideological basis of the old order. The changes of 1828 and 1829 are to be considered as an integral part of the history of reform, not as a prelude to it.

ECONOMIC DISTRESS AND POLITICAL ORGANIZATION, 1829–30

Events in Parliament in the years 1827–30 seriously weakened the anti-reformers, but the background to parliamentary reform cannot be understood only from a Westminster perspective. It is true that the cause appeared quiescent until 1829. While petitions about Catholic Emancipation and Corn Laws were received in large numbers in the later 1820s, no petitions concerned uniquely with parliamentary reform were presented in the years 1825–9 (Hilton, 2006. 411). By contrast, politicians during the reform crisis of 1830–2 constantly referred to public opinion and to the extent of disaffection 'out of doors'. Radical pressure for parliamentary reform intensified only at the very end of the 1820s. This owed something to the higher food prices which resulted from deficient harvests in 1829 and 1830 and something to trade depressions. Cobbett's dictum that only people with empty stomachs were receptive to radical political argument, though an obvious exaggeration, had basic validity. Reform flourished against a background of worsening economic hardship. Nevertheless, it should be remembered that the economic crisis of 1826, though shorter, was sharper. It was accompanied by no significant radical revival.

Two other factors, however, were at work. Pressure on behalf of working people became both more extensive and more confident in these years as the lessons of past failures were assimilated. Also, middle-class activity reached new levels of intensity, partly for intellectual and partly for economic reasons. The writings of Jeremy Bentham and the Utilitarians had drawn pointed attention to the irrationality of a political system which offered no uniform voting franchise, and which gave under-populated and economically stagnant Cornwall 44 seats in the House of Commons while industrially and commercially buoyant Lancashire had only 14 (Brock, 1973; Cannon, 1980; Evans, 1994).

Some middle-class opinion, also, was dissatisfied that economic growth was so frequently punctuated by periods of sharp recession, accompanied not only by unemployment but also by widespread bankruptcy. The textbook accounts of these years, which tend still to stress a growing 'working-class consciousness', usually fail to notice the extreme volatility of middle-class entrepreneurship. Only the largest and most fortunate employers survived periods of recession. In Manchester, 85 per cent of firms employing between one and 150 workers went bust in the years 1815–30 and more than a third of those employing between 150 and 500 did so (Daunton, 1995: 198]. A glance at trade directories of midland and northern towns over ten-year periods shows how fast was the turnover both of factory owners and master manufacturers. Never was business such a hazardous activity as in the first half of the nineteenth century. The general trend was towards fewer firms employing more workers but, even among the larger organizations, failure rates were high.

Working classes Term used to describe those who subsist by selling their labour for wages. In the early nineteenth century, they had little, or no, savings, property or investments. During the industrial revolution, a larger proportion of workers were engaged in repetitive work in factories or as building labourers or dockyard workers.

It is frequently observed that the reform crisis saw a conjunction of middle- and **working-class** pressure against the aristocracy. This observation is over-simple in itself, since it assumes that a coherent middle class and a coherent working class existed in 1830–2. Neither did. It also fails adequately to explain the reasons for middle-class dissatisfaction with the existing political structure. The obvious inequalities pointed out by Benthamites and by artisan radicals only take us so far. Birmingham and Manchester businessmen had long voted in the country constituencies of Warwickshire and Lancashire, and had exerted considerable influence in the selection of county members there (Thorne, 1986; Clark, 1985). They were not, therefore, 'unrepresented' in the old system. What needs much greater emphasis is the *economic* incentive for political change. Profit-making in early industrial Britain was a risky business and an important section of the middle-class came to believe that the level of risk had much to do with unwise government policy.

Fierce debate, which divided middle-class opinion, raged about the reasons for the apparent inefficiency of the economy. The classical political economists (see above, p. 12) looked to removing existing restraints on freedom of trade and commerce. If these were to be removed, unfettered economic growth was confidently expected. Others, of whom the Birmingham banker **Thomas Attwood** was the leading exponent, emphasized 'under-consumption'. This theory held that full employment and maximum productivity could be guaranteed only when the amount of currency in circulation matched the productive capacity of the economy. Since orthodox economic policy now dictated balanced budgets, currency restrictions and free trade, it challenged this theory at almost every point.

It was but a short step for Attwood's followers to agree with the artisan radicals (see above, pp. 17–19) that high taxes set by a landowners' Parliament were used to support the government's bloated army of place-holders and 'stockjobbers'. Indirect taxation on basic necessities like foodstuffs reduced the potential for domestic consumption. People were paying so much in indirect taxation that they had insufficient surplus to buy manufactured goods in the quantities needed to sustain the livelihoods of businessmen and labourers alike.

Thus was forged a potent alliance between one section of the middle class and much the most articulate and literate section of working people – the artisans – to secure a political remedy for economic grievances. The common target was 'Old Corruption' and the struggle was characterized as one between the 'productive' and the 'unproductive' classes of society. Such a characterization was a travesty of the truth, but the point about political slogans is not whether they are true (which is rarely the case) but whether they are believed (which they frequently are). True or not, the alliance alarmed parliamentary opinion as it had not been alarmed since a French invasion seemed imminent in 1797. Unlike 1797, or even after Peterloo in 1819 (see above, pp. 24–6), however, far fewer MPs now believed that the appropriate response should be further repression.

Unease about the continued viability of the political system was increased by the 'Swing Riots', which broke out in the late summer of 1830 and continued until the autumn of 1831. These disturbances (named after the mythical Captain Swing whose name appeared at the bottom of threatening letters, and who was supposed to be the movement's leader) took place in the rural south and east of England where, despite previous disorders in 1816 and 1822, levels of popular political consciousness were far less high than in London or the industrial towns. 'Swing' was a movement of labourers and rural craftsmen brought to the edge of despair by recent price rises in a society afflicted by structural under-employment and a consequential downward pressure on wages.

More than 'hunger politics' was involved, however. Labourers were selective in their targets. Threshing machines, which threatened one of the few

Attwood, Thomas Radical politician and currency reformer. He founded the Birmingham Political Union in 1830 to press for parliamentary reform, particularly in order to improve representation of the wealth-creating middle classes. He was MP for Birmingham from 1832–9 and presented the first Chartist petition to Parliament.

sources of winter work, were destroyed; the hay ricks of farmers who paid wages below the local odds were set aflame. Among the 1,400 or so reported 'Swing' incidents were many examples of community activity against local leaders accused of failing to discharge traditional obligations (Hobsbawm, 1973). Clergymen who, in their dual capacity as Justices of the Peace, fined or imprisoned local poachers, and Poor Law overseers who adopted harsh or inquisitorial methods, were likely to receive threatening letters or to be burned in effigy (Evans, 2001, 1975). The Swing Riots were a violent asser-tion that paternalism, which many MPs saw as the foundation of a social and political order dependent on hierarchy and reciprocal obligations, had broken down. Thus was a political message conveyed in sub-political ways.

In the towns, more structured collective activity was taking place in the late 1820s, especially among the skilled workers. **John Doherty** used the greater scope provided by the repeal of the Combination Acts (see above, pp. 55–6) to organize the cotton spinners of Lancashire and Cheshire in an effective union before the combined effects of trade depression and concerted employer opposition caused its collapse in the autumn of 1829. Doherty responded with a 'Grand General Union of Operative Cotton Spinners', active in 1829 and 1830, and then with his real objective, a union of workers across the trades. The 'National Association for the Protection of Labour' was founded in September 1829. Though it recruited overwhelmingly from the textile trades, it claimed about 70,000 members at its peak in 1830. Doherty used the potential of general unionism to advocate political reform in his trades journal *Voice of the People* in 1830 and 1831 (Rule, 1986).

Doherty, John Radical politician and trade union organiser who tried to establish general unions of working men across the trades. He organised the Grand General Union of Operative cotton spin-ners in 1829, an import-ant landmark in the development of national, rather than merely local, trade unions.

Cooperation also grew very rapidly between 1825 and 1830, partly as an alternative strategy when strikes collapsed. By 1830, about 300 cooperative trading associations were in existence with about 20,000 members (Royle, 1997; Hunt, 1981). Robert Owen, who returned to Britain in 1829 after the failure of his cooperative community of New Harmony in Indiana, encour-aged cooperators, especially in their growing links with trade unions. By 1832, a Union Exchange Society had been established for workers to swap the products of their labour without resort to an entrepreneur, and the National Equitable Labour Exchange had been established in London where the trading currency was the 'labour-value note' rather than coin of the realm in shillings and pence.

Implicitly or explicitly, cooperation involved educating working people to the potential of collective action, and the opportunity was not lost by the cooperative journals. The leading theorist of cooperation in these years was the physician Dr William King, who had been a Fellow of Peterhouse in Cambridge before moving to Sussex where he helped to establish a Mechanics' Institution in Brighton. Between 1828 and 1830 he edited *The Co-operator*, which attacked the wastefulness of capitalist competition. The first edition asserted: 'At present we work one against another – when one of us gets work, another loses it'. The lesson was clear: 'Let us therefore begin to work for OURSELVES . . . Every member of the Society will work, there will be no idlers. All the property will be common property.'

Cooperation, not surprisingly, had the greatest attraction for those in permanent work. It thrived for a few years among the London artisans. William Lovett, a cabinet maker from Cornwall, and the Yorkshire bookseller and publisher James Watson, both of whom later helped to draft the Democratic People's Charter, founded the *Co-operative Magazine* and helped to establish the British Association for Promoting Co-Operative Knowledge in 1829. *The Weekly Free Press*, edited by William Carpenter and John Cleave, also advocated cooperation. By mid-1830, more than 10 **cooperative** societies were known to exist in the capital and about 500 throughout the country were active early in 1831 (Prothero, 1979).

The resurgence of political radicalism in London was threatened by routine squabbles among its leaders. The Radical Reform Association, founded by Henry Hunt and William Cobbett, was riven with disagreement. Hunt favoured a direct attack on the old political system; Cobbett preferred currency reform and went off to tour the country in support of both his favoured solution and a seat for himself in Parliament. The anti-clerical Richard Carlile had become even more strident in his hatred of priests and in his advocacy of self-improvement through education and discipline. He attacked the Reform Association's lack of intellectual rigour. He harangued his hearers in his journal *Lion*: 'You cannot be free, you can find no reform, until you begin it yourselves . . . abstain from gin and the gin-shop, from ale and the ale-house, from gospel and the gospel-shop, from sin and silly salvation' (Belchem, 1985: 198). The lectures given by Carlile and his more scurrilous and less scrupulous colleague **Robert Taylor** at the Rotunda attracted large crowds to London's Blackfriars Road in the summer of 1830. They raised the political temperature during a year of distress in the capital (Prothero, 1979).

By the autumn of 1830, London was also reacting to a new French Revolution in Paris, which put the revival of 'liberty politics' into a European context for the first time since the French wars (Quinault, 1994). Since March it had also had a Metropolitan Political Union, formed by Hunt with support from Daniel O'Connell, which called for 'a real Radical Reform'. This organization was a response to the establishment two months earlier of the Birmingham Political Union. The success of the Birmingham organization emphasized, as had much extra-parliamentary pressure since 1815, the growing importance of the urban provincial centres in national political life (Read, 1961).

The political unions are often held to have generated and sustained, by their insistent petitioning campaigns in 1830 and 1831, that critical mass of

Cooperative movement A movement, whose members were mostly from the working classes, which encouraged people to trade for their mutual benefit and not for profit. One of the earliest Co-Operative Societies was founded in Rochdale in 1844.

Taylor, Robert Deistical writer, lecturer and radical politician. He was strongly influenced by Richard Carlile in the 1820s. He was imprisoned both for debt and for blasphemy in the late 1820s and the early 1830s. He preached regularly on deistical themes in London. His unorthodox religious views alienated him from many radicals.

extra-parliamentary pressure which convinced MPs that parliamentary reform was at last unstoppable. Thomas Attwood, founder of the Birmingham Political Union, used a similar metaphor. He claimed in January 1831 that his organization 'had condensed the moral power of this great population, and gathered it . . . into an electric mass, which is powerful to every good purpose, and utterly impotent to every bad one' (Hutton, 1836: 106). Certainly, the Political Unions were numerous and very noisy. About 130 were established in the period from January 1830 to June 1832. They organized large public meetings which welcomed all-comers. They called for radical reform to rid the nation of corrupt government and excessive indirect taxation which bore so heavily on working people. They asserted that their pressure harmonized with much older demands to uphold an ancient (if unwritten) English **constitution** which would safeguard the people's ancient liberties (LoPantin, 1999). In this way, they linked hundreds of thousands of people who attended the meetings and waved their 'liberty banners' back into a long-established radical tradition.

Constitution The body of rules, codes and practices which govern how a state is organized, how power is exercised and how its laws are formulated and put into practice. In the United Kingdom, although codes and practices are extensive, there is no overall written constitution.

The motivations of the Whigs in passing reform are considered below (pp. 89–92) but it is important to stress here the diverse nature of the political unions. The Birmingham Political Union (BPU) – 'a general political union between the Lower and the Middle Classes of the People' formed to achieve 'an effectual Reform in the Commons House of Parliament' (Brock, 1973: 60) – was hardly the model for a national agitation. It was established only when a petition for currency reform (Attwood's hobby horse) was denied, and its radical critics insisted that Attwood remained more interested in currency than in democracy.

Though he claimed much for its later influence, Attwood had no initial intention of using the BPU as a model for other political unions. Its middle-class leaders, in fact, were representatives of a local Tory group who opposed 'Whig' political economy. The early activities of the Union were publicised only in the Tory-controlled *Birmingham Journal*. The Metropolitan Political Union, drawing on a deep vein of artisan awareness, had a more democratic programme. Concerted pressure encompassing skilled workers, manufacturers and commercial figures was much easier to sustain in towns like Birmingham, which retained small workshops, an apprenticeship system and personal relations between masters and men, than in factory towns. Thus, while Sheffield developed a union of similar social structure to Birmingham's, the Manchester Union, organized by Archibald Prentice, the radical editor of the *Manchester Times*, drew support mostly from the intellectual middle-classes and from skilled artisans rather than from cotton manufacturers or labourers. It attacked government waste and called for free trade. In Leeds, three separate unions emerged with little in common.

The cumulative effect of these various activities, warring and contradictory though many of them were, outweighed their shortcomings. By the time that Grey took office, the overwhelming feeling 'out of doors' was that the old political system neither could nor should be sustained. More alarming to MPs at Westminster was the range of interests apparently reaching a similar conclusion. A landowners' Parliament could not risk flouting middle-class opinion. The belief that continued resistance to reform would provoke violence and the forcible imposition of a democratic political structure persuaded many MPs to support parliamentary reform, though more out of fear than conviction.

THE RETURN OF THE WHIGS AND THE REFORM CRISIS, 1830–2

The government formed by the second Earl Grey in November 1830 was agreed from the outset that a measure of parliamentary reform was essential. Despite Grey's long-term reputation as a reformer, this conclusion was not reached in order to fulfil some manifest Whig historical destiny. It was a reaction to short-term political developments both inside parliament and 'out of doors'. The combination of growing extra-parliamentary pressure (see above, pp. 81–7) and the instant focusing of opinion on the issue as a result of Wellington's anti-reform pronouncement **[Doc. 29, p. 123]** made it inconceivable that the government could take any other course.

The government was not uniformly enthusiastic either about the immediate prospect for reform or the longer-term consequences if a Reform Bill negotiated the parliamentary minefield without being blown up. Grey's reputation is that of a long-term parliamentary reformer, but he had hardly been staunch in the cause. More important, many senior Whig ministers, notably the Home Secretary, Viscount Melbourne, and the Lord President, the Marquis of Lansdowne, were paternalist landowners who saw reform as, at best, a necessary nuisance. The prospect of increasing the political influence of the Midland and northern towns they regarded with olympian distaste. They silently shared the prejudices of Horace Twiss, a junior minister in Wellington's recent ministry. In 1831, Twiss lamented the prospect of calling in 'shopkeepers and attorneys, persons of narrow minds and bigotted views . . . to counsel the nation' (Cannon, 1980: 215).

Furthermore, the government was described as 'Whig' only for convenience. It was in reality a coalition between the old Whig landed connection and mostly Liberal Tories who had left Wellington and Peel in 1827 and

1828 (see above, p. 73). Their leader after the death of Canning was William Huskisson, who had never been on close terms with the Whigs. During the last, tottering, months of Wellington's administration, Grey and Lansdowne believed that Huskisson would prefer to refashion a broader Tory governing group rather than unite with the Whigs. In any event, Huskisson died in September 1830 – the world's first fatality in a railway accident. This eased coalition negotiations between the Liberal Tories and the Whig grandees. In November 1830, therefore, Palmerston happily accepted the Foreign Office and Charles Grant the Board of Control with responsibility for Indian administration. Palmerston, in particular, had been influenced in the direction of modest change by the recent 'July revolution' in France (Milton-Smith, 1972; Quinault, 1994) which had replaced Charles X with the 'citizen king' Louis Philippe. By no stretch of the imagination, however, could the Whigs' coalition partners be called fervent parliamentary reformers. They had been followers of Canning who, whatever his other liberal predilections, was never an advocate of parliamentary reform.

A further complication presented itself in the self-regarding and irascible shape of Henry Brougham. Brougham had won a well-publicised victory in the country constituency of Yorkshire at the General Election of 1830, advancing what he called 'the great cause of parliamentary reform' (Stewart, 1985). Brougham had long been the leading Whig spokesman on legal and humanitarian reforms. Adding the franchise question to his bulging quiver of reformist 'issues' seemed like a hostile pre-emptive strike to colleagues already resentful of his ambition and suspicious of his motives. Before the Wellington government fell, he had already presented the Commons with his own outline proposals for parliamentary reform.

Brougham's influence outside Parliament was such that he could not be denied a senior post. Grey could keep him out of the House of Commons but only at the price of offering his disliked colleague the Lord Chancellorship. Brougham, fearing both a loss of political independence and the opportunity for developing his populist talents with his Yorkshire constituents, accepted only reluctantly. Grey was, however, determined not to be bounced into a parliamentary reform of Brougham's devising. The delicate task of formulating the Reform Bill for presentation to Parliament in the spring of 1831 was given to a small committee of four from which Brougham was deliberately excluded. Its chairman was John Lambton, Baron Durham, Grey's brother-in-law and inheritor of an immense landed and mining fortune in the north-east. He had, in 1819 and 1821, introduced two radical but unsuccessful parliamentary reform motions into the Commons. Lord John Russell, third son of the Duke of Bedford, earned his inclusion because of his experience with the Bill to disfranchise small boroughs which he had launched in 1822. His father had also been a radical Whig supporting reformer as a member of the aristocratic Society of the Friends of the People in the 1790s. Viscount Duncannon was another prominent member of a landed Whig family who would inherit its substantial Irish estates in County Kilkenny as the Earl of Bessborough in 1844. Sir James Graham, the Cumberland county landowner and, from 1829, MP for that county, had important connections to the Huskissonite camp and had played an important role in establishing the coalition. He was the fourth member (Brock, 1973; Cannon, 1980; Milton-Smith, 1972).

This predominantly blue-blooded committee was selected in part, no doubt, to convince country gentlemen that the Whigs could be trusted to remember where the solid propertied interests of Britain lay. Tactical considerations also came into it. Duncannon's good relations with the Irish leader Daniel O'Connell might prove useful in tight votes when the government depended on support from the large number of Irish MPs. Graham's strong links with the country gentry were also considered to be significant. Perhaps not surprisingly, it was he who wanted fewest changes in representation. Grey himself emphasized the importance of continuity in the exercise of power and of property as the necessary basis for the exercise of political influence. He wanted 'a greater influence to be yielded to the middle classes who have made wonderful advances both in property and intelligence, and this influence may be beneficially exerted upon the Government' (Milton-Smith, 1972: 64).

The nuts and bolts of the first Reform Bill were discussed in great secrecy, first within the committee and then by the Cabinet. The committee had favoured the introduction of a secret ballot and also the reduction in the maximum time between general elections from seven years to five. Grey squashed both proposals. The secret ballot was dismissed as 'unmanly' and 'unEnglish'. Nevertheless, the boldness of the Bill presented to Parliament in March 1831 shocked MPs **[Doc. 34, p. 126]**. It proposed the partial or total disfranchisement of 107 boroughs and the redistribution of 163 seats to the main urban centres of population and to the most densely populated counties. A uniform franchise was proposed for the boroughs, which would give the vote to householders occupying property valued for rental purposes at £10 a year or more. Some extensions to the county vote were also proposed, though the 40-shilling landed freehold remained the basic franchise.

No one knew by how much this would increase the electorate, but any measure which proposed to remove the parliamentary constituencies of a quarter of existing MPs was bound to be highly contentious. **Althorp** said that he saw Peel turn 'black in the face' as he listened to Russell's speech defending the reform proposals. The Whig backbencher and historian Thomas Babington Macaulay reported sardonically that 'the face of Twiss was as the face of a damned soul'. Even moderate reformers were taken aback:

Althorp, Viscount Whig politician. Born into one of the most aristocratic families in Britain, he followed family tradition by becoming a Whig politician. As Chancellor of the Exchequer and leader of the Whigs in the House of Commons, he did much to facilitate parliamentary reform during the crisis of 1830–2.

'They were like men taking breath immediately after an explosion', Brougham's secretary Denis Le Marchant reported (Brock, 1973: 163). One historian has characterized contemporary parliamentary reaction as seeing in the Bill 'reform at its most extreme, teetering on the verge of revolution' (Blanning, 1999: 167). During debates on this first Bill, opponents defended the historical integrity and efficiency of the existing composition of the House of Commons, while reformers urged the importance of a wider franchise to gain the confidence of increasingly important sections of public opinion. In these debates, Macaulay made his reputation as a great orator **[Docs 32, 33 and 35, pp. 125–6 and p. 127]**. When it came to the voting, on 22 March 1831, the House of Commons had never seen such a large division. The Bill's second reading was passed by a single vote, 302 to 301.

This vote precipitated the next, and constitutional, phase of the reform crisis. Such an equal division of opinion in the Commons guaranteed defeat for the government when the detailed proposals were considered in committee. This duly occurred at the end of April, once the opposition forces had had time to re-group. Grey could either persevere with a diluted bill or request the King to dissolve Parliament and call a general election. **William IV** had supported the Whigs to this point, but he required persuasion, verging on coercion, to agree to a dissolution with the 1830 Parliament still less than a year old. The forthcoming election, moreover, could be nothing but a **plebiscite** on a particular issue. The existing political nation would be asked simply to declare for or against the government's reform proposals. The King knew that general elections on one 'issue' were exceedingly rare and of doubtful propriety, especially when Parliament had more than six years to run. He was persuaded by **Durham** to dissolve for fear of widespread public disorder if he resisted but he extracted a pledge from ministers that, if they won, the Bill would not become still more radical.

The 1831 election produced the anticipated massive pro-reform majority. In almost all constituencies where voting was open enough to test propertied public opinion, reformers swept the board. Only the counties of Shropshire and Buckinghamshire returned two anti-reforming Tories. More than a third of the 82 English county members had declared against reform in the debates of March and April 1831. Only six re-appeared after the election (Brock, 1973). The Duke of Devonshire's agent wrote to his employer that, even in the Ashbourne and Wirksworth districts of Derbyshire, traditionally considered one of the most conservative parts of the county, 'nine-tenths of the freeholders have declar'd for reform' (O'Gorman, 1984: 425). The Tories had held about 60 seats in the larger, 'open' boroughs in the 1830 election; two-thirds of these were lost in 1831. The government's majority stood at between 130 and 140, guaranteeing a smooth passage for the Reform Bill in the Lower House.

William IV Monarch from 1830–37. He was the third son of George III and did not expect to become King. He was a sailor for much of his life. He had limited talent but his social standing helped him to become both Admiral of the Fleet in 1811 and Lord High Admiral in 1827. He was widely criticized for his handling of the Reform Crisis.

Plebiscite The putting of a specific political question to the people at large. Figuratively, it means the formal sounding out of public opinion. Literally, it requires a voting process. There was no provision for a plebiscite in the British political system in our period.

Durham, Baron Whig politician from a wealthy landed family in County Durham. Known as 'Radical Jack', he produced his own parliamentary reform proposals in 1816. He helped draft the Whig reform bill, but his plans for a secret ballot failed.

The Upper House was a different matter. Here the hereditary peers, not needing to concern themselves with the tiresome and demeaning chore of getting themselves elected, could exercise their opinions free of constraint, or so most of them thought in the autumn of 1831. A new bill, similar to its predecessor in all essentials save one, passed the Commons in September 1831, piloted skilfully, as in March, by Althorp and Russell. The exception was the addition to the franchise of £50 tenants-at-will. This was at the instigation of two anti-reformers, the Marquis of **Chandos** and Colonel Charles Sibthorp, who saw in the enfranchisements of substantial tenants a means whereby 'legitimate' landed influence could be preserved in county seats. It was widely assumed (though subsequent research has not invariably confirmed the impression) that tenants would support their landlord's candidate for fear of eviction. The 'Chandos Amendment' was significant. It increased the county electorate by about 30 per cent more than the Whigs had originally intended – and in the types of constituency where they normally did least well.

Chandos, Viscount Tory politician. He opposed Catholic Emancipation and supported agricultural protection. He is best known for 'the Chandos Amendment' to the Whigs' parliamentary reform bill. It gave votes to tenants of medium-sized and larger farms and proved a significant factor in the Tories' political revival after 1832.

On 8 October, the Lords threw out the amended Bill by a comfortable majority of 41, thus precipitating the second stage of the constitutional crisis. Public opinion was already heavily committed to reform, although the more perceptive working-class leaders already realized how little ordinary folk might expect from it (Thompson, 1963; Prothero, 1979; Brock, 1973). The effects of economic depression and higher food prices (see above, pp. 81–4) had already provoked some disturbances. In June a full-scale riot – its historian calls it an 'armed insurrection' – broke out in the South Wales iron town of Merthyr Tydfil. For several days the town was held against the troops by reformers; more than 20 people were killed in the conflict (Williams, 1978). It was a bloodier and more serious affair than Peterloo. Had it occurred in London, it would have probably have gone down as the most critical event of the whole crisis. It deserves wider notice than it has received.

The authorities might, therefore, have anticipated popular reaction to the Lords' rejection of the Bill. Their anxieties were fully justified. London radicals organized a grand procession in support of the Bill, in which more than 70,000 participated. Francis Place acted as midwife for a new National Political Union, which attempted – with considerable difficulty – to harmonize the interests of the smaller property owners with those of working people. The National Union of the Working Classes, also based in London, was not hampered by considerations of compromise. It bluntly petitioned the Lords to grant universal manhood suffrage and annually elected parliaments.

In several provincial cities, hostility to the House of Lords was expressed in more violent ways. The Duke of Newcastle's castle at Nottingham was burned during a riot. Nearby Derby also experienced rioting crowds. Bristol was held against the authorities for three days at the end of October 1831;

the Bishop's palace and several gaols were sacked before order was restored. In many places, anti-clericalism was a pronounced feature. Rioters were well aware that most (in fact 21 of the 26) Church of England bishops had voted against reform. They thus played a decisive role in securing a majority against reform in the Lords **[Docs 36 and 37, p. 128]**. Perhaps more significant than the disturbances, which excessive quantities of drink exaggerated in their later stages, was the enormous growth of support for the Political Unions (see above, pp. 85–6) and the discovery of plans, which alarmed men like Attwood as much as they did Melbourne, for the collection of arms and for drilling.

As the temperature rose, established and 'respectable' political unions in some towns became less confident of their ability to control pro-reform forces. *The Times* asserted that the troops were not sufficient to deal with 'occasions of sudden and very general emergency. We say then to our fellow subjects – organise and arm' (Brock, 1973: 253). By November 1831, the prospect of a total breakdown of public order appeared real. Cabinet disagreements surfaced and Grey contemplated resignation in order to let Wellington try to persuade the recalcitrant Lords to pass reform when the Whigs had failed.

Sterner counsels prevailed and a fresh Reform Bill was presented by Russell in mid-December. It differed little from its predecessors, except that the anticipated horse-trading provided some reprieves for small boroughs. In an attempt to neutralize the increased landowner influence which the Chandos Amendment presaged, a second seat was proposed to be given to a few of the new boroughs. In its final version, the Reform Bill deprived 56 English boroughs of representation; 30 more lost one of their two members. Seventy-seven new borough seats were created, 63 in England, eight in Scotland, four in Ireland and two in Wales. County seats in England and Wales were increased from 92 to 159 (Evans, 2001: 483).

The prospect of re-fighting a battle so recently lost disheartened the Cabinet in the early months of 1832. Grey had great difficulty in preventing wholesale resignations. Success in the Lords was far from assured, and some feared that the recent disturbances had stiffened the resolve of the diehard opponents of reform rather than the reverse. Durham was the first to support the creation of sufficient Whig peers to carry the measure. This third deviation from the unwritten constitutional code, following the premature dissolution of Parliament and a 'one-issue' election, was too much for William IV. When the Whigs were defeated on an amendment in the Lords early in May, Grey, having been refused 50 new Whig peers, resigned. The Tories under Wellington were charged by the King with the responsibility of trying to form an administration to carry some sort of reform. Grey confided to a friend:

'Never was a captive more desirous of escaping from prison than I am from my present situation' (Cannon, 1980: 234).

Wellington's attempt lasted less than a fortnight. It foundered largely on Peel's refusal to join a government which would have to pass reform. Peel was recognized on all sides as second only to Wellington in seniority within the Tory party. A Tory ministry without him in it would lack credibility. Knowing what damage had been done to his reputation in the party by his conversion to Catholic Emancipation (see above, pp. 74–5), however, he feared that association with parliamentary reform in 1832 would destroy his remaining political ambitions, which were substantial. Of more moment, however, was the enormous extra-parliamentary outcry that the prospective return of Wellington caused. Hostile petitions flooded into Westminster. The political unions organized massive demonstrations and threatened civil disobedience. Francis Place devised a scheme for reformers to withdraw deposits from the banks simultaneously: 'To stop the Duke, go for Gold'. Protest marches from the northern and Midland towns to London were organized **[Doc. 39, p. 129]**. It is unlikely that these 'Days of May' altered the course of events but they did confirm the tenacity of extra-parliamentary agitation during the reform crisis.

After Wellington's admission that he could not form a government, resistance to reform crumbled. The King was forced to promise new peers as a condition of Grey's return, but they were not needed. Most of the Tories absented themselves from further debates in the Lords and the Bill was quickly carried. William IV made a final, impotent, gesture on 7 June 1832 by refusing to attend the House of Lords to give the royal assent in person. It did not matter. The most dangerous political crisis of modern times had been peacefully resolved.

Precisely how close to revolution Britain came during the reform crisis is unknowable. It is never possible to make precise judgements about developments which could have occurred – but in the event did not. In this case, matters are complicated because it was central to the extra-parliamentary reformers' strategy to predict what dire consequences would follow from continued parliamentary intransigence. Thus, evidence about communication across communities, of arming, drilling and other preparations for combat was not likely to be underplayed, either outside Parliament or by those Whigs whose purpose was to frighten 'reform-sceptics' in the Commons and Lords into submission by asserting that sensible concessions were the only safe way to proceed. As indicated above (see pp. 85–6), the political unions which were both driving and orchestrating protest by 1831–2 had different compositions, different objectives and evinced different potential for armed militancy. Had revolution been attempted, it is likely that it would have had no more widespread or integrated support, even in the urban areas, in 1832 than in 1819. Indeed, a plausible case can be made for saying that Britain was nearer revolution in the wake of Peterloo than after the Lords' defiance of popular opinion in October 1831.

Certainly, it is not difficult to find evidence of *fear* of revolution in 1831–2, not just in the shires, but in Parliament itself. How the no-nonsense, soldierly Wellington of Waterloo would have reacted had he been able to form a government in May 1832 and had his reform plans proved so insultingly modest that they sparked militant protest, is one of the more fascinating 'what ifs' of British history. Perhaps the nation has reason to be grateful that it did not need to find out. That Britain was in a highly agitated, even neurotic, state during the last few months of the reform crisis is beyond dispute. Whether it was on the verge of revolution is much more dubious.

The consequences of the Great Reform Act lie outside the scope of this book and have been considered by the present author elsewhere (Evans, 1994, 2000, 2001). Some debate has taken place, however, about the true intentions of those who passed the Reform Acts of 1832. We should first note that there were three: separate bills were introduced for Ireland, for Scotland and for England and Wales. The broad objectives were the same – 'to amend the representation of the people' as the titles had it – but Parliament was well aware that it was legislating for separate nations within the still new United Kingdom of Great Britain and Ireland. The impact, in terms of both the percentage increase of adult males enfranchised by the legislation and the proportion of adult males entitled to vote, was very different (Evans, 2000: 129–31]. In both Scotland and Ireland, where pre-1832 franchises were extremely restricted, large percentage increases occurred but far fewer men were entitled to vote after 1832 than in England and Wales. Put very crudely, after 1832 less than 5 per cent of adult male Irishmen were entitled to vote, about 10 per cent of Scotsmen and just short of 20 per cent of English and Welshmen.

We should secondly be secure in our use of terms. These were not so much 'Whig reforms' as parliamentary changes passed by a loose coalition of pro-reformers, comprising not only the Whig political 'establishment' and the Liberal Tories but also some Irish and radical MPs normally well outside governing circles – whether the government was predominantly Tory or Whig. Many analyses, especially from the early twentieth century, ignored this important point. Earlier students of the Act tended to conclude that the Whigs had made judicious concessions to popular pressure (Butler, 1914). In the later nineteenth century the socialist thinker and historian Karl Marx saw the Act not as a concession to pressure but as a party political stratagem played out within the landed elite intended to increase Whig patronage at the expense of the Tories (Phillips, 1982). Neither of these explanations for the passing of Reform Acts is implausible but both are monochrome. Since 'the reformers' constituted a complex, heterogeneous, group, analyses of motivation also need to be multi-faceted.

As has recently been stressed, the old landed Whigs, including Grey himself, believed that it was the duty of politicians to follow 'the people's instincts', albeit converting these instincts into practical politics and, where appropriate, guiding and fashioning what might be either inchoate thoughts or wilder instincts and generally acting as a beneficial moderating influence (Blanning, 1999: 25–41). For this group, the bloodless revolution of 1688, which they believed had seen the removal of a tyrannical Catholic monarch and his replacement with a regime which worked with Parliament and consulted the people, was the perfect example of beneficial Whig intervention. For some, the absence of Whig influences in France was the reason why its own revolution a century later degenerated into bloodshed and terror, to be rescued only by a new form of military dictatorship. Even after Napoleon fell from power, political stability was not guaranteed. The July Revolution in Paris (see above, p. 88) was a significant element in the growing tensions over parliamentary reform at Westminster. Many Whigs reminded themselves of a simple lesson: if the people want reform, then they must have it. The duty and responsibility of the Whigs was to provide beneficent leadership, practical guidance and, crucially, a moderating influence.

Questions are, of course, begged here. How did Whig leaders define 'the people' and how moderate was this 'moderating influence' intended to be? For Grey, it was clear that the answer to the first of these questions turned on the question of property. He believed that the people he should be particularly listening to were property owners. His concern in framing the Reform Act was, therefore, to preserve the interests of property by extending the franchise to all, or almost all, of those who were possessed of property. He noted in November 1831 that the middle classes of society had shown a 'praiseworthy alacrity in supporting the government' and were 'actuated by an intense and almost unanimous feeling in favour of the measure of reform' [Doc. 31, p. 125].

What the middle classes wanted was a more uniform franchise defined in terms of a property qualification and this is exactly what the Whig leadership meant by 'a moderating influence'. There was to be no truck with household suffrages, still less that universal manhood suffrage for which so many artisan radicals in London and Manchester were calling. Macaulay was reflecting dominant Whig opinion when he told the Commons in March 1831 that universal suffrage would produce 'a destructive revolution'. Extending the franchise to those possessed of 'property and intelligence' [Doc. 33, p. 126] – by which last he meant detailed knowledge of political affairs – on the other hand would win the approval and confidence of 'the middle classes'. The old constitution would therefore be enhanced, rather than a new one constructed.

Those Liberal Tories who joined in the Coalition either took the same view or were more sceptical about the value of Reform at all. Palmerston, for example, wanted to allow the least change that it was practical to concede. The unequivocal evidence of substantially growing extra-parliamentary agitation in favour of reform, however, convinced him and others of like persuasion that token gestures would not serve. Granting no reform threatened revolution. Something substantial was required and he thus supported the substantial destruction of small parliamentary boroughs which so alarmed MPs when the Bill was first introduced.

The governing coalition, therefore, albeit for different reasons, favoured a substantial reform, but one grounded in property rights, in order to win over the middle classes and – perhaps even more important – to detach them from that threatening alliance with the working classes which was a feature of numerous political unions (Gash, 1979; Evans, 1994; Milton-Smith, 1972). Those who wanted more – a household franchise, perhaps, or the kind of parliament which might look kindly on pro-Catholic policies in Ireland – were marginalized. More radical parliamentary reformers had to decide in 1832 whether any reform was better than none. Most decided that it was. After all, with a new 'Representation of the People' on the statute book further battles could be fought at a later date. Most of those battles were won, in the less fraught years of mid- and late Victorian Britain (Evans, 2000). That is why it is possible still to argue that, although very few MPs intended it, 1832 did indeed set the nation on a tortuous path which would eventually lead to democracy.

Some time ago, a quite different perspective on Whig motivation for reform was offered. D.C. Moore saw the Act not as a concession to mounting external pressure, or as a feature of any wider Whig 'mission', but as a 'cure' which, by clever manipulation of electoral boundaries, was intended to solve problems of conflicting influence. Those without property remained excluded from political influence, but the distinctions between county and borough seats were intended to prevent 'seepage' of middle-class commercial influence into the county seats. The increase of county representation was a means of retaining landed influence after 1832 (Moore, 1976, 1966).

The Moore thesis is ingenious but it is too calculating by half. The Whigs, as we have seen, were anything but united. They had neither the statistical nor psephological evidence to make fine calculations about relative middle-class or landed influence in the different types of constituency. Beyond that, there was no consensus. Brought up to believe that their strength derived from an established, and effective, track record in listening to the views of 'the people', aristocratic Whigs had little alternative in 1830–2 but to respond to popular pressure. In the crisis of 1831–2 the passage of *some* reform bill and the preservation of property were more important considerations than arcane juggling over what, and who, was to be included and excluded. The Great Reform Act was an imperatively necessary concession to pressure which otherwise threatened to destroy not only a political system but an entire culture. Its intentions were conservative. It was left to Grey's successors to ponder at leisure how successful his concessions had been.

6

Conclusion

PUTTING PARLIAMENTARY REFORM IN CONTEXT

This book's title, *Britain Before the Reform Act*, should not be taken to imply that the years 1815–32 be read as some kind of extended prelude to the major change in the franchise enacted in 1832. The Great Reform Act was, of course, a watershed. In the short-term crisis that preceded it, parts of Britain were seriously disturbed and some historians believe that the country came closer to revolution (at a time, be it remembered, of European revolutions) than at any time in the eighteenth, nineteenth or twentieth centuries (Thompson, 1963). Parliamentary reform must, therefore, bulk large in any study of this period. It was, however, part of a much wider pattern of change which can only be appreciated by looking in some detail at the whole of the period 1815–32.

Britain's ability to effect a massive political and social transition in the first half of the nineteenth century without revolution had important implications for its development in the next century and a half. Some critics argue that Britain actually *needed* a revolution to pull it out of an attitude towards ancient institutions and traditions at once self-satisfied, sentimental and superior. What might be termed a culture of complacency grew up which deprived the country of a crucial cutting edge in world competition. Thus it is not self-evidently true that Britain's avoidance of political revolution in the early industrial period was, to use Sellar and Yeatman's magically simple phrase in *1066 and All That*, 'a good thing'. With that debate we are not concerned, though readers should know that it exists.

Parliamentary reform needs to be put in context. It was by no means the only issue on the agenda between 1815 and 1832. To those contemporaries who opposed radical change, it took second place to religion as the issue on which the ending of the old world of deference and authority turned. Liverpool and his ministers gave close attention to questions of taxation, government debt, overseas trade and commercial policy. These issues much more directly affected the lives of most contemporaries than did debates about rotten boroughs, franchise qualifications and the political status of Manchester or Birmingham. Debates in Parliament in the years 1815–31 increasingly concentrated on taxation, the cost of government and how public business might be more efficiently managed. Foreign policy continued to occupy much time as, from the early 1820s, did issues related to religious toleration. Only in the last 18 months covered by this book was Parliament's attention fixed upon parliamentary reform.

ASSESSING THE WHIG INTERPRETATION OF 'BRITAIN 1815–32'

Past events and controversies need to be seen, as far as possible, from the perspective and understanding of those who lived through them. History is not, or should not be, the story of progress from a lesser to a greater state to be plotted almost as a line moving steadily upward on a graph. The cruder varieties of such writing have been termed 'Whig history'. The phrase is intended to be dismissive. In fact it traduces a generation of meticulous and imaginative scholars active in the later nineteenth and early twentieth centuries whose work is no longer much read (hence the crude facility with which it can be misleadingly parodied), but who laid secure foundations for the development of history as a scholarly profession in the twentieth century.

The phrase 'Whig history', though misused, should nevertheless warn against concentration on issues only in the context of their significance for later generations. Thus 1832 should not be studied as one of a progression of dates which, when set alongside 1867, 1872, 1884, 1885, 1918 and 1928, charts the emergence of a democratic franchise. In its time, the first Reform Act is best characterized as a consciously anti-democratic measure. One of its main purposes was to frustrate the plans of working-class radical leaders for an assault on the citadels of privilege from which would emerge a democratic franchise and government by what they termed 'the productive classes'.

Contemporaries – a few atypical individuals like Major John Cartwright, Henry Hunt, and T. J. Wooler apart – were not obsessed with parliamentary reform throughout the period 1815–32. Even Earl Grey, who had introduced earlier reform motions in 1793 and 1797, thought parliamentary reform a confounded nuisance from the end of the French Wars until about 1829. He believed that it had split the Whig party and, on more than one occasion, prevented its return to office. Even William Cobbett, the best-remembered radical writer of the age and a staunch proponent of parliamentary reform, offered his readers other targets than the restricted franchise. He lambasted 'misgovernment' and blamed a landowners' parliament for the savage and inhumane consequences of a currency policy which harmed the employment prospects and lowered the wage levels of working people. His famous attacks on the 'bloated' Church of England and his defence of the rural poor were not invariably linked to his case for democracy.

Ordinary folk, it is safe to assume (then as now), were much more concerned with material matters like the size and purchasing power of family incomes and the prospects for employment than they were with the heady rhetoric of representation served up by Orator Hunt. The obstacles in the way of political literacy were substantial. The poorer areas of early industrial cities, where lived the great majority of urban citizens, were citadels of squalor: festering and pustulant affronts to a civilized nation. Here, mere survival was an achievement, an achievement, moreover, denied to about a quarter of the children born in British cities in the 1820s. Naturally, in such an environment, 'hunger politics' had an immediate appeal. The sustaining of any kind of deeper political consciousness required discipline, dedication, self-education, and self-denial of an order which compels admiration irrespective of one's political views.

In addition to issuing warnings against the fallacies of Whig history, historians have of late placed less stress on 'important dates'. This is part of a general retreat from historical research which, many believe, used to concentrate far too much on military and diplomatic history and on the doings of the wealthy and influential. As most students would readily agree, there is no special value in memorizing dates. They can always be looked up. However, a developed sense of chronology – a very different matter – is both a higher-grade skill and intrinsically more important than knowing that the Battle of Waterloo was fought in 1815 rather than 1814. This book began by urging that the importance of 1815 be not exaggerated. It ends with a plea to understand 1832 in its contemporary context. It is, however, proper to add a codicil to rectify the revisionist balance somewhat.

TRANSITION TO A 'NEW ORDER'?

Historians study the process of change over time. Even in such a short period as 1815 to 1832 changes took place of critical importance in understanding the longer-term transition from what might be termed the 'old' world of hereditary privilege, localism, paternalism and protection to a 'new order' encompassing representation of interests, liberalization, free trade and cheap government. The new order was managed by the same social groups as before. Victorian government at Westminster was barely less aristocratic than eighteenth-century government, at least until the 1880s. Local government, however, whose responsibilities had greater impact on the lives of ordinary citizens, underwent a greater transformation from the 1830s onwards. This produced a wider representation of interests and greater influence enjoyed by the propertied middle classes.

A little of the money saved on fighting large-scale wars, which Britain did much less of in the nineteenth than the eighteenth century, was transferred to the development of a regulatory regime over aspects of what the Victorians would call 'the social question'. Boards, commissions and inspectorates sprang up from the 1830s to deal with such issues as education, factory legislation and public health. The administration of an increasingly far-flung empire was also costly. Nevertheless, the tax burden falling on ordinary citizens began to diminish significantly from the 1820s. This new order also stressed economic growth as essential both to feed and to find employment for a population which was growing much more rapidly in the first 30 years of the nineteenth century than ever before. Political economists and other proponents of trade liberalization in the 1820s had their own version of the 'there is no alternative' assertion so effectively used by Margaret Thatcher in the 1980s. Free trade policies were the only way to secure growth. Industrialization provided a greater diversity of wealth-creation, not only in urban but also in rural society. A balance needed to be achieved between interests which would otherwise conflict.

This new order also responded to the quickening pace of life. It is of more than symbolic importance that this period witnessed the opening of the world's first passenger railway. Those who opposed the Reform Act did so only in part because they disliked its specific terms; they had a deeper reason for concern. The old political system, they believed, had grown both organically, if not mystically. It had been fought over bloodily in the seventeenth century and had achieved both stability and maturity in the eighteenth. It should not now be tampered with on the coarse warrant of calculations about Birmingham's population or the swollen number of MPs who represented mostly very small constituencies in Cornwall. Opponents of parliamentary reform were in no doubt: to amend was to destroy.

In one sense, these 'die-hards' were right. Though Lord John Russell thought it necessary to assert that the Reform Bill was 'the final solution of a great constitutional question' in order to persuade parliamentary doubters to support the measure in 1831–2, neither Russell nor Grey believed their own rhetoric. It was ludicrous to suppose that Manchester should return two MPs, but not three or four, until the last syllable of recorded time, or that the social composition of that collective representational artefact, the ten-pound householder, would remain unimpeachably respectable as election succeeded election and the value of money fell. As the Bill's opponents well knew, what had once been amended could be changed again as circumstances, or pressure, dictated. On this line of argument, and despite all the assurances of the Bill's supporters, 1832 was no 'final solution'. It did prove to be the thin end of a democratic wedge.

A similar train of thought had guided opposition to the religious concessions of 1828–9. To grant political equality to dissenters or the vote to Catholics was to imply that the state church did not now stand confident and unchallenged as an integral part of a confident, secure polity. Rather, the Church of England had become, at best, first among equals in a pluralist regime. These religious reforms, opponents argued, removed protection for the state church, and Ultra-Tories had a strong aversion to any free trade in faith on both historical and practical grounds. The primacy of a distinctively Anglican church had been a sure stronghold against Catholic insurgents and foreign invaders since the reign of Elizabeth I. Not only had it earned the continuing protection of the state; Ultras believed in the mystical bond between church and state. Their cosmos was sustained by dual, and equally weighted, pillars. Pull down one, and the edifice collapsed.

It is possible even here to find some justification for Ultra fears. Toleration for Dissenters and Catholics was further extended when the ancient universities were opened to them in the 1870s. By the end of the nineteenth century, toleration, if scarcely yet respectability, had been extended to atheists and agnostics. Though the conclusion is open to the charge of Whiggish determinism, that secularisation which is characteristic of the modern British political and social order might be traced back to crucial decisions about the nature of the relationship between church and state made by Wellington and Peel in 1828–9.

Political decisions on both Catholic Emancipation and political reform were strongly influenced by growing pressure outside Westminster. This is perhaps the most significant indicator of the transition from an old political world to a new. If Parliament was seen to bow to pressure 'out of doors', then the doctrine of 'virtual representation', by which the old world set such store, was fatally undermined. This idea held that all interests were 'virtually' represented in a legislature which put the wider national interest before selfish or class-based considerations. All that was needed to agitate the pure, if narrow, stream of political accountability was a steady flow of parliamentary petitions which brought local grievances to public notice for appropriate action and redress.

This doctrine reeked of preciousness and it had been mercilessly exposed in lampoons and satires from the middle of the eighteenth century onwards. Radicals believed that it had been killed by the self-interest of landowners when they introduced a fiercely protective Corn Law in 1815 which artificially inflated prices to consumers while helping to preserve the value of aristocratic rent-rolls. Nevertheless, virtual representation retained vitality in Tory circles until the disasters of 1828–32. To concede to threats was fatal to the old concept of representation and also a sign of weak government. In Ultra eyes, the government acted under duress both in 1829 and 1832 and thus legitimated unrepresentative, threatening extra-parliamentary action. Modern political structures recognize extra-parliamentary pressure groups and, though the Anti-Corn Law League of the late 1830s and early 1840s offers the best-developed example, earlier precedents can be found in O'Connell's Catholic Association in the 1820s and in the provincial political unions of 1829–32.

It would be foolish to assert that what has been termed 'the new order in politics and society' emerged fully-developed and triumphant between 1815 and 1832. The old political world proved remarkably tenacious for at least another half-century after 1832, most notably in the continued power exercised by the landed classes and in the measure of 'influence' which landowners enjoyed at parliamentary elections (Evans, 2001; Gash, 1985; Perkin, 1969; Evans, 1994). We are, after all, discussing peaceful transition not violent change. Apocalyptic Tory visions – 'The reform bill is a stepping stone in England to a republic' (J.W. Croker); 'We shall be destroyed one after the other . . . by due course of law' (Wellington) – seem on the face of it only to confirm the follies of those who dared to obstruct the march of progress.

Facile jibes, however, are out of place. Grey and Russell, even more obviously than Croker and Wellington, were representatives of a long-established but introverted social and political world based on great wealth (mostly landed), family connection, deference and clientage. Over the course of a half-century or so, that world was slowly strangled. The life was choked out of it by the pressures of modernity. These were the social consequences of unprecedentedly rapid industrial change. Among much else, they brought an increasingly informed and sophisticated extra-parliamentary political consciousness. The student looking for the origins of the new order must look not just to the reform crisis but to the teeming and turbulent years from 1815 which preceded it. The years covered by this book do indeed witness the birth of a new age.

Part 2

DOCUMENTS

Document 1   LORD LIVERPOOL DEFENDS THE CORN LAW, 1815

The imposition of a strongly protective tariff in 1815 was the subject of much criticism. It is generally depicted as class legislation enacted by a landowners' parliament. Liverpool here argues that protection is in the interests of consumers as much as producers. Compare this defence of protection with the Liverpool government's moves towards freer trade in other areas [Doc. 8, p. 109].

Lord Liverpool . . . now came to the principle of the Bill, with respect to the policy of rendering ourselves as independent as possible of foreign supply . . . It was not a question in this case as to the interests of the English landlord or the Irish landlord. . . . The great object was the interest of the Consumer; and this, he contended, would be effectually promoted by the present measure, the effect of which would be to render grain cheaper instead of dearer. The important point to attain was a steady and moderate price . . . where the supply was fluctuating, a year of extraordinary cheapness of grain must necessarily be followed by one of dearness, unless measures were adopted to insure a regular domestic supply, and by this means a uniform steady and moderate price.

Source: Hansard, 1st series, vol. xxx, col. 181, 15 March 1815.

————◀●▶————

Document 2   A PETITION AGAINST THE INCOME TAX, 1816

The government sustained an embarrassing defeat over its attempt to keep income tax in peacetime. Lord Althorp, Whig MP for the county of Northamptonshire from 1806 to 1832, here presents a petition drawn up not by him but by his constituents.

Lord Althorp, on presenting the petition from the borough of Wellingborough, in Northamptonshire, against the property tax . . . said, he was particularly instructed to support that part of the petition which referred to the pledges of economy given in the Speech from the throne at the opening of the session. He therefore invited the House to the most strict and rigid system of economy, as the only means of saving the country. He was aware that it might not be possible to satisfy the wishes of the people, groaning beneath their burthens, by any practicable reduction that was consistent with the honour and safety of the nation; but he was convinced, at the same time, that great savings might be made, and that it was the duty of the House to carry them immediately into execution.

Source: Hansard, 1st series, vol. xxxiii, col. 123, 11 March 1816.

————◀●▶————

GEORGE IV CONSIDERS DISMISSING LORD LIVERPOOL, 1820   **Document 3**

This letter was never sent. It must be read in the context of the developing crisis over the Queen Caroline divorce case and it indicates, beneath a veneer of civility, how disenchanted the King had become with his ministers for, as he considered it, failing him on a vital matter. It is a draft reply to what, in normal circumstances, would have been a purely formal request from prime minister to monarch to prorogue Parliament for the Christmas period.

16 November 1820

THE KING will no longer delay acquainting Lord L. with the result of the deep and anxious consideration he has given to the measure of prorogation so strongly pressed upon the King by Lord L. The King acquiesces in this measure . . . But it would not be at the same time consistent with that honor and fairness, with which the King has always acted towards his confidential servants, if the King were not to declare to Lord L. that, however painful it may be to the King's feelings, he considers himself under the necessity of taking measures for the formation of a new Administration.

Source: A. Aspinall (ed.), *The Letters of George IV*, 3 vols, Cambridge, 1938, vol. 2, p. 380.

SIR JOHN SINCLAIR DEFENDS THE AGRICULTURAL INTEREST, 1822   **Document 4**

This is an extract from an address delivered by the President of the Board of Agriculture to the landlords and farmers of Great Britain. Its immediate context is the depression of arable prices. Notice the extravagance of Sinclair's language and his plea to the government to consider land as a special form of property.

The crisis has at last arrived; and the question now at issue, is, whether the agricultural interests, forming, with those of the various classes dependent on British agriculture, by far the most important part of the community . . . are to be sacrificed, to gratify the wild speculations of dealers in foreign corn . . . or the mercantile and manufacturing enterprises of foreign traders. . . . It is not to be doubted, that commercial and manufacturing industry, when resting on, and combined with, agricultural prosperity, cannot be too much promoted; and this union of the three branches [land being the third] has been the means of elevating Great Britain to such a height of power as has rarely been equalled. But, on the other hand, those endless, and often ruinous speculations in manufactures and foreign commerce, which cannot be successfully carried on *without the depression of British agriculture*, ought not to meet with the slightest legislative encouragement. . . . to render this country permanently independent of foreign supplies, the means of promoting the extension and improvement of agriculture shall be considered the *most important department of government.*

Source: Farmers' Magazine, vol. xxiii, 1822, pp. 22–3, 46–7.

Document 5   A STATEMENT FROM BUCKINGHAMSHIRE ON THE AGRICULTURAL DEPRESSION, 1822

This is an extract from the quarterly report on the state of agriculture county by county published in the Farmers' Magazine. *Compare its message and its tone with those of Sir John Sinclair* [**Doc. 4, p. 107**] *and the Earl of Thanet* [**Doc. 6, p. 108**]. *This article was written for publication in a magazine read overwhelmingly by landowners and the larger farmers.*

Our Corn markets have been, and still are, ruinously low; and, without any prospect of a considerable advance; many have been obliged to thrash out, and turn their corns into money at any price they would bring. Stock of every kind being proportionably low in price, has brought the farmer low in circumstances; and many respectable agriculturalists, who were lately considered as opulent, are now selling off to prevent utter ruin, or are sold up by their landlords under a distress of rent. So many and frequent are the instances of such distress, that it has become a common topic of conversation – 'Who will fall next?'

Source: Quarterly Report for Buckinghamshire, *Farmers' Magazine*, vol. xxxiii, February 1822, p. 121.

Document 6   THE EARL OF THANET'S UNSYMPATHETIC VIEW OF THE AGRICULTURAL DEPRESSION, 1822

The Earl of Thanet was a prominent Whig landowner. Here he writes in a sardonic tone to Thomas Creevey, the diarist and MP for Appleby, which constituency he represented on Thanet's patronage.

I am just returned from Kent, more disgusted than usual at the language and temper of those I saw, which I take for a sample of the rest; everybody complaining, without an idea that they could do anything towards attaining relief. Landlords and farmers seem to have no other occupation than comparing their respective distresses. They ask what is to happen. I answer – you will be ruined, and they stare like stuck pigs. I could not hear of one Tory gentleman who had changed. One booby says it is the Poor Rate – another the Tithe – another high rents – all omit the real cause, taxation, the mother of all evil.

Source: Earl of Thanet to Thomas Creevey, September 1822, H. Maxwell, (ed.) *The Creevey Papers*, 2 vols, John Murray, 1904, vol. 2, p. 51.

THE *ANNUAL REGISTER* CELEBRATES BRITISH COMMERCIAL ADVANCE, 1824   **Document 7**

The Annual Register, *as its name implies, provided a yearly review of major events together with a critical commentary. It was not, however, neutral in its observations. It was generally firmly in support of Tory policies.*

Fifty years ago, an economist, who should have ventured to predict the present developement [*sic*] of English commerce, capital, revenue, or debt, would have been laughed at as the most frantic of a visionary tribe; and it is by no means impossible that the next half century may work perhaps even a greater change than that which the preceeding one has witnessed. A whole hemisphere of the globe has, within the last ten years, been in a manner opened to our industry – an event of magnificent promise, and which may ultimately change the aspect of the civilized world. All the relics of the commercial code, constructed with such perverse ingenuity by our barbarous ancestors – for such, in these matters, may we consider the statesmen of the eighteenth century – are fast being demolished under the new enlightened policy of their present successors; and we cannot but be assured, that the wisdom of this change of system will yearly make itself more sensibly felt in the progressive expanding developement of the unrestricted energies of our trade.

Source: *Annual Register*, vol. lxvi, 1824, p. 5.

WILLIAM HUSKISSON EXPLAINS THE VALUE OF TARIFF REDUCTIONS   **Document 8**

This document is taken from a speech delivered by Huskisson in the House of Commons when he was President of the Board of Trade and thus responsible for the formulation of commercial policy. Notice how Huskisson tries to disarm possible criticism of his trade liberalization policy.

We furnish, in a proportion far exceeding the supply from any other country, the general markets of the world, with all the leading articles of manufacture, upon which I have now proposed greatly to lower the duties. I own that I am not afraid of this country being overwhelmed with foreign goods. Some, I know, will come in . . . but they will not interfere with those articles of more wide and universal consumption, which our own manufacturers supply cheaper and better; whilst they will excite the ingenuity of our artists and workmen to attempt improvements, which may enable them to enter the lists with the foreigner in those very articles in which he has now an acknowledged superiority.

Source: *Speeches of William Huskisson*, 3 vols, London, 1831, vol. ii, pp. 344–6, 25 March 1825.

Document 9   *BLACKWOOD'S EDINBURGH MAGAZINE* ATTACKS FREE TRADE IDEAS, 1830

It is easy to lose sight of the fact that the economic philosophy of laissez-faire, *though it became dominant in the 1820s and 1830s, attracted many critics. Such critics are not to be dismissed as cranks or reactionaries merely because their views did not win. The document comes from a much longer discussion of the impact of free trade on the labouring classes. It was written, not by a radical politician urging parliamentary reform, but by a Tory defender of protection and paternalism. Read it in conjunction with Document 8.*

There is indeed nothing in the conduct of the advocates of Free Trade so deserving of reprehension, as the hypocritical pretences with which they attempt to disguise or conceal the real object of their measures. If we credit their professions, this amiable and enlightened tribe of philosophers has nothing in view but the common good, and the improvement of the condition of the industrious classes. There is, however, room to think, that they overestimate the ignorance and blindness of the community in supposing that the mass of our population can be much longer hoodwinked by this flimsy pretence . . . Recent and dear bought experience has taught the working classes, that the free competition of foreign labour *must* diminish the compensation which they can expect to receive for their toil. The artisans and mechanics of this country have probably by this time become pretty well convinced, that the importation and consumption of the produce of foreign labour has no tendency to ameliorate their condition and that they at least form no portion of that public whom the Free Trade system is said to benefit.

Source: *Blackwood's Edinburgh Magazine*, vol. xxvii, 1830, p. 561.

GEORGE CANNING EXPRESSES HIS RESERVATIONS ABOUT THE CONGRESS SYSTEM, 1818

Document 10

This letter was written to Castlereagh – in Aix-la-Chapelle for the Congress of 1818 – by Lord Bathurst, Liverpool's Secretary for War and a close associate of Wellington. It reveals Canning's disquiet over Congress diplomacy and, as so often with Canning, it reflected a wider public unease.

Downing Street, 20 October 1818

The objections which Canning feels on this subject are not confined to the inexpediency of announcing a decision of meeting at fixed periods, but to the system itself . . . He thinks that system of periodical meetings of the four great Powers, with a view to the general concerns of Europe, new, and of very questionable policy; that it will necessarily involve us deeply in all the politics of the Continent, whereas our true policy has always been not to interfere except in great emergencies, and then with a commanding force. He thinks that all other States must protest against such an attempt to place them under subjection; that the meetings may become a scene of cabal and intrigue; and that the people of this country may be taught to look with great jealousy for their liberties, if our Court is engaged in meetings with great despotic monarchs, deliberating upon what degree of revolutionary spirit may endanger the public security, and therefore require the interference of the Alliance.

Source: Marquis of Londonderry (ed.), *Correspondence, Letters and Despatches of Lord Castlereagh*, 12 vols, London, 1853, vol. xii, pp. 56–7.

THE CASTLEREAGH STATE PAPER OF MAY 1820

Document 11

This much-quoted document marks Castlereagh's official recognition that Congress diplomacy was not working as he had intended. He had had a very different 'System' in mind from that envisaged by Tsar Alexander I and this paper reasserts the need for pragmatic responses. It can also be read as a response to Canning's reservations, expressed in 1818 [**Doc. 10, above**].

The principle of one State interfering by force in the internal affairs of another, in order to enforce obedience to the governing authority, is always a question of the greatest possible moral as well as political delicacy, and it is not meant here to examine it. It is only important on the present occasion to observe that to generalize such a principle and to think of reducing it to a System, or to impose it as an obligation, is a Scheme utterly impracticable and objectionable. There is not only the physical impossibility of giving execution to such a System, but there is the moral impracticability arising from the inaptitude of particular States to recognize, or to act upon it.

Source: H. Temperley and L.M. Penson (eds), *Foundations of British Foreign Policy, 1792–1902*, Cambridge, 1938, p. 61.

Document 12   THE *ANNUAL REGISTER* IDENTIFIES THE BENEFITS OF CLOSE RELATIONS WITH SOUTH AMERICA, 1825

Prefaces to the Annual Register *in the early nineteenth century highlighted what the editor considered to be the most important political themes for a given year. His selection of South American diplomacy for 1825, therefore, needs to be read as a commentary on the importance of Canning's policies in the area.*

While the greater part of the Continent exhibits an aspect little cheering to the friends of the human race, consolation may be found in contemplating the state of England and the course of events beyond the Atlantic. Throughout the South American continent, not only has the cause of independence been victorious in the field, but some progress has been made in the establishment of regular government, and in laying the foundations of those institutions upon which well-ordered systems of freedom may be erected hereafter. Relations, too, of amity and commerce, with every likelihood of permanence, have sprung up between the new states and the parent and guardian of freedom in the old world, which must exercise a most beneficial influence both on their moral and on their political destiny.

Source: *Annual Register*, vol. lxvii, 1825, p. v.

Document 13   CANNING BRIEFS THE CONSUL-GENERAL OF BUENOS AIRES, 1823

This document is dated 10 October 1823. It neatly encapsulates the main points of Canning's South American policy. Note Canning's anxiety that Britain's representative in this newly independent state should stress his country's commercial, as opposed to imperial, concerns. Note also the implication in the final sentence that Britain could be a guarantor of Spanish American liberties.

It may be unnecessary to state to you, but it is very material, that it should be understood by the persons with whom you communicate in Buenos Aires;

that so far is Great Britain from looking to any more intimate connection with any of the late Spanish Provinces, than that of friendly and commercial Intercourse, that His Majesty could not be induced by any consideration to enter into any engagement which might be considered as bringing them under His Dominion. Neither, on the other hand, would His Majesty consent to see them (in the event of their final separation from Spain) brought under the Dominion of any other Power.

Source: Public Record Office, F.O./6/1, Letter of Instruction, quoted in H.R. Ferns, *Britain and Argentina in the Nineteenth Century*, Arno Press, New York, 1977, p. 111.

CANNING'S REASONS FOR INTERVENTION IN PORTUGAL, 1826 **Document 14**

This document should be read alongside Documents 10 and 11, where the role of Britain in Europe is also debated. Canning saw British intervention in Portugal as necessary not only to bolster the government of a long-term ally but also to deter the other great powers. Note the use by Canning of the word 'umpire', perhaps an appropriate encapsulation of Britain's role in European diplomacy in the 1820s.

It is one thing to have a giant's strength, but it would be another to use it like a giant. The consciousness of such strength is, undoubtedly, a source of confidence and security; but in the situation in which this country stands, our business is not to seek opportunities of displaying it, but to content ourselves with letting the professors of violent and exaggerated doctrines on both sides feel, that it is not in their interest to convert an umpire into an adversary . . . Let us fly to the aid of Portugal, by whomsoever attacked, because it is our duty to do so; and let us cease our interference where that duty ends. We go to Portugal, not to rule, not to dictate, not to prescribe constitutions, but to defend and preserve the independence of an ally. We go to plant the standard of England on the well-known heights of Lisbon. Where that standard is planted, foreign dominion shall not come.

Source: *Hansard*, 2nd ser., vol. xvi, cols 367–9, 12 December 1826.

TORY UNCERTAINTIES AFTER THE DEPARTURE OF LORD LIVERPOOL, 1827 **Document 15**

This document provides a glimpse of a troubled and perplexed political world in the long hiatus between Liverpool's stroke in January and the formation of

Canning's government in April 1827. The succession was by no means certain and the contentious issues which Liverpool's presence had held in check, most notably the Catholic emancipation issue, divided old political colleagues. Here one supporter of Canning's claims to succeed Liverpool writes to another about the burning issue of the day. The letter is a good example of informed political gossip and, like many of its ilk, its predictions were largely falsified by subsequent events.

London, 23 February 1827

The two principal speculations are – Canning avowedly head over all – with Robinson sent to lead in the Lords – & then in the event of Canning's clinging (wh. he will in any event be much dispos'd to do) to the F[oreign] Office – Robinson to be First Lord – & Huskisson of the Exchequer. 2nd. speculation. Robinson to be a peer – *First Minister* & First Lord – Huskisson Chancellor of the Exchequer. Other things as they are. This is founded on the notion that in the existing state of matters in the Cabinet there would be as great a difficulty in making some consent to serve under Canning – as it would be to make him serve under them & that this is your only safe compromise. This might be consider'd a patching up *pro tempore* – & indeed it would not have anything very solid in it. Some who speak of this (wh. is a very common speculation) seem to think that Peel & the Duke of Welln. would object to Canning's being Premier – the former on the ground of the Cath. question.

Source: Letter from Lord Bining to Sir Charles Bagot in A. Aspinall (ed.), *The Formation of Canning's Ministry*, Camden Society, 3rd series, vol. lix, 1937, pp. 23–4.

Document 16   SAMUEL BAMFORD ON THE INFLUENCE OF WILLIAM COBBETT IN 1816

Samuel Bamford, a weaver from Middleton, near Manchester, was a leading working-class politician who was twice imprisoned for his radical activities between 1815 and 1821. His story of political activity in Lancashire is both rich in detail and extremely rare. Few working men left such a vivid account. It is a useful corrective to the far larger number of sources which write about working-class activity (whether sympathetically or not) from the outside.

At this time [December 1816] the writings of William Cobbett suddenly became of great authority; they were read on nearly every cottage hearth in the manufacturing districts of South Lancashire, in those of Leicester, Derby and Nottingham; also in many of the Scottish manufacturing towns. Their influence was speedily visible; he directed his readers to the true cause of their sufferings – misgovernment; and to its proper corrective – parliamentary reform. Riots soon became scarce . . .

Instead of riots and destruction of property, Hampden clubs were now established in many of our large towns, and the villages and districts around them; Cobbett's books were printed in a cheap edition form; the labourers read them and thenceforward became deliberate and systematic in their proceedings. Nor were there wanting men of their own class, to encourage and direct the new converts; the Sunday Schools of the preceding thirty years, had produced many working men of sufficient talent to become readers, writers and speakers in the village meetings for parliamentary reform.

Source: Samuel Bamford, *Passages in the Life of a Radical*, Oxford University Press edn, 1984, pp. 13–14.

COBBETT'S ADDRESS TO THE JOURNEYMEN AND LABOURERS, 1816   **Document 17**

This is the kind of appeal which Bamford [Doc. 16, p. 114] alleged moved its readers and hearers to dignified but committed protest. Cobbett was no socialist but he had a clear idea of the dignity of labour which he passed on to his readers in direct, vigorous prose.

As it is the labour of those who toil which makes a country abound in resources, so it is the same class of men, who must, by their arms, secure its safety and uphold its fame. Titles and immense sums of money have been bestowed upon numerous Naval and Military Commanders. Without calling the justice of these in question, we may assert that the victories were obtained by you and your fathers and brothers and sons in co-operation with those Commanders, who, with *your* aid have done great and wonderful things . . .

With this correct idea of your own worth in your minds, with what indignation must you hear yourselves called the Populace, the Rabble, the Mob, the Swinish Multitude; and with what greater indignation, if possible, must you hear the projects of those cool and cruel and insolent men, who, now that you have been, without any fault of yours, brought into a state of misery, propose to narrow the limits of parish relief, to prevent you from marrying in the days of your youth, or to thrust you out to seek your bread in foreign lands, never more to behold your parents and friends?

. . . As to the cause of our present miseries, it is the *enormous amount of the taxes*, which the government compels us to pay for the support of its army, its placemen, its pensioners, etc. and for the payment of the interest of its debt . . . The *remedy* is what we have now to look to, and that remedy consists wholly and solely of such a *reform* in the Commons or People's House of Parliament, as shall give to every payer of *direct taxes* a vote at elections, and as shall cause the Members to be *elected annually*.

Source: Cobbett's Political Register, 2 November 1816, reprinted in G.D.H. Cole and A.W. Filson (eds), *British Working Class Movements: Select Documents, 1789–1875*, Macmillan, London, 1967 edition, pp. 122–3.

Document 18   AN ATTACK ON COBBETT, 1817

The recent resurgence of interest in working-class politics has uncovered a treasure-trove of radical literature which is becoming ever more widely available in reprints and new editions. It must not be forgotten that, though few could rival Cobbett's journalistic abilities, he did not lack for combatants. The following document is almost totally unknown. It shows how his opponents tried to reduce Cobbett's influence among the poor by asserting the impracticality of Cobbett's schemes and the damage their implementation would do to the very folk he was aiming to persuade. Note the author's reference to what would become known as the March of the Blanketeers (see above, pp. 21–2). The last sentence refers to Cobbett's early career as a pro-Tory and anti-reformer in the 1790s.

To the MANCHESTER WORKMEN

MY GOOD FRIENDS – Do not believe, that in addressing you, I am not moved by the most sincere and heartfelt interest in your distresses. I can too well conceive, how much you have of late had to struggle against, to keep yourselves, your wives, and families, from the very extremity of suffering – perhaps from sinking under the pressure of the times; but let me beg you to reflect on the absurd and preposterous method that you have been persuaded to adopt for your relief. You have been advised to set off, by thousands, to walk to London, in order to present your Petitions to the Prince Regent. Now, my good Friends, let me first tell you how, and by whom, and for what purposes, this foolish notion has been put into your heads. You are not aware who it is, that is making fools of you, in this manner; still less do you suspect with what view it is done; but I will detect the villain, I will drag him from his hole. It was COBBETT . . . it was he who first proposed a scheme which, he knew, must turn all those who listened to it into Vagabonds, or Rioters, or Thieves . . . Whether you may be starved to death on the road, or taken up and hanged, he does not care a doit. He would only call you *silly* and *misguided* people, for your pains; but his end would have been answered; he would have made you dance to his fiddle, and pay him for the music too, though it was leading you to the gallows here, and to eternal torment hereafter. For, my Friends, this greedy grasping wretch, after having written for the rich against the poor, till no respectable person would read his writings any longer, is now trying to squeeze the last farthing out of the pockets of the Poor, by writing against the Rich.

Source: Anti-Cobbett or The Weekly Patriotic Paper, vol. i, no. 5, 15 March 1817, pp. 130–1.

ADVERTISING THE SPA FIELDS MEETING OF DECEMBER 1816   **Document 19**

This placard advertised one of the most famous of radical meetings. Notice the directness of the language. The radicals were not abashed at invoking Nelson's famous call to his sailors to do their duty at Trafalgar in 1805. Not also the centrality of the contrast between the state of the many and the 'splendid Luxury' enjoyed by the few. Contrast both the language and the message of this placard with that of the 'call to arms' [**Doc. 20, p. 118**] *and then with that of the Report of the Committee of Secrecy* [**Doc. 21, p. 118**].

ENGLAND
Expects every Man to do his Duty

The Meeting in Spa Fields
Takes Place at 12 o'clock
On Monday, December 2nd. 1816

To receive the answer of the PETITION to the PRINCE REGENT, determined upon at the last meeting held in the same place, and for other important Considerations.

THE PRESENT STATE OF GREAT BRITAIN
Four Millions in Distress !!!
Four Millions Embarrassed !!!
One Million-and-half fear Distress !!!
Half-a-million live in splendid Luxury !!!

Death would now be a relief to Millions –
Arrogance, Folly, and Crimes – have brought affairs to this dread Crisis.
Firmness and Integrity
can only save the Country!!!

Source: State Trials, vol. xxxii, 1817, p. 86.

Document 20   A CALL TO ARMS IN 1816

Documents like the following, which was circulated before the Spa Fields Meeting of December 1816 and reprinted in the Committee of Secrecy report, could be used by the authorities to justify legislation which suspended the normal liberties of the subject for protest and peaceable assembly. The tenor of the report suggests, however, that, although there was indeed a 'project' for 'raising an insurrection' at the end of 1816 the threat which this announcement seems to offer was well under control. Notice the specific targets listed by the author of the handbill.

Britons to Arms!

The whole country waits the signal from London to fly to arms! haste, break open gunsmiths and other likely places to find arms! run all constables who touch a man of us; no rise of bread; No Regent; no Castlereagh, off with their heads; no placemen, tythes or enclosures; no taxes; no bishops.

Source: Reprinted in *Hansard*, 1st ser, vol. xxxv, 1817, cols 440–1.

Document 21   THE REPORT OF THE COMMITTEE OF SECRECY, FEBRUARY 1817

This Report followed very similar procedures to those of the Secrecy Committees established by the younger Pitt in the 1790s. It provided abundant evidence of disaffection, sufficient to justify, at least to a majority of MPs, legislation concerned to strengthen public order. The blame, of course, could be laid at the door of hotheads and trouble-makers conveniently known to the authorities. Ordinary Britons could thus be absolved from blame and, indeed, praised for their forbearance in the face of economic hardship.

On a review of the whole it is a great satisfaction to your Committee to observe that, notwithstanding the alarming progress which has been made in the system of secret societies, its success has been confined to the principle [sic] manufacturing districts where the distress is more prevalent, and numbers more easily collected; and that even in many of these districts, privations have been borne with exemplary patience and resignation, and the attempts of the disaffected have been disappointed; that few if any of the higher orders or even of the middle class of society, and scarcely any of the agricultural population, have lent themselves to the more violent of these projects. Great allowance must be made for those who, under the pressure of urgent distress, have been led to listen to plausible and confident demagogues, in the expectation of immediate relief. It is to be hoped, that many of those who have engaged, to a certain extent, in the projects of the disaffected, but in whom the principles of moral and religious duyty [*sic*] have not been extinguished or perverted by the most profane and miserable sophistry, would withdraw themselves before those projects were pushed to actual insurrection.

Source: *Hansard*, 1st ser., vol. xxxv, 1817, cols 446–7.

A RADICAL ATTACK ON LEVELS OF TAXATION, 1819   **Document 22**

This article, by one of the most gifted of radical jounalists, T.J. Wooler, is in the mainstream of extra-parliamentary opposition. It argues that government taxation policies exaggerate the already wide gulf between rich and poor. Notice the reference to the recent Corn Law as only one of a number of punitive taxes. In Wooler's view, the much-vaunted 'liberties' of the freeborn Englishman had, in fact, been systematically shackled by the corrupt men who ruled Britain in their own interest.

France offers brandies to all the world, at less than *three shillings* a gallon; but an Englishman is not at liberty to drink it, unless he can pay six or seven and twenty shillings a gallon. And if the plenty of the world were to bring its superfluous corn to the British shores, and offer it at *twenty* shillings a quarter, the masters of the freeborn Englishman would insist upon it that he should not have it at a less price than *eighty*. His salt costs him six times what it is worth, as salt . . . his tea pays a hundred per cent duty; in short I am tired of enumerating all his *privileges* . . . the *real* and *only freedom* of an Englishman, is *money* and *money* alone. If rich, what he can *buy* he may have. If great, what he can *take* is his; but your poor free-born Briton is one of the most miserable of human beings. He labours more, and earns less than any other labourer. His skill and enterprize are only equalled by his want and misery – his freedom, is the liberty of seeking his only refuge from calamity – the grave!

Source: *The Black Dwarf*, 8 December 1819.

RADICAL FREETHOUGHT IN THE 1820s   **Document 23**

Richard Carlile was a disciple of Tom Paine who took his master's writings several stages further by attacking organized religion as a servile prop to the system of old corruption. He was frequently imprisoned for articles which were widely considered blasphemous and seditious. Though atheism was an import-

ant strain in radical political thought at this time, Carlile's work embarrassed many extra-parliamentary radicals who believed that he alienated potential sympathisers in both the middle and the working classes with his trenchantly unfashionable views. Contrast the message here with that offered by Wooler [Doc. 22, p. 119].

Since nature has not furnished mankind with Kings, Lords and Priests . . . it follows, that their existence must be the result of good policy in the whole, or of trick in a few of the more cunning and powerful . . . Where you see a rich and powerful aristocracy and priesthood you are sure to find a poor people . . . you cannot shake the power of the aristocracy by any insidious means, it must be done by open attack; and to attack the Priests is to attack the aristocracy at their weakest point. In fact, it is attacking them at all points at once; for the ignorance arising from superstition is the stronghold of all the unjust distinctions, and of all the splendid idlers of society.

Source: Republican, 21 May 1824.

Document 24   THE REPEAL OF THE TEST AND CORPORATION ACTS ATTACKED, 1828

While Catholic emancipation [Doc. 25, p. 120] aroused the wider political passions, it would be wrong to think that the long-delayed measure which granted equality in most spheres to Protestant dissenters passed without controversy. Some zealous defenders of the Church of England saw it as a fundamental breach of the constitution.

. . . a more complete subversion of the principles upon which our Constitution has been founded, we cannot imagine; a more ridiculous, inconsistent, and irrational attempt at argument, is not to be found out of Bedlam; and we grieve to say, that it is not to Lord John Russell, or his supporters, that we apply these epithets; . . . with sincere and poignant grief, we must confess, that they are applicable to those whom we had hoped would have proved themselves the constant and uncompromising defenders of the Established Church.

Source: John Bull, 21 April 1828, p. 124.

Document 25   SIR ROBERT PEEL CONCEDES ROMAN CATHOLIC EMANCIPATION, 1829

Peel had made his early political reputation not only as an effective minister and administrator but also as a zealous defender of Protestant rights in Ireland

– hence the sardonic epithet 'Orange Peel'. The speech from which this docu-
ment is a brief extract had momentous political consequences both for Peel and
the future Conservative party. It ensured the passage of emancipation and it
earned Peel the undying hostility of a large proportion of Tory backbenchers.
For some, indeed, the collapse of Peel's government in 1846 was a long-
delayed and richly merited retribution for his 'betrayal' in 1829. Note how
Peel explains his change of mind. Many of his Tory opponents found his
explanation inadequate.

Sir, I approach this subject, almost overpowered by the magnitude of the
interests it involves, and by the difficulties with which it is surrounded. I am
not unconscious of the degree to which those difficulties are increased by the
peculiar situation of him on whom the lot has been cast to propose this
measure, and to enforce the expediency of its adoption . . . I believe that the
time has come when less danger is to be apprehended to the general interests of the empire and to the spiritual and temporal welfare of the Protestant
Establishment, in attempting to adjust the Catholic Question, than in allowing it to remain any longer in its present state . . . I do not think it was an
unnatural or unreasonable struggle. I resign it, in consequence of the conviction that it can be no longer advantageously maintained; from believing
that there are not adequate materials or sufficient instruments for its effectual
and permanent continuance. I yield, therefore, to a moral necessity which
I cannot control, unwilling to push resistance to a point which might
endanger the Establishments that I wish to defend.

Source: Hansard, 2nd. ser., vol. xx, 5 March 1829, cols 728–30.

PERSPECTIVES ON THE FIGHT FOR NORWICH DURING THE 1830 GENERAL   **Documents**
ELECTION   **26–28**

This election gives the flavour of the hustings when opinion was growing in
favour of parliamentary reform. It saw the defeat of Robert Peel's 'high' Tory
brother, Jonathan. His letter requesting the electors' continued support [**Doc. 26,**
p. 122] *was typical of many sent by retiring members who were confident*
of re-election. The attack on him, written anonymously [**Doc. 27, p. 122**],
makes standard radical charges of nepotism and excessive spending of public
money in an embarrassingly ad hominem *fashion. Peel's defeat was a signi-*
ficant straw in the wind. Norwich, though a constituency in which money
frequently changed hands to buy votes at elections, was one of the largest
freemen boroughs in the county. As such, it had an electorate which exceeded
3,000 and was indicative of any changes in public opinion. Robert Grant was

a Huskissonite Tory. As such, he was the target of a campaign mounted by Wellington's government to defeat as many of their former political allies as possible. Grant's victory over Peel [Doc. 28, p. 123] was indicative of the limited support for Wellington in the contested constituencies. The candidate who came top of the poll, Richard Gurney, was a wealthy Whig banker who was reputed to have spent more than £3,000 a year on maintaining his support in the constituency.

Document 26   To the Worthy the Clergy, Freemen and Freeholders of the City of Norwich, 28 June 1830

Gentlemen . . .

I lose not a moment in communicating to you my intention of again soliciting the favour of your suffrages in the honourable and distinguished situation which I now occupy as one of the Representatives of your ancient and populous city.

I refer you to my conduct in Parliament for the fulfilment of the promises I made when first you committed to me the important trust. It has been my earnest desire to merit your confidence and esteem, and to re-deliver that Trust unsullied into your hands. Should I again have the honour of representing you in Parliament, it is my intention steadily to pursue the same line of public policy which I have hitherto adopted, believing it to be best calculated for supporting the real and permanent Interests of the Country . . .

Your most obedient humble servant, Jonathan Peel

Document 27   'No Grumbling' to the Independent Electors of the City of Norwich, June 1830

Mr. Peel and his family too, fully understand real and permanent interests, but it is for you to say whether the real and permanent interests he speaks of and is so well acquainted with are in the interests of the country or not.

'A Well Paid Family'

	Per Ann
The Right Hon. R. Peel is a Secretary of State, with a Salary of	£6,000
Mr. W. Peel is under Secretary of State, with a Salary of	2,000
Mr. Lawrence Peel is a Commander for the affairs of India, probably of considerable profit, but no Salary.	
Mr. Dawson, their Brother-in-Law Secretary to the Treasury, with a Salary of	4,000

Besides the following appointments held by their immediate followers

Mr. Gouldbourn [sic], Chancellor of the Exchequer	5,000
Dr. Loyd, Bishop of Oxford, Mr. Peel's private tutor	4,000

Mr. Jonathan Peel, a Young Brother of Mr. Secretary Peel, and Sir Henry Floyd, Mrs. Peel's Brother, Lieut. Colonels in the Army, although we believe neither the one nor the other ever distinguished themselves in the Service of the Country.

Brother Electors – It must be in your memory, that many virtuous attempts to reduce items in the Enormous Taxation, have been made in the present Session of Parliament, and you are hereby informed that Mr. Jonathan Peel uniformly voted for their continuance, and he tells you, that so long as he is your Representative, he will pursue the same policy, yes, and so he has a right, if you again elect him to represent you, after seeing how his interest is identified with the system, and should the Aristocracy demand it, you will have a right to pay double the amount of Taxes which you now pay without grumbling, should Mr. Peel be returned.

The rapidity with which the Polling proceeded, astonished even the oldest **Document 28** campaigner. The state of the Poll at Six o'Clock will bear us out in this remark: – For

Mr. Gurney	2032
– Grant	1963
– Peel	1699
– Ogle	1560

Majority in favour of Mr. Gurney, 340 – Mr. Grant, 264

Source: The Norwich Election Budget, Containing a Narrative of the Proceedings, Norwich, 1830 and 1831, pp. 10–11, 31, 40–1, copy in British Library.

WELLINGTON MISJUDGES THE PUBLIC MOOD, 1830 **Document 29**

This speech, it is generally agreed, hastened the collapse of Wellington's government. Taken at face value, its assertions were clearly nonsensical at a time of mounting public agitation (see above, pp. 75–6). As a way of rallying Tory support, the speech also missed its mark. The speech amounted to a public declaration of ministerial suicide.

He had never read or heard of any measure . . . which could in any degree satisfy his mind that the state of the representation could be improved, or be rendered more satisfactory to the country at large . . . He was fully convinced that the country possessed at the present moment a Legislature which answered all the good purposes of legislation, and this to a greater degree than any Legislature ever had answered in any country whatever. He would go further and say, that the Legislature and the system of representation possessed the full and entire confidence of the country . . . as far as he was concerned, as long as he held any station in the government of the country, he should always feel it his duty to resist such measures [of reform] when proposed by others.

Source: Hansard, 3rd ser., vol. i, 2 November 1830, cols 52–3.

Document 30   A HOSTILE VIEW OF POLITICAL UNIONS, 1831

This document encapsulates the distaste felt by many property owners for the direct forms of agitation which the political unions fostered after 1830. Notice the references to 'physical power' and the assertions about the intimidatory tactics of the unions.

Besides the usual machinery of petitions, permanent political associations had already begun to be formed in different parts of the country, for the purpose of organizing large numbers of individuals into one body, to act on the mind of the public around them and press upon the government. These self-constituted organs of popular opinion took the name of Political Unions . . Their objects were, to push on political changes to any extent, by any means; to insist on whatever they chose to demand, as a right which could not be refused without a crime; to repress, by their display of force, any expression, in their neighbourhood, of opinions of an opposite tendency; and to make even the government, which they pretended to be supporting, feel, by their violence, that they existed in order to dictate, not to obey. They did not even conceal the effects which they would produce by their mere physical power, and used language of abuse and intimidation which had no meaning except upon the idea that they were prepared and resolved to extort by force the possession of that power which, in their hands, was to save the country. The great object of all their deliberations was to excite incurable enmity in the middling and lower classes against those who stood above them in the order of society.

Source: Annual Register, 1831, p. 5.

EARL GREY USES THE MIDDLE CLASSES TO PRESS HIS CASE FOR
PARLIAMENTARY REFORM, 1831

Document 31

*This appraisal of the importance of the political unions might usefully be con-
trasted with that of the Annual Register [Doc. 30, p. 124]. Grey's letter is to
William IV's private secretary and is designed to inform the King of the importance of middle-class opinion in the government's determination to press ahead
with parliamentary reform despite the recent defeat in the Lords (see above,
pp. 91–3). Behind the bland, respectful tone of the letter there lurked the threat
that William IV might have to create peerages in order to coerce Tory opinion
in the Upper House. This idea was anathema to the King.*

Earl Grey to Sir H. Taylor, 8 November 1831

These Unions have received a great impulse and extension from the rejection of the Reform Bill; and . . . many persons, not otherwise disposed to
do so, have been induced to join them for the purpose of promoting that
measure. It is also undeniable that the middle classes, who have now shown
so praiseworthy an alacrity in supporting the government, are actuated by an
intense and almost unanimous feeling in favour of the measure of reform.

Source: Earl Grey (ed.), *Correspondence of Earl Grey and William IV*, 2 vols, London,
1867, vol. i, pp. 410–11.

SIR ROBERT INGLIS AND T.B. MACAULAY DEBATE THE REFORM QUESTION,
1831

**Documents 32
and 33**

*These extracts come from debates in the House of Commons on the second
reading of the first Reform Bill. Inglis was MP for Oxford University and a
strong opponent of reform. Macaulay was rapidly making a name for himself
as a leading writer and orator on the Whig side [Doc. 35, p. 127]. Notice
the appeals, respectively, to precedent and to pragmatism. Inglis celebrates
a historically ordered entity which represents all of what to him were the
important interests. Macaulay similarly rests his case on the enfranchisement
of property, not numbers, yet contests the effectiveness of the existing parliamentary system.*

Sir Robert Inglis:

Document 32

Such, generally speaking, as the House of Commons is now, such it has
been for a long succession of years: it is the most complete representation of the interests of the people, which was ever assembled in any age

or any country. It is the only constituent body that ever existed, which comprehends within itself those who can urge the wants and defend the claims of the landed, the commercial, the professional classes of the country: those who are bound to uphold the interests of the lower classes, the rights and liberties of the whole people. It is the very absence of symmetry in our elective franchises which admits of the introduction to this House of classes so various.

Document 33   T.B. Macaulay:

I oppose Universal Suffrage, because I think it would produce a destructive revolution . . . We say, and we say justly, that it is not by mere numbers but by property and intelligence that the nation ought to be governed. Yet, saying this, we exclude from all share in the government vast masses of property and intelligence – vast numbers of those who are most interested in preserving tranquillity, and who know best how to preserve it. We do more. We drive over to the sin of revolution those whom we shut out of power.

Monarchy and aristocracy, valuable and useful as I think them, are still useful and valuable as means, and not as ends. The end of government is the happiness of the people; and I do not conceive that, in a country like this, the happiness of the people can be promoted by a form of government in which the middle classes place no confidence, and which exists only because the middle classes have no organ by which to make their sentiments known.

Source: *Hansard*, 3rd ser., vol. ii, 2 March 1831, cols 1108–9, 1192–3 and 1199–1200.

Document 34   AN IMMEDIATE RESPONSE TO THE PRESENTATION OF THE GOVERNMENT'S REFORM BILL, 1831

This document derives from the diary of a cabinet minister in Wellington's government of 1828–30. Despite the impression given in this extract, Baron Ellenborough was not rootedly opposed to parliamentary reform. He even favoured a household suffrage at one point. Here we see Ellenborough's immediate, rather than his considered, judgement on the reform proposals when they were first unveiled before Parliament. Both the surprise and alarm at the radicalism of the Bill and the expectation that it could not pass were typical. The extract neatly conveys both the main strengths and weaknesses of diaries as a historical source.

March 2nd, 1831

The Reform proposed is much more extensive than was expected. Parts of it are very absurd. There was no little laughter as they were detailed. The feeling in the Gallery was against it, as absurd. In the House, Ld. John [Russell] seems to have been little cheered and to have spoken miserably . . . I rather gather . . . that the opponents of Reform are thrown aback by the extent of the proposed change, & alarmed. The feeling, however, is that the Bill cannot pass.

Probably the Ministers wish to be beat upon Reform, & so to go out. How to form any strong Government in their place I know not, but perhaps, for Providence seems always to save us when we are in real danger, the alarm of the influential classes may create a support.

Source: A. Aspinall (ed.), *Three Early Nineteenth-Century Diaries*, Williams and Northgate, London, 1952, pp. 61–2.

AN APPRAISAL OF MACAULAY'S DEBATING STYLE, 1831   **Document 35**

By December 1831, with reform the only important political question, Macaulay had established himself as the pre-eminent debater on the Whig side. This document offers an informed view of his oratory. Debating skill swayed votes in the 1830s, before the days of tight party organization and the advent of powerful party 'Whips', and Macaulay's skills were important as well as ornamental. E.J. Littleton, from whose diary this extract is taken, was one of the two county MPs for Staffordshire. Like Palmerston, he had been a supporter of Canning and Huskisson in the 1820s and supported the Whigs from November 1830. Unlike Palmerston, however, his ministerial career was brief and inglorious. He served unsuccessfully as Chief Secretary for Ireland in 1833 and 1834.

December 17, 1831

Macaulay made one of those brilliant speeches, his third on the Reform question, which carried the House away in the same furious whirlwind of mixed passions which seemed to seize himself. Never was a more extraordinary compound of deep philosophy, exalted sentiments, and party bitterness, enunciated with a warmth, a vigour, and rapidity inconceivable. The public can collect but little of its character from the papers. It is like the course of a meteor, never to be forgotten by those who have the fortune to see it, but seen by a few.

Source: A. Aspinall (ed.), *Three Early Nineteenth-Century Diaries*, 1952, p. 171.

Document 36   THE POLITICAL INFLUENCE OF THE ESTABLISHED CHURCH, 1831

The radical writer John Wade is best remembered for his painstaking researches into the extent of what the radicals called 'Old Corruption'. His most vulnerable target was the Church of England and the analysis which follows seemed particularly relevant during the demonstrations which followed the rejection of the second Reform Bill in October 1831 (pp. 91–2). These had a strongly anti-clerical flavour.

The clergy, from superior education, from their wealth and sacred profession, possess greater influence than any other order of men, and all the influence they possess is as subservient to government as the army or navy, or any other branch of public service. Upon every public occasion the consequence of this influence is apparent. There is no question, however unpopular, which may not obtain countenance by the support of the clergy: being everywhere, and having much to lose, and a great deal to expect, they are always active and zealous in devotion to the interests of those on whom their promotion depends. Hence their anxiety to attract notice at county, corporate, and sessional meetings. Whenever a loyal address is to be obtained, a popular petition opposed, or hard measure carried against the poor, it is almost certain that some reverend rector, very reverend dean, or venerable archdeacon, will make himself conspicuous.

Source: John Wade, *The Extraordinary Black Book*, London, 1831, pp. 20–1.

————————◄●►————————

Document 37   AN ATTACK ON ESTABLISHED AUTHORITY WITHOUT CONTEMPORARY UNDERSTANDING, 1832

A growing element in the radical critique of the old political system was the argument that those in authority were ignorant of conditions in the rapidly growing industrial areas. This line of reasoning enabled radicals to concentrate on 'lords and parsons', both of whom were in short supply in the early nineteenth-century city. The Poor Man's Advocate was published from Manchester and embraced a wide range of radical causes. Note the reference to 'moral regeneration' in Europe.

There are two classes of men in this country who enjoy the greatest facilities for acquiring, and yet who, in reality, possess the least amount of real knowledge. These are lords and parsons. The one class are set apart to instruct, and the other to rule the people; yet both are lamentably ignorant of the actual state of society. The rank and habits of one class shut them out from that intercourse with the rest of mankind, which is essential to their properly discharging the duty they have undertaken. The supercilious pride and sectarian hostility of the other have rendered them obnoxious rather than acceptable to the people, and both are in equal danger of being swept away by the swelling tide of moral regeneration which has already inundated Europe.

Source: The Poor Man's Advocate, no. 11, 31 March 1832.

THE DAYS OF MAY AND THE LIKELY RETURN OF WELLINGTON AS PRIME MINISTER, 1832 **Document 38**

This document is taken from a provincial newspaper which is trying to analyse the likely consequence of Wellington's resuming office in May 1832. References to the financial implications of the reform crisis were very common both in the London and the provincial press at this time.

We learn that the Duke of Wellington consents to be Premier again! We learn, too, that he will go on with the Reform Bill, and that he proposes to make very little alteration in it!! Parliament will, it is believed, be dissolved immediately, therefore, let the people prepare forthwith. Stocks have fallen one per cent more! . . . The greatest alarm is entertained lest the 100,000 men at Birmingham should not be kept from an outbreak. It is felt to be the duty of the Tories to take their post without delay, so that if there should be a conflict between the government and the people, it may not be between the people and Earl Grey . . . There is a panic in the city.

Source: Buckinghamshire Gazette, 12 May 1832.

JOHN WILSON CROKER ENCOUNTERS MANCHESTER WORKING MEN, 1832 **Document 39**

This account by a leading Tory writer and intellectual has its unintentionally humorous side, but it is useful to reflect on the cultural chasm which separated the writer from the people he is evidently so reluctant to meet. The incident took place during the 'Days of May' when some, at least, feared imminent revolution.

May 18th, 1832

I remained at Molesey [Surrey], and was surprised at finding that a body of workmen from Manchester (who had been marched up, it seems, to intimidate the King and the new government, but were stopped and ordered back in consequence of the restoration of the Whigs) had quartered themselves in this and the neighbouring villages, and were, like sturdy beggars, insisting on getting food and money. Two of them came to my gate and made some noise, and I could hardly get rid of them. Each carried a small skein of cotton yarn, which they pretended to sell; but when I showed them the absurdity of such a pretence . . . they confessed that they had come up *many thousands* to carry the Reform Bill which was to put down machinery, and enable the poor man to earn a livelihood . . . They wore a kind of workman's uniform – a flannel jacket, trimmed with narrow blue ribbon. One was an Englishman, and civil; the other an Irishman, and very much inclined to riot and rob. But his companion listened to reason, and when he heard that there was a lady dangerously ill in the house, he half forced away his troublesome comrade. I have no doubt that they were part of a body of workmen which have been brought up from Birmingham and Manchester to help the Whigs. I thought it right, however, to apprise Lord Melbourne, Secretary of State for the Home Department, of this migration of the northern hives.

Source: L.J. Jennings (ed.), *The Correspondence and Diaries of J.W. Croker*, 3 vols, London, 1884, vol. ii, pp. 169–70.

Document 40   THE DUKE OF WELLINGTON CONSIDERS THE LIKELY CONSEQUENCES OF REFORM, 1832

Wellington remained defiantly pessimistic about reform up to and beyond the passage of the Reform Act. This letter to a fellow Tory peer, the Duke of Buckingham, indicates his state of mind. Though it is easy to poke fun at predictions which were proved wildly wrong, it is more important to try to understand why they were so widely shared in Tory circles in 1832. For many, the passage of the Reform Act genuinely meant the end of civilisation as they had known it. Less fevered calculations more than a century and a half later still conclude that the Reform Act was one of the most important events in modern political history.

23 June 1832

My dear Duke,

    I quite concur with you respecting the symptoms of the times of the last week. They have occasioned a little apprehension in London and elsewhere; but the impression is only temporary. It is not in my power to prevent the consequence of what has been done. The Government of England is destroyed. A Parliament will be returned, by means of which no set of men will be able to conduct the administration of affairs, and to protect the lives and properties of the King's subjects.

I hear the worst accounts of the elections; indeed, I don't believe that gentlemen will be prevailed upon to offer themselves as candidates.

Source: Duke of Buckingham, *Memoirs of the Courts and Cabinets of William the Fourth and Victoria*, 2 vols, London, 1861, vol. i, p. 5.

Further Reading

The pace of historical scholarship renders all bibliographies out of date as soon as they are published and many now prefer to search online. The Royal Historical Society's online *Bibliography* www.rhs.ac.uk/bibl/, which is regularly updated, can be safely recommended and is equipped with excellent author and topic search facilities. The best of published bibliographies are now beginning to show their age. However, L.M. Brown and I.R. Christie (eds), *The Bibliography of British History, 1789–1851*, Oxford, 1977, is exhaustive on material published before the mid-1970s. D. Nicholls, *Nineteenth-Century Britain, 1815–1914*, Folkestone, 1978, is what is termed a 'critical bibliography'. This appears to mean that it is more selective, while offering some judgements on the works which are chosen for inclusion. In the nature of things, such judgements are subjective. More up-to-date bibliographical aids can be found in *The Routledge Companion to Britain in the Nineteenth Century, 1815–1914*, London, 2005, and via the formidable bibliographical essay which concludes Boyd Hilton's *A Mad, Bad and Dangerous People? England 1783–1846*, Oxford, 2006. The Royal Historical Society produces an *Annual Bibliography of British and Irish History*.

Documents and Contemporary Sources

Fortunately there is no shortage of good documentary collections for this period. The biggest is A. Aspinall and E.A. Smith (eds), *English Historical Documents*, vol. xi, 1783–1832, London, 1959. See also H.J. Hanham, *The Nineteenth Century Constitution*, 2nd edn, Cambridge, 1969.

On foreign policy the best collections, with commentary, are H. Temperley and L.M. Penson, *The Foundations of British Foreign Policy from Pitt to Salisbury*, Cambridge, 1938, and K. Bourne, *The Foreign Policy of Victorian England, 1830–1902*, Oxford, 1970. Readers are advised not to be deterred either by the title's eccentric definition of the Victorian period or the book's apparently marginal relevance to the period 1815–32. The first section has some excellent material on Castlereagh and Canning.

Chapters 1 and 2 of Norman Gash, *The Age of Peel*, Arnold, 1968, contain some useful documentary material on religion and on parliamentary reform. The best collection of documents concerned with radicalism, working-class politics and trade unionism remains G.D.H. Cole and A.W. Filson, *British Working Class Movements, 1789–1875*, Macmillan, 1967 edn, though P. Hollis, *Class and Conflict in Nineteenth-Century England, 1815–1850*, Routledge, 1973, is also valuable. See also the Seminar Studies by D.G. Wright, *Democracy and Reform*, 1970, and E.J. Evans, *Parliamentary Reform c. 1770–1918*, 2000.

The political culture of the age ensured a flourishing supply of sophisticated commentators and diarists on the fringes of power who knew their restricted world well and wrote about it brilliantly. Their works offer an excellent quarry for the historian. The commentators and diarists are frequently as unintentionally revealing about themselves and the assumptions they harboured about their inbred society as they are perceptive about their contemporaries. The best for this period are F. Bamford and the Duke of Wellington (eds), *The Journal of Mrs. Arbuthnot*, 1950; A. Aspinall (ed.), *Three Early Nineteenth-Century Diaries*, 1952; H. Maxwell (ed.), *The Creevey Papers*, 1923; L.J. Jennings (ed.), *The Correspondence and Diaries of J.W. Croker*, 3 vols, 1884; L. Strachey and R. Fulford (eds), *The Greville Memoirs*, 7 vols, 1938; L. Melville (ed.), *The Huskisson Papers*, 1931; and C.D. Yonge (ed.), *The Life and Administration of the Second Earl of Liverpool*, 3 vols, 1868.

Diaries of the less privileged are naturally much sparser, so Martin Hewitt and Robert Poole (eds), *The Diaries of Samuel Bamford*, Sutton Publishing, Stroud, 2000, is a welcome edition to accessible radical literature. A new paperback edition of Samuel Bamford's *Passages in the Life of a Radical*, Cosimo Classics, 2005, is also well worth consulting, especially for a close and sympathetic view of the Lancashire agitations of 1816–21. Mary Thale (ed.), *The Autobiography of Francis Place*, Cambridge, 1973, is an interesting statement by one of the great upwardly mobile political organizers and fixers of the age. The radical writers of the period are best examined in the journals referred to in Chapters 2 and 5 but special attention may be drawn to the assiduous researches about 'Old Corruption' published by John Wade as *The Extraordinary Black Book* in 1831. His entertainingly tendentious *British History Chronologically Arranged*, 1839, gives a graphic, one-sided account of the reform crisis. If students are in need of an antidote, the yearly introductions to the *Annual Register* rapidly reveal the real sympathies beneath the misleadingly neutral title.

Secondary Sources

Please note that, when articles are cited in the list below, the following abbreviations are used:

HJ   Historical Journal
JBS   Journal of British Studies
JMH   Journal of Modern History
EHR   English Historical Review
Econ. HR   Economic History Review
P & P   Past and Present
ESR   European Studies Review
PH   Parliamentary History

General works

Much the best detailed survey of the period is Hilton, B., *A Mad, Bad and Dangerous People: England, 1783–1846*, Oxford, 2006 – a volume in the New Oxford History of England. It is an excellent read as well as offering the most detailed guide to the period. It is especially good on the ideas which generated the policies. Briggs, A., *The Age of Improvement, 1783–1867*, Longman, 2nd revised edn, 2000, is still worth reading, while Cannon, J. (ed.), *Aristocratic Century*, Cambridge, 1984, shows fine understanding of the political motivation of the landed elite. Evans, E.J., *The Forging of the Modern State: Early Industrial Britain, 1783–1870*, 3rd edn, Longman Pearson, 2001, has been extensively used by students seeking a useful, yet detailed, introduction. It includes an extensive Compendium of Information. Gash, N., *Aristocracy and People, 1815–1865*, Arnold, 1979, is also worthwhile, though much better on the aristocracy than the people. Royle, E., *Modern Britain, 1750–1985: A Social History*, 2nd edn, Arnold, 1997, provides perhaps the best survey of the social structure of early industrial England. Despite its age E. Halevy, *The Liberal Awakening, 1815–1830*, Benn, 1926, is still worth reading not least for its fine-grained detail and well-chosen examples.

Government, Politics and Parties

Useful introductions to this theme are provided by Turner, M.J., *British Politics in an Age of Reform*, Manchester, 1999, Derry, J.W., *Politics in the Age of Fox, Pitt and Liverpool*, 2nd edn, Palgrave, 2001, and Evans, E.J., *Political Parties in Britain, 1783–1867*, Routledge, 1983. Burns, A. and Innes, J. (eds), *Rethinking the Age of Reform: Britain, 1780–1850*, Cambridge, 2003, offer a stimulating collection of essays. These deliberately define 'reform' broadly and examine what the idea of reform meant to contemporaries. A number of useful studies of party politics have been produced and the reader can be safely directed to Hill, B.W., *British Parliamentary Parties, 1742–1832*, Allen and Unwin, 1985, for an overview. Brock, W.R., *Lord Liverpool and Liberal Toryism*, 2nd edn, Glasgow, 1967, and Cookson, J.E., *Lord Liverpool's Administration, 1815–1822*, Scottish Academic Press, Edinburgh, 1975, in their different ways, argue for a change of course in the Liverpool administration when the 'new men' come in, a view which has increasingly come under challenge. Stewart, R., *The Foundation of the Conservative Party*, 1830–67, Longman, 1978, is a reliable guide to the end of our period while Hay, W.A., *The Whig Revival, 1808–30*, Palgrave Macmillan, Basingstoke, 2005, argues that the Whigs were in better shape during their long period in opposition than most have accepted. Jupp, P.J., *The Governing of Britain, 1688–1848: the executive, Parliament and the people*, Routledge, 2006, is a splendid, archivally based, overview of the governing process, written by someone who immersed himself in the detailed politics of the period throughout his career. His *British Politics on the Eve of Reform: the Duke of Wellington's Administration, 1828–30*, Macmillan, Basingstoke, 1998, is now by some distance the best detailed study of the politics of the Wellington government, which are expertly set into the wider context of British politics. Thorne, R., (ed.), *The History of Parliament, 1790 1820*, 5 vols, Secker and Warburg, 1986, provides the reader with biographies of all MPs who served in the parliaments of these years and details of every election fought in every constituency. The long-awaited companion volumes of the *History* on the period 1820–32 is promised for 2009. The *History of Parliament* has established itself, in effect, as the location of ultimate resort on the facts concerning parliamentary history. The introductions and analyses of constituencies and members of parliament are of very high quality also. Finally, Moore, D.C., *The Politics of Deference*, Harvester, 1976, remains worthy of attention for his carefully argued case that the Whigs intended to put the parliamentary reform issue to bed for good and all in 1832 – although few historians now agree with him.

One article has received particular attention for arguing that British government and society were conservative in their composition and attitudes: Clark, J.C.D., 'A General Theory of Party, Opposition and Government, 1688–1832', *HJ*, xxiii, 1980, pp. 295–325. The best synoptic discussion of debates concerning government, political parties and changing policy emphases is Harling, P., 'Equipoise Regained? Recent Trends in British Political History, 1790–1867', *JMH*, lxxv, 2003, pp. 890–918.

Two articles by Frank O'Gorman argue that party divisions were well established before 1832, O'Gorman, F., 'Electoral Deference in "Unreformed" England, 1760–1832', *JMH*, lvi, 1984, pp. 391–427 and 'Party Politics in the

Early Nineteenth Century, 1812–32', *EHR*, cii, 1987, pp. 63–84. A contrary view is presented by Fraser, P., 'Party Voting in the House of Commons, 1812–27', *EHR*, xcviii, 1983, pp. 763–84.

Harling, P. and Mandler, P., 'From "Fiscal-Military" State to Laissez-Faire State, 1760–1850, *JBS*, xxxii, 1993, pp. 44–70, suggest ways in which the commitment to high-spending by governments was significantly reduced once the wars ended and ideas about free-trade and minimal government interference took hold. An excellent summary of key political developments in our period is provided by Eastwood, D., 'The Age of Uncertainty: Britain in the Early Nineteenth Century', *TRHS*, 6th ser., viii, 1998, pp. 91–115.

Biography

Preliminary note: the appearance of the *Oxford Dictionary of National Biography*, Oxford, 2004–7, has transformed the landscape for those who wish to make serious first acquaintance with the leading figures of the period, not least in view of its wide availability online at www.oxforddnb.com/. Students are recommended to make use of it, not least for the bibliographies which conclude each entry.

Biographies of prime ministers in the period, or those who would become prime ministers later, are in ready supply. The most authoritative and influential is that on Peel, which appears in two volumes, Gash, N., *Mr. Secretary Peel: The Life of Sir Robert Peel to 1830*, 2nd edn, Longman, 1985, and *Sir Robert Peel: The Life of Sir Robert Peel after 1830*, 2nd edn, Longman, 1986. The same author's biography of Liverpool: Gash, N., *Lord Liverpool*, Weidenfeld, London, 1984, is slighter and less consistently archivally based. Two useful introductory biographies of Peel are Jenkins, T.A., *Sir Robert Peel*, Macmillan, Basingstoke, 1999, and Evans, E.J., *Sir Robert Peel: Statesmanship, Power and Party* 2nd edn, Routledge, London, 2006. For Palmerston, the pre-eminent Whig foreign secretary and later prime minister, see Chambers, J., *Palmerston: the people's darling*, Murray, London, 2004, and Bourne, K., *Palmerston: The Early Years, 1784–1841*, Allen Lane, 1982. Jones, W.D., *Prosperity Robinson: The Life of Viscount Goderich, 1782–1859*, Macmillan, 1967, makes the most of an unpromising subject who somehow never quite contrived to quit the political scene. Smith, E.A., *Lord Grey*, Oxford, 1990, and Mitchell, L.G., *Lord Melbourne, 1779–1848*, Oxford, 1997, are both well-researched and effective biographies. It is a pity that Canning has received relatively little attention from biographers. Nevertheless, Hinde, W., *Canning*, Collins, 1973, is worth consulting. Jupp, P., *Lord Grenville, 1759–1834*, Oxford, 1985, is an authoritative and lucid biography of a man who is difficult both to capture as an individual and to explain in terms of his beliefs and his tortured relationship with the Whig party. The most recommendable studies of Wellington emphasize different aspects of his life: Thompson, N., **Wellington after Waterloo**, Routledge, 1986, is concerned with Wellington's chequered political career while Holmes, R., **Wellington: the Iron Duke**, Harper Collins, London, 2002, concentrates more on his military prowess. There are likewise two contrasting treatments of Lord John Russell: Prest, J., **Lord John Russell**, Macmillan, 1972, and Scherer, P., **Lord John Russell: a biography**, Susquehanna, 1999.

Castlereagh has attracted more biographical attention than most senior British politicians in this period. Derry, J.W., **Castlereagh**, Allen Lane, 1976, is a good starting point. Bartlett, C.J., **Castlereagh**, Macmillan, 1966, Geoghegan, P.M., **Lord Castlereagh**, Dundalk, 2002, and Hinde, W., **Castlereagh**, Collins, 1981, are all recommendable. Much of Robins, J., **Rebel Queen: The Trial of Queen Caroline**, Simon and Schuster, London, 2006, offers a biographical assessment of a caricature figure while her equally unlovely husband is given serious, but never too respectful, treatment in Smith, E.A., **George IV**, Yale, 1999. Two useful recent studies on important, if not attractive, figures – both of whom became Lord Chancellor – are Melikan, R.A., **John Scott, Lord Eldon, 1751–1838: the duty of loyalty**, Cambridge, 1999, and Stewart, R., **Henry Brougham: His Public Career, 1778–1868**, Bodley Head, 1985.

Finally, three biographies of leading radical figures shed much fresh light on their influence and their importance: Belchem, J., **'Orator Hunt': Henry Hunt and English Working-Class Radicalism**, Clarendon, Oxford, 1985, Burton, A., **William Cobbett, Englishman: a biography**, Aurum, London, 1997, and Miles, D.H., **Francis Place 1771–1854: The Life of a Remarkable Radical**, Harvester, Brighton, 1988.

Society

The books mentioned below cover a wide range of themes. The first two need contextualizing carefully. Cannon, J. (ed.), **The Whig Ascendancy**, Arnold, 1981, contains much orthodox political history, although the book is concerned with explaining the social, and in this case predominantly landed, context within which political change took place. By contrast, and despite its title, Clark, J.C.D., **English Society, 1688–1832**, Cambridge, 1985, is more concerned with political than with social history. His remains an enormously controversial interpretation. Clark argues – against much compelling evidence – that British state and society before about 1828 was pre-modern and conservative. It has, however, attracted much attention and its spiky writing makes it a rewarding, if challenging, read. The key works on rural society in this period are Dunbabin, J.P.D., **Rural Discontent in Nineteenth-Century Britain**, Faber, 1974, Hobsbawm, E.J. and Rudé, G.F.E., **Captain Swing**, Pelican edn, 1973, and Peacock, A.J., **Bread or Blood**, Gollancz, 1965. All are good at explaining why rural society was in crisis for much of this period.

Two formidable books about the emergence of an industrial society in the early nineteenth century appeared first in the 1960s and both assume that the Industrial Revolution created a new kind of 'class' relations. Other means of social categorization have been given greater prominence in recent years but Thompson, E.P., *The Making of the English Working Class*, Gollancz, 1963, and Perkin, H.J., *The Origins of Modern English Society, 1780–1880*, Routledge, 1969, remain indispensable works – not only for their scholarship but for their commitment and their literacy. Both are controversial, opinionated, joys to read. There are a number of useful books about urban society in the early industrial period. See, for example, Glen, R., *Urban Workers in the Early Industrial Revolution*, Croom Helm, 1984, Hunt, E.H., *British Labour History, 1815–1914*, Weidenfeld, 1981, Price, R., *Labour in British Society*, Croom Helm, 1986, and Rule, J., *The Labouring Classes in Early Industrial England*, Longman, 1986. Henriques, U.R.Q., *Before the Welfare State*, Longman, 1979, is good on changing legislative responses to the emergence of 'the social question' in early industrial England, while Poynter, J.R., *Society and Pauperism*, Routledge, 1969, remains useful for an understanding of how the poor coped, or failed to cope, with the pressures of change. Cunningham, H. and Innes, J., *Charity, Philanthropy and Reform from the 1690s to 1850*, Macmillan, Basingstoke, 1998, offer a useful corrective to the widespread, but misleading, assumption that it was the poor law which coped with the problems of poverty. Charities and charitable giving were crucial.

Stevenson, J., *London in the Age of Reform*, Blackwell, 1977, and Stevenson, J., *Popular Disturbances in England, 1700–1870*, Longman, 1979, are useful studies of societies undergoing rapid change. Williams, G., *The Merthyr Rising*, Croom Helm, 1978, is a very useful corrective to the assumption that the main challenges to authority mostly took place in London, or if not there then in provincial, industrial English cities. The influence of the press in shaping and changing public opinion is very well explained in Read, D., *Press and People, 1790–1850*, Arnold, 1961. Emsley, C., *Crime and Society in England, 1750–1900*, Longman, 1987, should be the first port of call for anyone wishing to understand criminal behaviour and how emphases on criminal behaviour changed over time. Tranter, N.L., *Population and Society, 1750–1940*, Longman, 1985, is an accessible, non-technical introduction for students wishing to understand the process of rapid population change.

Among the periodical literature, two articles on the so-called standard of living controversy (now largely resolved) remain valuable: Flinn, M.W., 'Trends in Real Wages', *Econ. HR*, 2nd ser., xxvii, 1974, pp. 395–413, and Lindert, P.H. and Williamson, J.G., 'English Workers' Living Standards during the Industrial Revolution: A New Look', *Econ. HR*, 2nd ser., xxxvi, 1983, pp. 1–25. For a corrective to the view that industrial enterprises were nearly always large, see Gatrell, V.A.C., 'Labour, Power and the Size of Firms in Lancashire Cotton in the second quarter of the nineteenth century', *Econ. HR*, 2nd ser., xxx, 1977, pp. 95–139.

Trade, Economics and Finance

The best general assessment currently available is Daunton, M., *Progress and Poverty: An Economic and Social History of Britain, 1700–1850*, Oxford, 1995. A volume now showing signs of its age in the light of more recent computer-aided quantitative research remains worth consulting not least for its clarity and identification of key themes, namely Deane, P. and Cole, W.A., *British Economic Growth, 1688–1959*, 2nd ed., Cambridge, 1961. More specialist texts which bring the results of econometric research to a wider audience include Crafts, N.F.R., *British Economic Growth during the Industrial Revolution*, Oxford, 1985, Floud, R. and McCloskey, D. (eds), *The Economic History of Britain since 1700*, 3 vols, 2nd edn, Cambridge, 1994, and Floud, R. and Johnson, P. (eds), *The Cambridge Economic History of Modern Britain*, Cambridge, 2004. For recent thinking both on the nature, and indeed the validity of the concept, of the Industrial Revolution, see Mokyr, J. (ed.), *The British Industrial Revolution: An Economic Perspective*, Westview Press, Boulder, Colorado, 1998. Four extremely valuable texts on the development of political economy as a science and on its application to practical politics are Gordon, B., *Economic Doctrine and Tory Liberalism, 1824–30*, Macmillan, 1979, Gordon, B., *Political Economy in Parliament, 1819–23*, Macmillan, 1976, Hilton, B., *Corn, Cash, Commerce: The Economic Policies of the Tory Governments, 1815–1830*, Oxford, 1977, and Thompson, N.W., *The People's Science: The Popular Political Economy of Exploitation and Crisis, 1816–1834*, Cambridge, 1984.

Religion

The more recent textbooks now offer a reliable introduction to the religious history of the period and recognize its importance in explaining change in both political and religious history. The most ambitious of the more specialist works is Hilton, B., *The Age of Atonement: the influence of Evangelicalism on Social and Economic Thought, 1785–1865*, Oxford, 1986, which offers an intriguing, and well-argued, thesis on the links between evangelical religion and changing priorities in politics. For Roman Catholicism in this period, see Bossy, J., *The English Catholic Community, 1570–1850*, Darton, Longman and Todd, 1975, and Machin, G.I.T., *The Catholic Question in English Politics, 1820–30*, Oxford, 1964. The best accessible study on Methodism and its growth is Hempton, D., *Methodism and Politics in British Society, 1780–1850*, Hutchinson, 1984. Royle, E.,

Radical Politics, 1790–1900: Religion and Unbelief, Longman, 1971, is very useful in explaining the links between protestant nonconformity and political radicalism.

In the article literature, there is a good study of the nature of opposition to Dissenters' claims for equality of civil rights in Machin, G.I.T., 'Resistance to the Repeal of the Test and Corporation Acts', *HJ*, xxii, 1979, pp. 115–39. On the coming of Catholic Emancipation, see Davis, R.W., 'The Tories, the Whigs and Catholic Emancipation, 1827–9', *EHR*, xcvii, 1982, pp. 89–98, and Machin, G.I.T., 'Canning, Wellington and the Catholic Question, 1827–29', *EHR*, xcvii, 1984, pp. 94–100. For weaknesses in the Church of England during this period, see Evans, E.J., 'Some Reasons for the Growth of Rural Anti-Clericalism in England, c. 1750–1830', *P & P*, lxvi, 1975, pp. 84–109, and Evans, E.J., 'The Church in Danger? Anti-Clericalism in Nineteenth-Century England', *ESR*, xiii, 1983, pp. 201–23.

Foreign Policy

We live in an era when orthodox diplomatic history and the history of relations between nation states are much less studied than they were. Not surprisingly, therefore, the heavy-duty detailed accounts of foreign policy have stood the test of time. Seton-Watson, R.W., *Britain in Europe, 1789–1914*, Cambridge, 1937, is, therefore, still recommendable, despite its age, as is the volume by Temperley and Penson cited in the 'Documents and Contemporary Sources' section above. There is, however, much more interest in the history of the British Empire and for this Bayly, C.A., *Imperial Meridian: the British Empire and the World, 1780–1830*, Longman Pearson, 1989, can be safely recommended as the best introduction, concentrating as it does on the impact of imperial outreach and imperial thinking. As relatively recent treatments of British foreign policy, Chamberlain, M.E., *British Foreign Policy in the Age of Palmerston*, Longman, 1980, Clarke, J.C., *British Diplomacy and Foreign Policy, 1782–1865: The National Interest*, Harper Collins, London, 1989, and Hayes, P., *The Nineteenth Century, 1814–80*, A&C Black, 1975, are all recommendable. It is also good to welcome an interesting modern selection of essays in Thomas, G. (ed.), *The Making of British Foreign Policy: from Pitt to Thatcher*, Basingstoke, Palgrave, 2001. The general works by Hilton and Evans cited above have useful chapters on foreign policy.

Radical Politics

Probably the best introductions in this field are Belchem, J., *Popular Radicalism in Nineteenth-century Britain*, Macmillan, 1996, Royle, E. and Walvin, J., *English Radicals and Reformers, 1760–1848*, Harvester, 1982, and Dinwiddy, J.R., *From Luddism to the Reform Act*, Blackwell, 1986. Royle, E., *Revolutionary Britannia? Reflections on the Threat of Revolution in Britain, 1789–1848*, Manchester University Press, 2000, re-examines the critical question of how near to success the various revolutionary attempts of this period came. More detailed studies with a specific geographical focus are Flick, C., *The Birmingham Political Union, 1830–39*, Dawson, 1978, and Prothero, I., *Artisans and Politics in Nineteenth-Century London*, Dawson, 1979. Blanning, T.C.W. and Wende, P. (eds), *Reform in Great Britain and Germany, 1750–1850*, Oxford, 1999, offers a useful comparative insight while Harling, P., *The Waning of 'Old Corruption', 1779–1846*, Clarendon, Oxford, 1996, presents a lucid explanation of why so many radicals considered the state irredeemably 'corrupt' and why that line of attack had lost purchase by the middle of the nineteenth century. LoPantin, N.D., *Political Unions, Popular Politics and the Great Reform Act of 1832*, St Martins, New York, 1999, re-examines the short-term importance of the Political Unions, while Wood, M., *Radical Satire and Print Culture, 1790–1822*, Clarendon, Oxford, 1994, explains why visual attacks on the establishment were at least as effective as those using the written medium.

Useful scholarly articles on the importance of the Queen Caroline affair are Hunt, T.L., 'Morality and Monarchy in the Queen Caroline Affair', *Albion*, xxiii, 1991, pp. 697–722, and Fulcher, J., 'The Loyalist Response to the Queen Caroline Agitations', *JBS*, xxiv, 1995, pp. 481–502. A piece which argues that Liverpool's government was more complicit in the Peterloo affair than has recently been assumed is Poole, R., ' "By the Law or the Sword": Peterloo Revisited', *History*, xci, 2006, pp. 254–76. For an interesting perspective on the reform process, see Davis, R.W., 'Toryism to Tamworth: The Triumph of Reform, 1827–35', *Albion*, xii, 1980, pp. 132–46.

Parliamentary Reform

Two volumes by the present author may act as useful introductions: Evans, E.J., *The Great Reform Act*, Routledge, 2nd edn, 1994, and *Parliamentary Reform, c. 1770–1918*, Pearson Education, 2000. The most detailed, if now ageing, study of 1832 is Brock, M., *The Great Reform Act*, Hutchinson, 1973, though Cannon, J., *Parliamentary Reform, 1640–1832*, 2nd edn, Cambridge, 1980, in taking a longer chronological view, is able to identify long-term causes as well as discussing the various reform crises. Butler, J.R.M., *The Passing of the Reform Bill*, Cass edn, 1914, was the benchmark study for more than half a century. Though it tends to see the Bill in Whiggish terms as a major step towards modern democracy, and has been widely criticised for so doing, it remains a very useful reference point. Lawrence, J. and Taylor, M., *Party, State and Society: Electoral Behaviour in Britain since 1820*, Scolar Press, Aldershot, 1997, incorporate much recent research. Anyone wishing to gain an insight into how elections work and what issues were at stake needs to consult it.

The article literature on reform is rich. From a very wide selection, see McCord, N., 'Some Difficulties of Parliamentary Reform', *HJ*, x, 1967, pp. 376–90, and Phillips, J.A., 'The Many Faces of Reform: The Reform Bill and the Electorate', *PH*, i, 1982, pp. 115–35. Milton-Smith, J., 'Earl Grey's Cabinet and the Objects of Parliamentary Reform', *HJ*, xv, 1972, pp. 55–74, and Quinault, R., 'The French Revolution of 1830 and Parliamentary Reform', *History*, lxxxix, 1994, pp. 377–93, each deal with particular aspects of the reform crisis. Milton-Smith evaluates a range of Whig perspectives while Quinault urges us to look abroad – as did so many contemporary politicians – for reasons to treat reform pressures seriously. Moore, D.C., 'Concession or Cure: The Sociological Premises of the First Reform Act', *HJ*, ix, 1966, pp. 39–59, argued the case that the Whigs intended the Act to be a cure for constitutional ills, rather than merely a necessary concession to growing extra-parliamentary pressure for change.

References

The following abbreviations are used:

Econ. HR	*Economic History Review*
EHR	*English Historical Review*
ESR	*European Studies Review*
HJ	*Historical Journal*
JBS	*Journal of British Studies*
JMH	*Journal of Modern History*
P & P	*Past and Present*
PH	*Parliamentary History*

Bartlett, C.J., *Castlereagh*, Macmillan, 1966.

Bayly, C.A., *Imperial Meridian: the British Empire and the World, 1780–1830*, Longman Pearson, 1989.

Belchem, J., *'Orator Hunt': Henry Hunt and English Working-Class Radicalism*, Clarendon, 1985.

Belchem, J., *Popular Radicalism in Nineteenth-century Britain*, Macmillan, 1996.

Blanning, T.C.W. and Wende, P. (eds), *Reform in Great Britain and Germany, 1750–1850*, Oxford University Press, 1999.

Bossy, J., *The English Catholic Community, 1570–1850*, Darton, Longman and Todd, 1975.

Bourne, K., *Palmerston: The Early Years, 1784–1841*, Allen Lane, 1982.

Briggs, A., *The Age of Improvement, 1783–1867*, 2nd revised edn, Longman, 2000.

Brock, M., *The Great Reform Act*, Hutchinson, 1973.

Brock, W.R., *Lord Liverpool and Liberal Toryism*, 2nd edn, Glasgow, 1967.

Burns, A. and Innes, J., *Rethinking the Age of Reform: Britain, 1780–1850*, Cambridge University Press, 2003.

Burton, A., *William Cobbett, Englishman: a biography*, Aurum, 1997.

Butler, J.R.M., *The Passing of the Reform Bill*, Cass edn, 1914.

Cannon, J. (ed.), *Aristocratic Century*, Cambridge University Press, 1984.

Cannon, J., *Parliamentary Reform, 1640–1832*, 2nd ed., Cambridge University Press, 1980.

Cannon, J. (ed.), *The Whig Ascendancy*, Arnold, 1981.

Chambers, J., *Palmerston: the people's darling*, Murray, 2004.

Chamberlain, M.E., *British Foreign Policy in the Age of Palmerston*, Longman, 1980.

Clark, J.C.D., 'A General Theory of Party, Opposition and Government, 1688–1832', *HJ*, xxiii, 1980, pp. 295–325.

Clark, J.C.D., *British Diplomacy and Foreign Policy, 1782–1865: The National Interest*, Harper Collins, 1989.

Clark, J.C.D., *English Society, 1688–1832*, Cambridge University Press, 1985.

Cookson, J.E., *Lord Liverpool's Administration, 1815–1822*, Scottish Academic Press, 1975.

Crafts, N.F.R., *British Economic Growth during the Industrial Revolution*, Oxford, 1985.

Cunningham, H. and Innes, J., *Charity, Philanthropy and Reform from the 1690s to 1850*, Macmillan, 1998.

Daunton, M., *Progress and Poverty: An Economic and Social History of Britain, 1700–1850*, Oxford University Press, 1995.

Davis, R.W., 'The Tories, the Whigs and Catholic Emancipation, 1827–9', *EHR*, xcvii, 1982, pp. 89–98.

Davis, R.W., 'Toryism to Tamworth: The Triumph of Reform, 1827–35', *Albion*, xii, 1980, pp. 132–46.

Deane, P. and Cole, W.A., *British Economic Growth, 1688–1959*, 2nd edn, Cambridge University Press, 1969.

Derry, J.W., *Castlereagh*, Allen Lane, 1976.

Derry, J.W., *Politics in the Age of Fox, Pitt and Liverpool*, 2nd edn, Palgrave, 2001.

Dinwiddy, J.R., *From Luddism to the Reform Act*, Blackwell, 1986.

Dunbabin, J.P.D., *Rural Discontent in Nineteenth-Century Britain*, Faber, 1974.

Emsley, C., *Crime and Society in England, 1750–1900*, Longman, 1987.

Evans, E.J., *Parliamentary Reform, c. 1770–1918*, Pearson Education, 2000.

Evans, E.J., *Political Parties in Britain, 1783–1867*, Routledge, 1985.

Evans, E.J., *Sir Robert Peel: Statesmanship, Power and Party*, 2nd edn, Routledge, 2006.

Evans, E.J., 'Some Reasons for the Growth of Rural Anti-Clericalism in England, c. 1750–1830', *P & P*, lxvi, 1975, pp. 84–109.

Evans, E.J., 'The Church in Danger? Anti-Clericalism in Nineteenth-Century England', *ESR*, xiii, 1983, pp. 201–23.

Evans, F.J., *The Forging of the Modern State: Early Industrial Britain, 1783–1870*, 3rd edn, Longman Pearson, 2001.

Evans, E.J., *The Great Reform Act*, Routledge, 2nd edn, 1994.

Flick, C., *The Birmingham Political Union, 1830–39*, Dawson, 1978.

Flick, C., 'The Fall of Wellington's Government', *JMH*, xxxvii, 1965, pp. 62–71.

Flinn, M.W., 'Trends in Real Wages', *Econ. HR*, 2nd ser., xxvii, 1974, pp. 395–413.

Floud, R. and Johnson, P. (eds), *The Cambridge Economic History of Modern Britain*, Cambridge University Press, 2004.

Floud, R. and McCloskey, D. (eds), *The Economic History of Britain since 1700*, 3 vols, 2nd edn, Cambridge University Press, 1994.

Fraser, P., 'Party Voting in the House of Commons, 1812–27', *EHR*, xcviii, 1983, pp. 763–84.

Fulcher, J., 'The Loyalist Response to the Queen Caroline Agitations', *JBS*, xxiv, 1995, pp. 481–502.

Gash, N., *Aristocracy and People, 1815–1865*, Arnold, 1979.

Gash, N., *Lord Liverpool*, Weidenfeld, 1984.

Gash, N., *Mr. Secretary Peel: The Life of Sir Robert Peel to 1830*, 2nd edn, Longman, 1985.

Gash, N., *Sir Robert Peel: The Life of Sir Robert Peel after 1830*, 2nd edn, Longman, 1986.

Gatrell, V.A.C., 'Labour, Power and the Size of Firms in Lancashire Cotton in the second quarter of the nineteenth century', *Econ. HR*, 2nd ser., xxx, 1977, pp. 95–139.

Geoghegan, P.M., *Lord Castlereagh*, Dundalk, 2002.

Glen, R., *Urban Workers in the Early Industrial Revolution*, Croom Helm, 1984.

Gordon, B., *Economic Doctrine and Tory Liberalism, 1824–30*, Macmillan, 1979.

Gordon, B., *Political Economy in Parliament, 1819–23*, Macmillan, 1976.

Green, D., *Great Cobbett, The Noblest Agitator*, Oxford University Press, 1983.

Halevy, E., *The Liberal Awakening, 1815–30*, vol. 2 of his *History of the English People in the Nineteenth Century*, Benn, 1926.

Harling, P., 'Equipoise Regained? Recent Trends in British Political History, 1790–1867', *JMH*, lxxv, 2003, pp. 890–918.

Harling, P., *The Waning of 'Old Corruption', 1779–1846*, Clarendon, 1996.

Harling, P. and Mandler, P., 'From "Fiscal-Military" State to Laissez-Faire State, 1760–1850', *JBS*, xxxii, 1993, pp. 44–70.

Hay, W.A., *The Whig Revival, 1808–30*, Palgrave Macmillan, 2005.

Hayes, P., *The Nineteenth Century, 1814–80*, A&C Black, 1975.

Henriques, U.R.Q., *Before the Welfare State*, Longman, 1979.

Hempton, D., *Methodism and Politics in British Society, 1780–1850*, Hutchinson, 1984.

Hill, B.W., *British Parliamentary Parties, 1742–1832*, Allen and Unwin, 1985.

Hilton, B., *A Mad, Bad and Dangerous People: England, 1783–1846*, Oxford, 2006 – a volume in the New Oxford History of England and a definitive, detailed guide to the period.

Hilton, B., *Corn, Cash, Commerce: The Economic Policies of the Tory Governments, 1815–1830*, Oxford University Press, 1977.

Hilton, B., *The Age of Atonement: the influence of Evangelicalism on Social and Economic Thought, 1785–1865*, Oxford University Press, 1986.

Hinde, W., *Canning*, Collins, 1973.

Hinde, W., *Castlereagh*, Collins, 1981.

Hobsbawm, E.J. and Rudé, G.F.E., *Captain Swing*, Pelican edn, 1973.

Holmes, R., *Wellington: the Iron Duke*, Harper Collins, 2002.

Hunt, E.H., *British Labour History, 1815–1914*, Weidenfeld, 1981.

Hunt, T.L., 'Morality and Monarchy in the Queen Caroline Affair', *Albion*, xxiii, 1991, pp. 697–722.

Hutton, W., *The History of Birmingham*, 6th edn, James Guest, 1836.

Hyam, R., *Britain's Imperial Century*, Batsford, 1976.

Jenkins, T.A., *Sir Robert Peel*, Macmillan, 1999.

Jones, W.D., *Prosperity Robinson: The Life of Viscount Goderich, 1782–1859*, Macmillan, 1967.

Jupp, P., *British Politics on the Eve of Reform: the Duke of Wellington's Administration, 1828–30*, Macmillan, 1998.

Jupp, P., *Lord Grenville, 1759–1834*, Oxford University Press, 1985.

Jupp, P.J., *The Governing of Britain, 1688–1848: the executive, Parliament and the people*, Routledge, 2006.

Lawrence, J. and Taylor, M., *Party, State and Society: Electoral Behaviour in Britain since 1820*, Scolar Press, 1997.

Lindert, P.H. and Williamson, J.G., 'English Workers' Living Standards during the Industrial Revolution: A New Look', *Econ. HR*, 2nd ser., xxxvi, 1983, pp. 1–25.

LoPantin, N.D., *Political Unions, Popular Politics and the Great Reform Act of 1832*, St Martins, 1999.

Machin, G.I.T., 'Canning, Wellington and the Catholic Question, 1827–29', *EHR*, xcvii, 1984, pp. 94–100.

Machin, G.I.T., 'Resistance to the Repeal of the Test and Corporation Acts', *HJ*, xxii, 1979, pp. 115–39.

Machin, G.I.T., *The Catholic Question in English Politics, 1820–30*, Oxford University Press, 1964.

McCord, N., 'Some Difficulties of Parliamentary Reform', *HJ*, x, 1967, pp. 376–90.

Melikan, R.A., *John Scott, Lord Eldon, 1751–1838: the duty of loyalty*, Cambridge University Press, 1999.

Miles, D.H., *Francis Place 1771–1854: The Life of a Remarkable Radical*, Harvester, 1988.

Milton-Smith, J., 'Earl Grey's Cabinet and the Objects of Parliamentary Reform', *HJ*, xv, 1972, pp. 55–74.

Mitchell, L.G., *Lord Melbourne, 1779–1848*, Oxford University Press, 1997.

Mokyr, J. (ed), *The British Industrial Revolution: An Economic Perspective*, Westview Press, 1998.

Moore, D.C., 'Concession or Cure: The Sociological Premises of the First Reform Act', *HJ*, ix, 1966, pp. 39–59.

Moore, D.C., *The Politics of Deference*, Harvester, 1976.

O'Gorman, F., 'Electoral Deference in "Unreformed" England, 1760–1832', *JMH*, lvi, 1984, pp. 391–427.

O'Gorman, F., 'Party Politics in the Early Nineteenth Century, 1812–32', *EHR*, cii, 1987, pp. 63–84.

Peacock, A.J., *Bread or Blood*, Gollancz, 1965.

Perkin, H.J., *The Origins of Modern English Society, 1780–1880*, Routledge, 1969.

Phillips, J.A., 'The Many Faces of Reform: The Reform Bill and the Electorate', *PH*, i, 1982, pp. 115–35.

Poole, R., ' "By the Law or the Sword": Peterloo Revisited', *History*, xci, 2006, pp. 254–76.

Poynter, J.R., *Society and Pauperism*, Routledge, 1969.

Priest, J., *Lord John Russell*, Macmillan, 1972.

Price, R., *Labour in British Society*, Croom Helm, 1986.

Prothero, I., *Artisans and Politics in Nineteenth-Century London*, Dawson, 1979.

Quinault, R., 'The French Revolution of 1830 and Parliamentary Reform', *History*, lxxxix, 1994, pp. 377–93.

Read, D., *Press and People, 1790–1850*, Arnold, 1961.

Robins, J., *Rebel Queen: The Trial of Queen Caroline*, Simon & Schuster, 2006.

Royle, E., *Modern Britain, 1750–1985: A Social History*, 2nd edn, Arnold, 1997.

Royle, E., *Radical Politics, 1790–1900: Religion and Unbelief*, Longman, 1971.

Royle, E., *Revolutionary Britannia? Reflections on the Threat of Revolution in Britain, 1789–1848*, Manchester University Press, 2000.

Royle, E. and Walvin, J., *English Radicals and Reformers, 1760–1848*, Harvester, 1982.

Rule, J., *The Labouring Classes in Early Industrial England*, Longman, 1986.

Scherer, P., *Lord John Russell: a biography*, Susquehanna, 1999.

Seton-Watson, R.W., *Britain in Europe, 1789–1914* Cambridge University Press, 1937.

Smith, E.A., *George IV*, Yale, 1999.

Smith, E.A., *Lord Grey*, Oxford University Press, 1990.

Stevenson, J., *London in the Age of Reform*, Blackwell, 1977.

Stevenson, J., *Popular Disturbances in England, 1700–1870*, Longman, 1979.

Stewart, R., *Henry Brougham: His Public Career, 1778–1868*, Bodley Head, 1985.

Stewart, R., *The Foundation of the Conservative Party, 1830–67*, Longman, 1978.

Taylor, A. (ed.), *The Standard of Living Controversy in the Industrial Revolution*, Methuen, 1975.

Thomas, G. (ed.), *The Making of British Foreign Policy: from Pitt to Thatcher*, Palgrave, 2001.

Thompson, E.P., *The Making of the English Working Class*, Gollancz, 1963.

Thompson, N., *Wellington after Waterloo*, Routledge, 1986.

Thompson, N.W., *The People's Science: The Popular Political Economy of Exploitation and Crisis, 1816–1834*, Cambridge University Press, 1984.

Thorne, R. (ed.), *The History of Parliament, 1790–1820*, 5 vols, Secker and Warburg, 1986.

Tranter, N.L., *Population and Society, 1750–1940*, Longman, 1985.

Turner, M.J., *British Politics in an Age of Reform*, Manchester, 1999.

Williams, G., *The Merthyr Rising*, Croom Helm, 1978.

Wood, M., *Radical Satire and Print Culture, 1790–1822*, Clarendon, 1994.

Index